Jason E. Hamilton

Life, the Yurt and Everything

Copyright © Jason E. Hamilton, 2015
Standard Edition
First Printing 2015
Published by Mazelton Estates Publishing
Mazelton Estates Publishing, 99 Wilson Road, Upper Rexton,

New Brunswick, E4W 3G6

All rights reserved. Without limiting the rights under copyright reserved above, no part of this publication may be reproduced, stored in or introduced into retrieval system, or transmitted in any for or by any means (electronic, mechanical, photocopying, recording or otherwise) without the prior written permission of both the copyright owner and the above publisher of this book.

ISBN: 0992118936
ISBN-13: 978-0992118936

Contents

1	A Yurt You Say	1
2	Backwards Jason	23
3	The Two Ministries	42
	Photo Gallery	60
4	A Backed Up System	78
5	To Sell Or Not To Sell	93
6	SOLD!	110
7	Setting Out	127
8	Getting To Know The Locals	146
9	The Disappearing Yurt Fiasco	163
10	Circle Power	180
11	The Birth Of A Yurt	197
12	Does It Have To Be Exactly 32 Feet?	215
13	Move In Condition	234
14	The Ghosts Of Toronto	253
15	Along Came Earl	274
	Epilogue	293

DEDICATION
While I dedicate this effort to Steve Spurrell, I derive the inspiration for it from my son Dustin and my common-law heterosexual life partner Sylvie.

ACKNOWLEDGMENTS

Mom and Dad (of course). Wendy for my first corporate gig. Fern and Flo for the encouragement. Countless friends and colleague's who heeded my call for initial feedback. But most importantly to all of those who, intentional or not, had a say in making me a better writer.

To learn more about Jason please visit:

www.jasonehamilton.co

1

A Yurt You Say

"Why did you call 911!?!" I pleaded. Her reaction was mute. I wasn't the first to go there.

"Hmm, that's funny, y'know our next door neighbor Mark. Yeah, he asked me the same thing," Sylvie retorted and continued. I listened and repeated her words. The hope of an inferno faded in her logic.

"Yeah, the fire could spread. It's been dry. The shed is close to the fence and the fence is attached to our house," my voice trailed into disappointment.

"But hold on, you didn't see any actual flame, you just saw smoke. Well, couldn't you have just waited a little longer before calling?"

It wasn't the measured voice of compassion she was expecting.

"Don't worry Jase, I thought of all those things. But remember, we have an infant son and I don't want to be homeless just yet. Believe me I wanted nothing more than to see that Crack shed go up in flames," Sylvie said apologetically.

I hurried home after the workday ended eager to know if the neighbors' garden shed had at least become inhospitable. As I peered over the fence from the safety of my patio the only indication of a fire was an outside wall darkened from water. No charcoaled wood, no charred remains, no hint of collapse or imminent danger. The twisted extension cords that wound around to provide electrical 'service' to the garden shed remained undisturbed.

"It looks like nothing happened!" I blurted.

"Quiet, they might hear you," Sylvie, with our infant son Dustin strapped to her hip, hauled me inside. He stirred momentarily at the changed equilibrium but otherwise remained comatose. Oh to sleep through such things.

Though she was two years my senior, I probably eclipsed Sylvie in height before I was a teenager. She packed a punch and her temperament was impossible to contain; her personality could charm a room or it could fell an empire…depending on her disposition.

Closing the patio door, Sylvie offered a summation of events, "She sure looked awfully scared though."

"Of what, being busted? She probably started the fire in the first place!"

"Yeah, trying to get a hit."

"At eight o'clock in the morning?"

"That's the best time."

"So what did you see?"

"I was having my coffee, still a bit foggy of course because Dustin was up half the night. I took a glance out the back door and thought, hmm, why is someone running a smoke machine in our backyard?"

"I know that feeling, when you're so tired you think you're still at work. I hate those dreams."

"So then I looked over and the neighbors' garden had a bunch of white smoke billowing out the back. Of course, after I saw that I snapped to attention. I still didn't think of what to do next…"

I chuckled under my breath: Sylvie in a crisis situation. A few years ago in our old apartment an incident occurred in a car in the driveway. A prostitute performed a service and the customer refused to submit payment. A disagreement turned into a fight until the woman started screaming blue murder: "HE'S GOT A GUN. HE'S GOING TO KILL ME. OH MY GOD!!!"

The entire house, four apartments in total, rose to attention and hustled about trying to find out/see/gawk/marvel at the situation before realizing it might actually be serious. The other inhabitants converged on our bedroom, peering down at the scene below and tried to figure out what to do. In heroic leadership of the resistance, Sylvie bellowed at the four other women, "What's the number for 911?!?"

After gaining her wits and punching the numbers she suddenly turned into a well-trained coordinator when she spoke to the dispatcher.

"Yes, it's a Caucasian male who so far as we know has the victim in the car. The vehicle is parked below us here at 105 Indian Road. The woman claims there is a firearm. I haven't seen anything to suggest that, but I think the suspect should be considered armed and dangerous…."

"Did you remember the number for 911 this time?" I teased. She chuckled, the old memory triggered by the mention of the numbers.

"I did, now fuck off. Anyway, the crack whore was running around in a mad panic, spinning this way and that. I thought it might be serious. And hey, they're only two houses over with a massive tree that covers half of Toronto, plus a dried out old fence and gawd knows what else could go up in flames. Because believe me, I'm pretty sure I was the only one home to be able to make the call. But the last thing I wanted was to have to bundle Dustin up and get out of the house because we were burning down."

"No big deal, you could've gone and stayed at your parents' in New Brunswick."

She considered the option before responding.

"Shit, I should've let it burn."

"Yup, it would've been a nice, easy, convenient way to get rid of the infestation."

"So anyway I called 911. I remembered this time. And of course between them, the police and the ambulance all being just up the road they were here in no time."

"They were probably on the radio just waiting for Shaky to fall off his porch."

"They certainly must've known where to go because they were here in like, two seconds. And no, they didn't go across the street to Shakey's house first.... Can I finish my story?"

I zipped my lips and stared at the floor.

Sylvie continued, "So when the firemen showed up that's when she really panicked. They kept on having to haul her away from the shed. Methinks some stash might have gone up..."

"Sounds like it. Where was the mighty Lurch in all of this?"

"Nowhere to be found. I didn't see the old couple there either. They hosed it down quick and that was that."

"That was that? The cops didn't go over the place with a fine tooth comb?"

"Guess it wasn't their priority."

I shook my head.

"What's it gonna take for them to do something? Have the whole goddamn neighborhood burn to the ground? Fuck me, I'm sick of this. I wonder if there's a way we can get in touch with our insurance company. What about by-law enforcement? Surely the city would want to know about a fire that took place in an illegal dwelling in someone's backyard. This is crazy. I suppose if we lived in Rosedale we wouldn't have any problems dealing with problems like these."

"Jase, if we lived in Rosedale WE would be the problem," Sylvie said.

I stewed in fruitless anger.

"Thank you Margaret," we said in unison.

Margaret, our real estate agent who counseled and coached us on our home purchase five years ago provided this summation of us and our new neighborhood: "It's an up and coming neighborhood (i.e. dodgy) and I wouldn't let you buy this home if I didn't think you could handle it..."

Handle it we have. It wasn't where we wanted to be, accustomed as we were to our old neighborhood in the west end of Toronto that gentrified before our eyes. In so doing, the opportunity to invest and reap the rewards of that transformation was lost. In the blink of an eye the average home in Roncesvalles Village jumped from $300K to over half a million.

The same thing occurred in all the 'desirable' Toronto neighborhoods. Though the bank would allow a couple of film bums like us to borrow to our maximum of $350K, I couldn't allow myself to fall victim to such empty promise. Yes, I understood a house was an investment. Yes, Toronto real estate was about as safe as it could get. But most of the housing stock in the downtown core was approaching a century old. Buying the investment was one thing, maintaining it was another. And yet, the lure of home ownership along with the frustration of throwing a thousand dollars a month away in rent was too tempting. When that move had to take place it would be in a less desirable part of the city in order to fit our budget.

Two months after taking residence in our new home, the gravity of that decision pierced the dark of early morning. A pitched wail reverberated off the bedroom walls.

"DON'T SHOOT. PLEASE GOD, I DON'T WANT TO DIE!!!"

Roused from slumber, we clamoured for the windows. On the street in front of our house a blockade of police cars closed traffic and littered the neighborhood with a hemorrhage of flashing lights. Behind our house a small squad of police subdued two young 'toughs' with little more than pathetic auditory diarrhea as a defense.

That bust, not a gift basket or flowers, was our introduction to the house of hell. We came to learn it was the grandson who was hauled away for dealing pot. His father (who we would affectionately call 'Lurch') was a recovering junkie being treated with methadone. (We assigned the name Lurch purely on physical characteristics. The skin around his cheeks and temple were unnaturally sunken with thinning grey hair and matching complexion. The deathly look was complete even without the hunched walk and tattered wardrobe. In Oprah years he was probably approaching a hundred.)

And then there was Denny, the grandfather. Denny was a slight old man often found in khaki's and a lightly checkered shirt. Himself a recovering alcoholic, Denny could be found on a mosey, never walking too fast despite the old greaser coating to his thinned hair, standing guard over the community he's called home for the past forty years. Three generations of trouble. They were entrenched and they weren't going anywhere.

But as much as they weren't the Brady's they were hardly the only problem spot on Coxwell Ave. Down the road at the corner was a little strip mall. That strip mall housed two equally dank and depressing bars that catered to, and whose existence depended on, the social assistance of their clientele. (A point driven home, not coincidentally, on the last weekend of the month.) On those days the street noise and arguments would get louder and later with occasional mayhem. Most times it would be just a fight, but the now-familiar wail of law enforcement sirens and the like would need to be called when extra-curricular activities had taken place (your stabbings, your muggings, your general assaults. It's doubtful the thin blue line raised their heart rate much over something as trivial as a 'disturbing the peace' complaint.)

Though it was a far from desirable establishment to our discerning tastes, the 'London Dock' and the 'Fleurs de Lys' bars were fairly contained problem spots that had a lot more legal coverage to squelch a problem if it got too far out of hand. Though a stabbing at your friendly neighborhood bar was not a welcome attraction, it tended to have the swift repercussions of the many arms of the legal system to deter its repeat occurrence. Those same avenues of punishment were not as easily enforced on sole proprietors in the drug and prostitution business.

An evolutionary U-Turn such as our good friend Lurch necessitated a side-kick: Lisa, a tiny wisp of a thing with Mick Jagger lips, the same sunken cheeks as her boyfriend (evidence suggests the cells of two people will start to mutate over time to make them look more like one another…the crystal meth helps) with a long, trifecta of colors in her hair: auburn tips, a grimy, greasy middle and white piano cord roots.

From having observed her behavior over the years, she had two distinct 'tells': when the eyes were fixed piercingly ahead and her body, stooped over, was speed walking to keep up with her purpose, she was scoring. Be it drugs or a john I could never be sure. That was her business posture.

When the walk was a less hurried or determined I believe she was focused less on immediate matters and more on the long-term side of things: marketing, branding, the stuff that would really make her mark in the vice business.

I knew this about her because after some time in our dream home and having lived through several domestic disputes where Lurch was threatening to kill the entire neighborhood, I felt then that they were a power couple worth watching.

Along with their own specialties, they'd raised a son who wasn't afraid of any young toughs either. Since his crown-imposed vacation from trafficking, he'd come back more determined than ever to reclaim his territory. In staking back that status he'd run afoul of an even worse measure than the law: in a quarrel with four other business acquaintances, Lurch's son was stabbed on the front lawn. We heard the tail end of the confrontation as four youths made for their car.

It seemed like just another day at the bargaining table when one voice on the street was overheard to be deliberating settling the impasse with a .45. But more so than chronicling their rise in the street-crime underworld, another vested interest pushed back this morbid curiosity. Our son Dustin entered the world.

****

Work, naturally, prevented me from attending the meeting. It was in the evening of some weekday night at the school just up the road. Our entire street was in attendance at the meet and greet. After the initial speech from our local councilor introducing the various members who served our community were made, Sylvie and the rest descended on the police representative.

The firing line began:

Millou: "How can we have two bars in the same corner?"

"Well ma'am that isn't uncommon in other parts of the city and it's out of our jurisdiction. Your best bet is to go through the liquor board if you have complaints, they're usually more than happy to flex their muscles on these matters. What's important here is that you keep on them..."

Sylvie: "We've got a crack whore living next door in the garden shed...."

"We have been aware of this problem. What we need from you is to be a witness. Whoever she deals with, comes in contact with, take down license plates, descriptions of characters..."

"My husband has been doing this for some time. Every time he calls the police the transaction is over too quick for you guys to do anything about it."

"Keep the record. We need to build a case. If you guys have been witnessing this, would you be afraid to testify?"

"No."

"Great, you're doing the right things. Here's my card, I'm the community liaison officer and you can contact me directly to keep in touch."

The voice of hope. Finally a contact in the bowels of power that could exact some influence more than the desk clerk I'd been calling repeatedly about the case. Her enthusiasm about my problem was never more than what a brother would show his sibling over a missing toy.

And yet, even after several years of observing the comings and goings, the various dealings of our neighbour who lived in the garden shed and reporting it directly to the police division....nothing. I could report and instruct them exactly as to how she dealt her drugs: Her head on a swivel, I would note the purposed, fast walk as she hustled down the street. Bent noticeably at the waist she looked like Elvis on speed. She would cross to the other sidewalk from her fortress. A car would pull up and in she'd get. The car would drive up the street, away from the pick up and stop at the side of the road for a few minutes to complete the transaction. The deal done, the car would pull a u-turn and drive back down the street a little distance from her base. She would get out, looking around suspiciously to see if anyone witnessed the transaction, before scurrying back to her hideout in the shed at the back of the house.

For a time, emboldened after the meeting and the potential for progress in the matter, I became more aggressive in observation: binoculars in hand at the front windows, note pad at the ready. I would peer around the blinds, trying to document as much information as I could. License plate, make and model of car, time and day of transaction. The basics. If time would allow and our friend became sloppy, I could get more details about the individuals involved.

I was building my case. I wanted this nuisance out of our neighborhood! Too bad they weren't the only issue. Along with the problem house, our immediate community had also witnessed a murder, the explosion of a meth lab, two stabbings, a few attempted abductions, not to mention the bar fights, the domestic screaming matches and a hodgepodge of break and enters, vandalism, graffiti and everything that country folk don't like about city folk. As the crime docket increased, the activity was hitting a little too close to home. On our own, Sylvie and I, while not particularly happy about the situation and admittedly a little protective of our best investment (our home) the degree of that acceptance changed dramatically when we found out we were pregnant.

****

I wish I could explain the change that happens to couples after giving birth. Attitude. Fundamental values. The nature of every individual relationship with friends and family. Security. Overall life direction. Self-worth. That's an approximation. A guesstimate. The degrees in the various avenues' are different. Some mothers and fathers (a small minority) are able to roll with the change without so much as a hiccup in their overall makeup. Fully 50 per cent of parents of newborn children move within the first year after the child is born. Others quit drinking, smoking and carousing. Others find the Lord. The best, most succinct description I can give for the reality of having children is it throws a grenade right into the middle of ALL your relationships.

And then it takes a while before the dust settles, you get comfortable in your own skin and you move on with how things are instead of clinging desperately to how they were.

The challenges of living in an up and coming neighborhood were one thing, but long before Dustin arrived I'd also had my fill of the film industry. If having a child is like throwing a grenade into your personal relationship with your spouse, then trying to leave the film industry is about as difficult as quitting smoking crack, drinking alcohol and doing heroin....all at once!

The film business was the only industry I'd known my entire adult life and I'd seen more than my fair share of ups and downs. It has been trivialized by many as being the 'best part time job you'll ever have' and there is a hair of truth in that statement. A lowly lighting technician, or grip or camera assistant, which doesn't require much more than a high school education, can earn twenty thousand dollars in six weeks. Guh, whu? Sounds great. But there's a catch: you are owned for that length of time and when you're done your next gig could be six days, weeks or months later. Not to mention that's GROSS pay. The high tax bracket means you get to escape with less than half that amount. Still pretty good for six weeks work.

I had been on the three-year plan by the time the pilot for *Fringe* came along. Three years of slowly weaning myself off of the film teat. After one grueling six-month TV series where our average day was 14 hours long, I vowed I would not work any show longer than eight weeks. It was too painful.

But making the bold proclamation and sticking with it were very different animals. Try going out into the real world, as I had on a couple of occasions, to make a go of it after being spoiled with film money for so long. "What, $15 an hour, it's gonna take me a whole week to make what I could make in a day in film!?!" And sure enough, after six months working as an electrical apprentice and getting nowhere, when the business picked up again, there I was eager for my dose. I still managed to avoid the long haul of a TV series, but I was a whore for any other scraps that came my way. One show led to another, to another and then the beast of them all: *Fringe*.

In my fifteen years working in the show business work dried up for any number of reasons: SARS, SAG strike, Writer's Strike, media and political pressure on runaway productions, tax credits, the high dollar, location burnout, studio space, time zone difference, union seniority, Teamsters...you name it. Each one a real, legitimate explanation for the ebb and flow of work...but about as easy to predict as a butterfly causing a hurricane.

Those ups and downs saw me leave town on five different occasions to find the work to fill the gap and keep me on the roller coaster: Halifax, Saint John (where I met Sylvie), Winnipeg, Vancouver, Saint John (again). And the longer you stayed on the roller coaster, the less apt you were to look outside of your situation to see just how zany it had become to find a semblance of normalcy. Crazy was normal. So exhausted from work your body buzzed as though you were high. So exhausted your emotional nerves were frayed to the point of numbness. Rendered, quite literally, too tired to feel. Too tired for a normal relationship with yourself, much less anyone else. Too tired to be sexually aroused.

At some point you either succumb to this existence and allow yourself to be swallowed wholly into its rhythm or something destroys that entire belief system in which the ebbs and flows of the industry is at the core.

2008 was the perfect storm: a low dollar, a favorable tax credit, wage certainty for actors, writers, crew and Starbucks coffee. And unbeknownst to us there was abundant cash looking for a place to be spent

Fringe was the meeting of those favorable factors: a dearth of content in studio vaults and too much money lying around. The previous years' docket of pilots had been wiped out do to the threat of yet another writers' strike. But not the money allocated to that docket. If

Hollywood does one things well, it's burn cash!

Because the ideas tied up into a single TV pilot episode are generally lost money, when one is approved it's with a modest budget and a tight deadline. As if to say, "we challenge you and your team to accomplish this with these restrictions." Most pilots are filmed in ten days and barely scratch the ceiling of $5 million. J. J. Abrams' team was given a budget approaching $20 million and a shooting schedule of six weeks.

We hit the ground running on a February afternoon that never seemed to finish with weather that never ceased to surprise: rain, slush, wind, and then a wet, heavy snowfall that stuck to your bones. All crammed into a tidy fifteen-hour day. It was only day one and I already felt like I'd been kicked in the groin. The next day was a handsome twelve and we finished our short, introductory week with a mere sixteen hours of work. Meeting the twilight, then the onset of the sun in the same shift during the long winter night was disheartening. The rest of the show did not improve.

It isn't the quantity of the hours that's the most devastating. It's the rotating shift situation that changes throughout the week. A body can get (somewhat) accustomed to the graveyard shift if they stay in those hours of say 11-7 for a stretch of time. But picture this: Monday, 7AM start (finish 11PM) Tuesday: 10 AM start (finish 12:30 AM) Wednesday: 1PM start (finish 3 AM) Thursday: 2 PM start (4 AM finish) and finally, the marathon that is Friday: 4 PM start (9AM finish).

And then repeat six more times with varying degrees. You get the picture: Ugly.

The very last day of filming, the last hurrah, went something like this: Thursday evening start: 8 PM. Finish: Friday 3PM. A nineteen-hour day. (Of course, young interns in the medical profession are introduced to their field with 24-hour shifts and other such nonsense that belies the seeming intelligence of the people involved, but we weren't saving lives.)

The caveat is this: you aren't working all that time. In fact, there are often several hours of little or no activity. In those moments there is ample opportunity to socialize, scheme, write (as I was known for) and dream the dream of the other side: out of film. Out of the city. Out of anywhere but the endless, gut wrenching wait that can and does slowly, progressively drive you mental. But getting out is one thing, staying out another.

You had to have a pretty good idea of what out was going to constitute and you had to be prepared for your enablers (i.e. film friends) to continue to harass you with the tales of big and easy money. Because ending one career and starting another meant you were going to be at the bottom of the heap trying to prove yourself all over again.

Those that did get out and stay out were celebrated, if only because we never got the cold hard truth about how difficult it was since they never returned. Even to muse aloud about the possibility was met with indifferent, or sometimes hostile reaction in my closest of friends. Especially since as much as I hated the ups and downs I had a lifestyle to match my earnings. I would be like an alcoholic who still hangs out with all of his old friends and still goes to bars. Sure, maybe I'd kicked the actual destructive part of the habit, but the pattern that led to it was still the same.

Getting out and starting again from scratch wasn't a realistic possibility. Not with a Toronto mortgage. Not after paying for my house for five years with the upkeep on said investment leaving us with the same balance on my mortgage as when we'd started. Not when the rumblings of a housing crisis south of the border threatened our own property values.

But what if we were to cash out entirely? Move to another part of the country where housing values weren't quite so inflated. Move to another province. Maybe closer to Sylvie's VERY extended family (who could help with things like babysitting and house repairs…)

As these events started to conflagrate, my musings started to turn into actual planning. Could it be done?

"What?" Pierre scoffed, "New Brunswick. What the hell are you going to do there? There's no film work there…"

"I don't want to work in film anymore."

He shook his head. The idea was still in its infancy, its percolating stage. The opposition to this sublime scheme was to be expected. There was no strict timetable, nothing to go to, no home, no job or career. But we had a piece of property. A space on a great, wondrous river that glowed a deep auburn in the dawn of the summer sun. Maybe we could put a small cottage or something on our property until we figured it out. Maybe that was how we could do it: "Build it and they will come…."

But build what?

"Where would you live, what would you do?"

"Anywhere but here, doing anything but this…"

It was AN answer, not a great one, the anything but was something, but it certainly wasn't concrete, planned or realistic. It was a flaky scheme in something of a life of them.

As I discussed this scenario with my very good friend, it dawned on me even if the idea was well constructed and thought-out (which at this point it wasn't) there would be resistance. Leave Toronto for New Brunswick? One of the world's great cosmopolitan cities for…the woods? Culture for wilderness? Opportunity for survival? Ideas, innovation, creativity, endless opportunity, growth and invention for 'Bud Light,' arrested development, hunting/gathering and a culture of defeat?

(The 'cough' esteemed 'cough' Prime Minister of the country labeled the entire East Coast of Canada as having a culture of defeat in one of his more noteworthy speeches about the area.)

He made a strong case. Toronto was a world-class city. (Just ask anyone who lived there!) It had theatre, film, sports and every kind of entertainment imaginable.

"Look, this is a good city but, c'mon, all the things I do here I can do in New Brunswick."

Pierre guffawed. My back got up.

"Oh please. Do you really think your kid is going to get half the education in the bush like he would here?"

"Moncton is a nice city I'll have you know…"

"Moncton, so it has a name now."

"Yeah, we want our son to go to French school."

"Of course. French will come in handy after the Chinese take over the world!!!"

We tried to make light, but humour has a best before date on how long it can hold the true emotions.

"Touché. So tell me, when WAS the last time you went to a hockey game?"

"The Leafs, I don't go to the Leafs. Even with free tickets it still costs a hundred bucks!!"

"Exactly. There I'll actually be able to afford to go to the game, and take the family."

"True, but its only junior hockey."

"Even better, nothing like seeing a bunch of testosterone-fuelled teenagers kicking the shit out of each other."

A shared laugh, a little more genuine but still a little hollow.

"I could never do it."

"I know YOU couldn't, but we're talking about me."

"I could only go to a bigger city like New York. Here I live right on top of my next-door neighbor and I don't have to have anything to do with them. That's just the way I like it. I can get everything I want on Roncesvalles. Hardware store, coffee, beer, pierogies….I bet'cha can't just get that at any old corner place in Monkeytown!"

"Nope, but you can get lobster and all the poutine you can handle. Real Acadian Poutine, not the fake Quebecois shit!"

We settled into an uncomfortable silence. What I failed to mention in the conversation, beyond the comparative merits and demerits of each locale, was I'd really grown sick of the incessant voice in my own head. The voice that was always fed up and objectionable to this career situation but who never actually got up the balls to go ahead and DO something about it. For as much as I whined about wanting to get out of the industry, I was really a mouse in the choir. The fact was almost ALL of us held the business in the affirmative love/hate relationship and no matter whether it was busy and eating us up or slow and doing the same, we were never happy.

For most of us the problem ceased to be what the industry was and what it represented: the death of dreams. Except for the hardcore few who either stumbled into the business or had a family tradition, most behind-the-scenes technicians strode wide-eyed into show business with the full intention of becoming the story and film-making gurus of their generation. But it didn't quite work out that way. Somehow, someway those dreams and that inspiration didn't materialize but the next best thing did: the chance to work on and be a part of the machine that created those dreams in the first place.

There were always occasions when an ultra-serene moment with a movie start or starlet had you believing what a cool and interesting job you had. But the fact remained you were living in the shadow of what you wanted to be. And in the space of those long hours spent idling away while working on someone else's film, you had all the time in the world to think about why it turned out that way.

Everyone had an excuse. Everyone had a great idea for a film that was never able to materialize. And once upon a time, we all had the gumption to bring up our amazing ideas to those who could make it happen. I was no different. And in the shadow of our great cultural overbears I could find solace in the hearts and minds of others who'd had similar dreams and shoddy outcomes. It was one large pity pot and I could only hear myself bemoan my lot for so long. Yet in taking back the gauntlet and making the determination this would not be my fate, was I not exposing those close friends and colleague's who were somehow happy in their misery?

****

As in other scenarios dealing with bureaucrats, it wasn't long before the hope fed to us from our community liaison officer vanished. He'd moved on to greener pastures. "Out of the field completely," I was told by the desk clerk.

Surveillance had been conducted on our drug-dealing neighbor, but nothing untoward, illegal, or otherwise worth bothering about was uncovered. And just like that the file was closed. We'd lost the one link to curtailing some of the escalating criminal activity that could leave collateral damage. As a couple we'd tolerated the situation and joked about possible outcomes. Being a new father who was now rendered impotent by the system was the last straw. Where once I'd advocated for the underdog and strongly believed that no matter how hard the addiction, every life was worth saving, my base instinct to protect my family had kicked into overdrive. Values I'd once deemed important were dumped to the curb.

"I want them out. I want them gone. I don't care if they were the first fucking people on the moon."

"Calm down, take it easy," Sylvie tried to assuage.

"No, she's skulking around, hustling and I'm just supposed to sit here and pretend it's not happening. Are you crazy? Y'know what, they've gotta sleep sometime don't they? Even junkie's need rest. I can cut the power off to the shed. Maybe when I'm driving home some night I can swing over to the wrong side of the road and take her out...."

Even in my saner moments the fire and then the stabbing drove home the point the fate of our neighbors wasn't good. An ill-gotten end was what lay in wait: either by their own hand or someone else's.

With Dustin now approaching his first birthday and no one in the upper echelon's of community willing to take action, the affection for our home was quickly vanishing.

With each wailing siren and howling domestic issue the peace and solitude of our vacant lot on the Richibucto River in New Brunswick was looking more appealing: The gently retreating tide exposing hidden sand dunes. The haunting call of a solitary loon. A bald eagle that soars and in whose shadow lesser creatures scatter.

Even the more ferocious times, like camping in a tent trailer when the tail end of hurricane Rita came whipping up the Bay of Fundy and had us feeling like a plastic bag in a car wash, were met with wide-eyed nostalgia. Because when the winds died and the skies parted, the most stunning full-figure rainbow I'd ever seen kissed the horizon and arrested our spirit.

Or maybe it was just because it was ours. Not something we were allowed to use in partnership with the bank, but ours lock, stock and barrel. And with no one quite sure how the housing crisis in the mighty United States would filter its way into our safe Toronto real estate investment perhaps it was looking like a good time to cash out after all.

But still, how could we do it? A full-sized house was too expensive to build from scratch. A camper trailer, while on the surface might be cheap, would still require a septic system, a well and electrical hook-up. A Bunkie was a possibility for a time. An easy way to make use of a structure we already had. For two people, while extremely claustrophobic, it was possible. With an infant the idea was profane. How could we construct something reasonably priced, efficient and environmentally friendly?

Then Sylvie remembered the yurt.

It was on her screen before I knew it.

"There. In Algonquin Park. We were supposed to stay in them for our winter photography expedition. They were something like twelve feet across."

"Huh. You were going to stay in them during the winter?"

"Apparently there's a wood stove and they can get quite warm."

"They. Are their others'?"

"Here, I'll Google it."

A vast array of examples, sizes, decoration ideas and historical information met our computer screen. "Hey look, you can buy them, they're a kit."

"Yurts in Alaska, Alberta, Montana...."

"Russia, Mongolia."

"I guess if they stand up in those climates, New Brunswick should be a piece of cake."

We looked at one another with the same mischievous grin. Our idea had been answered.

Before we could make an actual commitment, it was imperative we visit a real, living, functioning yurt. We managed to turn a family vacation to Ottawa into live research for the idea.

****

As the gravel slowly crunched under our car wheels I peered out from under the windshield. From the outside, though the round and smooth walls were unique, the structure was hardly inspiring.

"Wow, this is amazing…" Sylvie declared as she got out of the van.

I did not duplicate her gusto.

To be a barometer of our enthusiasm we invited our good friends to share their opinion.

I touched the fabric of the wall and marveled at the roof. Vinyl. 'I'm going to live in a fucking tent,' I thought to myself.

Jenn and Brad (the artist and the policeman) were quick to see the essence of the feng-shui of living in a round structure.

"How are you going to discipline Dustin, you can't tell him to go and stand in a corner," Brad snickered.

"And here I was hoping for a little constructive criticism…"

"Just trying to not point out the obvious."

"Oh?"

"That you're going to live in a fucking tent!" Jen chimed in not minding the tender ears of her daughter Sandra.

"Thanks," I muttered before following Sylvie inside.

As we stepped inside, the lattice walls gave way to log rafters that called your attention up to the round, domed hole in the middle of the roof. I don't know how, but the structure, despite being crammed full of antiques, had a way of feeling expansive yet cozy.

"It's great Jase, even bigger than I imagined." Sylvie was already committed: Hook, line and sinker. It didn't matter about other pesky practical matters like heat, hydro and water. It was a beautiful open space, a blank canvas and another venue for her to showcase her French flare. As I took up a conversation with the dealer on real matters, Sylvie was busy fulfilling a childhood fantasy.

"Oooh," she said out loud, "we could make it into a loft. Y'know Jase, ever since 'Flashdance' I've always wanted to live in a loft...."

'Right,' I thought to myself, 'and a farmhouse, and a Victorian, a boathouse, a lighthouse, oh, did I forget a church...'

But I was locked in my own dialogue trying to discern the nuts and bolts of the thing.

"How about wind, snow, y'know WEATHER?"

"Well, it's a round structure so you don't really have to worry about the wind catching on a corner of the yurt, it will just go around it. We also have the engineer's rating for snow loads. It's got a good enough pitch and with the vinyl, the snow will just slide off..."

Beside me, Brad managed another snicker.

"Okay, Sandra is freaking out, Brad we gotta go. Guys, love the yurt, see you at the house," and like a flash our barometer exploded out the door. Sylvie didn't miss a beat.

"Oh hun, is that a king sized bed? Could we fit a full-sized bedroom in here?"

"You can do anything you want. We've seen them with a loft. It's an open space that is only limited by your imagination..."

Sylvie beamed from ear-to-ear; they'd struck the chord of gratification my wife was only too happy to expose. I could envision a *Far Side* comic in my head: A woman on her back, hands and feet curled up like a dog as her tongue wagged with a blissful faraway look in her eyes. The caption reads: "The holy grail of sales. If she has a blank check you can sell her the horse she rode in on..."

My eyes rolled. Thankfully we didn't have access to quick cash right that instant.

"Alright, how do you attach a mast, how do you get your electricity hooked up. What about heat?"

"Well again, because it's a round structure, the heat doesn't get lost in the corners. And what's really cool about it is the insulation, while not much, at first, is meant to reflect back whatever heat you're generating. It's not a big R-value, but that's not the point. In traditionally built houses the insulation acts to keep the cold air out, it does nothing to enhance the heat you create…"

And now I was on the fishhook. Hearing Sylvie being so enthusiastic my guard and the need to remain rational had eroded and my mind could find no more questions on the potential flaws of the structure. Like, hey, if it reflects heat so well, how does it behave when the mercury climbs into the upper echelons of a desert summer?

"Just remember, the product is coming from BC, you need to give us enough notice to order it so the yurt arrives in time."

****

With Dustin sleeping in the back, the drive back to Toronto was noticeably quiet. Normally Sylvie was so stoked from inspiration I could barely get in a few words edge-wise. It was some time before the silence was broken. Evidently she was thinking the same thing I was:

"If we do this, our parents are going to think we're crazy…"

"Parents, family, friends, work-colleagues, neighbors…"

"Don't tell your family about it right away huh? We haven't decided anything. We haven't done anything. They're going to think I've got you under my witchy spell again. Like I make you do these crazy things…"

"They don't say that. I've been doing crazy things since a lot longer than I've been with you."

"C'mon, you remember the look on your Dad's face when you told them we were going to Vietnam and Thailand."

"Yeah, I know, they sounded encouraging but…"

"But I can still hear Jerry, 'what, why would you want to travel when anything you want to see you can see in Southern Ontario.…"

"Yeah, yeah, I know. But Jerry was a trucker. He spent half his life on the road, I can understand why he doesn't want to range too far from home now."

"Still, I think we should tell your mom first. Break the idea to them slowly."

"What, that we're building a yurt or we're going to move to New Brunswick?"

"Both, and that I'm taking their grandson away from them."

"Ouch, that's harsh, they don't think that, they'll understand."

"They'll understand, sure, but it won't make them like the idea any more."

2

Backwards Jason

Either they'd become accustomed to my bouts of madness over the years or they'd anticipated a move of some kind was imminent. When the time came to break the news to my family we were going to move to New Brunswick it wasn't the reaction I was expecting. I'd gone over the merits of what we were doing and why we were doing it. I'd practically broken down the entire situation into a spreadsheet. I rehearsed, I visualized, and I practiced breathing techniques. In short, I did everything humanly possible to be able to handle what I thought for sure was going to be an adverse reaction to our plans.

None of it was necessary.

"We kind of figured you might be moving," my mom said.

We sat in the quiet afternoon of a Canadian Thanksgiving deep in the heart of farm country. Sitting on the back patio of their Harriston home, a mere two-hour drive north of Toronto, I held my cheat sheet and took a deep breath. The stale muster of cow manure tickled my nose, diverting my concentration. Inside, my dad hauled in the scraps from our meal while preparing the supplementary course to the main: dessert. Dustin and Sylvie napped while I broke the news to my mother.

My mom wasn't taken aback, offended or otherwise upset by the move. This wasn't in any of the carefully planned skirmishes of my flight simulator. It was my turn to be flushed and surprised. Since it was going so well, I thought it best to press the attack for that element of shock and awe I was mining.

"And we're going to build a yurt."

"A what!?!" my Dad said as he stepped through the door. Now I'd gotten their attention. This was the fun I'd prepared myself for.

"It's a round canvas structure."

"Okay," they said together, their voices subtle. I'd baited them, only, canny as they were, the true, raw reaction I felt for sure existed wasn't yet uncovered. As much as it comforted me to know they were in support of whatever we decided to do, I could sense an unspoken reservation that needed unearthing. As Sylvie and I were in the giddy stages where the idea had no reality with which to bind it, no adversity of opinion yet existed. As much as I was expecting the familiar skepticism that has accompanied some earlier, youthful, folly stricken plans and projects since they didn't know anything about a yurt they remained silent until they did. It was an unexpected development, but a happy problem to have.

Instead, the concept of the yurt brought about intrigue. What does a round canvas structure look like?

Retreating to the computer, images for my mother to see and technical specs for father quickly shared the screen.

"Well, that's different," Jan said.

"It looks like a teepee!" Jerry exclaimed.

"No, not exactly, but kind'a. I guess the idea originated in Mongolia where the nomadic peoples would use these structures to live in while tending to their flock"

"I see. I still say it's a teepee," Jerry insisted.

"A teepee is just an upside down cone. The yurt we're getting has about seven foot high exterior walls and then the circular cone is the roof."

Mom cocked her head as she studied the wall structure.

"Okay, so, what's this, they just threw a bunch of sticks together and tied a bed sheet around it? That's like something your dear departed Aunt Dorothy would have built."

"I know, it kind'a looks like it doesn't it? I guess the nomads, because they tended to sheep, would harvest the wool to make quilts and such, would hang the finished product inside the yurt for both insulation and style."

"Will you too?"

"Uh, no, c'mon, Sylvie's all over the inside, whatever she's up to I guess I'll find out during the unveiling."

We all snickered. Sylvie was nothing if not entirely intimidating when it came to staking territory about decorating the yurt. We all knew better than to venture wise into her realm.

"Yeah, and so, to make the yurt portable, the frame is made of lattice walls that they just fold down, roll up and cart to wherever they're going next."

"Lattice walls!?"

"Yup, lattice. Now, mind you the one we're getting has snow studs around the outside."

"You'd better with where you're building. I hear they get a bit of snow out there."

"So I've been told. In New Brunswick they call it white gold because of how much snowmobiling and winter activities you can do. We'll see. But with the pitch and the outside being vinyl the snow should just slide off."

"Vinyl!?! Whoa now. If the outside is vinyl, what the hell is keeping this thing warm?"

"It has an r-foil insulation. It's supposed to reflect back whatever heat you generate."

I could see the tone change in my father's face. The skepticism had returned. The wheels turned as he computed how he would do things and how different they would be, but to both of our surprises, he swallowed alter ego Jerry and let sleeping dogs lie.

"I hope you didn't just order this off the Internet."

"Actually, we went to see one up in Ottawa a couple of weeks ago and I've gotta say, it was pretty cool…" I said.

"I'll bet," my Dad chimed and shook his body like a chill came over him.

"Not like that you knucklehead. There's something about the space. I can't quite put my finger on it. It was roomy yet cozy at the same time. There's a lightness to it."

As more pictures poured over the screen from different settings around the world, the curiosity factor still gripped them.

"Now what made you decide you wanted to do this instead of say, a regular cottage?"

"We could have done a camper trailer. We thought about turning the little 8'x12' shed that's already there into a Bunkie…thought about a log home…a cottage…a garage with a loft…should I go on?"

They both nodded their heads.

"Are you going to live in that?" they asked.

"For a time. Just until we get settled. After we build it then we'll come back to Toronto, work for the summer and sell the house in the fall."

"So how does it come?"

"It comes in a crate. You have to build the floor, but everything else, the walls, the insulation, the rafters, dome, lattice, comes with the package."

"How long d'ya think it's gonna take to build?"

"They said on the website and in the brochure's that it should take three people about two days to build the large yurt."

"I see…."

"Do you have any idea what you're going to build it on?"

"Probably wood."

"Yeah, I know smart-ass, but are you putting in a foundation? Are you building cement piers?"

"I haven't thought about it. I don't know what the building process is. From some of the people I've been talking to I can't start anywhere until I get a septic system. Then I can get a building permit."

"Have you started to look into that?"

"A little bit. I've been doing some of my own research and I think I can get away with a grey water system and a composting toilet. That way I can be more environmentally sound while also saving myself a few bucks. That's my goal."

"A grey water system?" my father asked. My mom could sense the deep recesses of a debate and two constantly diverging opinions about to clash. Seeing it hundreds of times before she took it as her cue to leave.

"I've been researching grey water systems. They're not quite as common but this way you don't have to put the pipes as deep into the ground. After all you're not putting any solid effluent into the earth. The black water goes into the composting toilet and all of your grey water can just filter away naturally."

"And what does the province say about that?"

"I don't know."

"I think I'd be checking that first before I made any decisions."

"I can't see it being a problem. It's New Brunswick. You can probably do whatever you want."

"No, well I can."

"Oh, do tell? I've done the research and they're perfectly legitimate. Your shit turns into compost that you can put into your flower garden. They don't recommend putting it into any garden where you'll eat the food. And the grey water, well, you don't have to put the pipes down as far, or build the ground up as much because there's no poop in it."

"I see. Well, you do what you want, but I think you'd be better off putting in a proper septic system and that way you know you'll never have a problem. Like, how is this going to work in the winter? If the pipes aren't in the ground too far aren't they going to freeze? Have you thought about that? Be an awful shame to put all that work into the yurt only to have the toilet backflow…"

"There would be no toilet."

"Or, or, the sink or the washing machine. Be terrible to want that old water to drain out of the tub and it just sits there. That would work great wouldn't it."

I don't know what frustrated me more, the fact I might be wrong or my old man might be right. As much as an intense debate was a common form of communication, no matter how futile or inconsequential the topic there was always a little something more at test. Like an old silver back eagerly accepting the challenger into his tribe to continue to test his ability to be dominant, my father and I constantly sparred.

Though there was mutual respect and occasional bouts of wisdom shared in our banter, there seemed to be an unspoken component festering below the surface. You know it's there because of the sifted ground that indents into the surface. The quiet whisper through the grass suggests that while, on the outside, it might appear safe, a quantum shift in the energy below the surface could trigger a massive earthquake. Among our challenges to harmony, my Dad and I were both of similar personality and temperament.

But perhaps the most distinct challenge we both faced was holding onto our thoughts and beliefs until they had a venue to be shared.

Sylvie, ever so observant to my habits and behaviours, could almost see a volatile thought process based on my body language. "You're having a conversation in you're head again," she started to tell me.

Cut from the same cloth, if my Dad were feeling a particularly strong emotion his body wouldn't rest until the thought was sent out into the world and he found the evidence to confirm his beliefs. He could take up a seemingly innocent conversation with a stranger and somehow turn it into a passionate political platform. (A terribly restless man, I think he's rationed an excess of daily physical energy that, if not expunged, backs up into his brain.)

But not always was the deep emotion that crafted the thought properly harvested.

Of course, I didn't help matters much when I sought their counsel in the incubation part of my planning.

The incubation aspect of planning is the brainstorming of any old kooky idea that may (or most likely MAY NOT) be utilized in the overall project. Unfortunately for me, many of my kooky ideas often meant a great deal of time and effort explored into their feasibility when anyone with half a brain would realize long before I did how stupid the idea really was. Fond of research, discovery and finding new ways of looking at things, the process of exploration was a reward unto itself. It was a gauntlet thrown into the accepted (i.e. common) methods of doing things.

And that gauntlet was borne of a necessity that saw a great deal of opportunity in what others might throw away. Sometimes those opportunities were seized on and the effort was worthwhile.

****

In an older frontier of Toronto an abandoned gaggle of Victorian era factory buildings were constantly used as various locations in the film industry. The Gooderham and Worts Distillery District has been cast in films as far ranging as *X-Men* to *Chicago* and plenty of forgettable straight to DVD movies in between. In the early 2000s, when a developer optioned the area for gentrification, several projects aimed at integrating the area with shops, living spaces and artists' lofts transformed the district overnight. No longer were the scores of tractor-trailers and movies run amuck allowed to monopolize this now valuable piece of real estate.

In the rush to complete the various stages of transformation, some valuable resources were quickly discarded in the renovations. Speaking with a work acquaintance about tools and other things, it was mentioned that a great deal of material could be had, literally, for the taking.

"Like what, what are we talking about here?" I asked Nikki.

"I grabbed a bunch of floor joists and put them into my truck. I don't know what I'm going to do with them just yet, but they're about fourteen feet long, straight,' Nikki replied.

"But what would I do with it?"

Up until this point my woodworking hobby had included an entertainment centre made from used plywood from the stage of *Chicago* and a rolling coffee table. No intricate carvings or ornate structures: just basic, square (mostly) functional furniture that was proof (to myself) that my downtime wasn't a complete waste.

I was slowly mastering some basic carpentry skills and looking to expand my repertoire. Not only did my scrounging provide me with free materials, I could invest in the tools to do the job with a clean conscience. And with each completed project under my belt, I gained more confidence to try my hand at bigger and more elaborate projects.

"What the fuck are you going to do with those?" Sylvie asked me when I carted my truck full of lumber into the shed.

As I deposited the last piece onto the floor with a heavy thud, billows of dust escaped into the air. Her nose scrunched.

"Never you mind. I've got an idea," I retorted quickly. We paused and stared at one another. She'd been through enough of these projects to know when to ask questions and when not. I wanted to keep her in suspense, but she didn't buy it. Her frustration quickly turned to fear and I didn't understand why.

Her right leg shot up to protect herself and her arms flapped like she was about to take flight.

Just as she was about to compose herself and explain the weird spasm a shiver went up my spine. From the innards of the 150-year-old wood a mammoth spider latched itself to my shoulder. Sylvie covered up while I flicked it away onto the floor.

Before I had a chance to stomp on it and save the life of my poor frightened wife, it shrugged back under the pile of lumber.

"You are not bringing THAT 'wood' into this house!" Sylvie thundered.

I turned the floor joist over in my hand and quickly appreciated her apprehension. Years of dust and sediment had deposited itself on the wood. A layer of soot, literally, harbored whatever type of wood remained intact underneath. The color was so rich it looked bluish black.

"Well no, of course it's not coming in like this, I'm not that stupid.

I've gotta plane it and sand it…" I said.

"You mean you've gotta buy more tools!?" she rebuffed.

"Well, yeahhhh."

She shook her head about to turn away.

"Lookit Hamilton, you're the one who's always complaining about money."

"Well you tell me then, how expensive would it be for us to go out and buy a new dining room table!"

There was no response.

"I picked all this wood up for free, do you know how expensive it would be if we bought the table new or paid for the new lumber to do it. Five times as expensive as buying the tools and working with what I have here. I've got time on my hands, this will keep me busy and I can always sell the tools if we need the money."

"You're making a dining room table….out of this!?!"

At that she brushed the lumber with her finger. A thick cake of grime wrinkled into her skin.

"You'll see, once I get it planed down…."

"You'd better be right because wouldn't it suck to buy all the tools and still have to buy the table…"

A last dig. I ignored her roundhouse. She followed up the combination.

"Just don't do it half-assed. Do it right!"

****

As I tore into the dining room table project and the layers bore back years of use, the wood came alive. The original thickness of the floor joist was a full two inches of wood. Punching the material through the planer, clouds of grime and soot filled the air. When the protective layer was breached, the heart of the wood revealed its' true story. So excited by the revelation, I took a smaller piece into the house to share the discovery.

"You do this every time. You're not even finished yet and you're dragging the wood into the house."

She barred me at the door, denying me entrance with the raw material.

"You've gotta check this out. Come here. Take a whiff of this."

Arms crossed, the body language of abject disbelief. My infectious grin tore through her defenses. She gave in and leaned over oh, so slightly. Her nostril barely shrugged. Without getting close her head jerked back immediately.

"Holy shit!" she said before digging in. This time she grabbed the wood and pulled it to her nose.

"It smells like whiskey!"

"Sure does. Try and get that from any old table you buy at Pottery Barn!"

Ka-Bam!

"Oh Ham," she said as she looked at the piece, now rich and flavorful. A hint of red blended with the creamy yellow of most of the texture. Sylvie pulled the wood from my hand and hauled it into the dining room. She laid it on top of the old, round, dining room table with its neat perfections. A little self-conscious I started to pick at a protruding rotting nail sticking out the side.

"I don't know if I'm going to putty in some of the nail holes…and some of the boards aren't exactly perfect…" I offered.

"Oh no," Sylvie admonished, "You can't do that! Leave it. Well, you know what I mean. Make it neat, don't let us get stabbed on a nail." She paused to laugh.

The finished project became a featured aspect of our home. Fully six feet long and nearly four feet wide with nooks, crannies and bumps the deep chocolate brown table was a crowning achievement in my hobby shop repertoire.

The confidence in my growing abilities hasn't always produced banner results. It's infectious to think you can turn any old piece of scrap into a functional, unique and artistic piece of your life. You end up driving by dumpsters for a pause as though at a shopping boutique, forever on the look out for that unique collection of wood your hands can magically manipulate. You imagine value in some of the most mundane objects simply because of past success. And for every "brilliant, one of a kind always to be talked about by new guests dining room table," there's a gigantic blunder like a massive skeleton in your closet.

Just when you think your hands can turn lead into gold and win fans out of the most ardent skeptics, you make a colossal misjudgment that calls into question your ability to judge the difference between brilliant art and garbage.

At or about the same time I forged my efforts into the dining room table, the same luxury of time I had to commit to that project meant I was once again out of work. When the film industry did pick up again the days were few, sparse and short. Even though I was 'earning' I certainly wasn't filling in the hole created by the several months of sporadic income.

We always tried to make the most of our time and Sylvie and I attempted to remain as active as possible. With the weather a little cooler in the fall of the year it was the perfect temperature to be active outdoors. Bike riding was on the agenda except Sylvie did not have a ride.

Mentioning this conundrum to a colleague at work the forces of attraction quickly went to action. Steve, a fifty-something laborer with years of hard living in his face but the heart of a saint caught wind of the situation and offered to help.

You always do your best to not reserve too much judgment on people, but the honest truth is we all do it. When we meet people we analyze, categorize and try to figure out a little bit about them based on how they act, dress and look. In a civilized society this is frowned upon because it seems to bestow a certain caste or reinforce racism and stereotype. True in many respects.

If you want to remain committed to whatever determination you make of someone even if they're the most kind-hearted and warm person you know you will overlook those qualities for the ones that reinforce your ardent beliefs. The fact is that 'judgment' of an individual is a survival instinct in our species that has, as yet, not evolved out of us.

When we encounter strangers we can discern a great deal about them to determine whether or not their relationship with us will aid us or endanger us. Friend or foe. Our intricate human nature has taken that basic survival element and attached all sorts of footnotes and appendages about race, culture and socio-economic status. Fun times.

Some work colleagues you form close bonds with and others remain friendly and cordial, but not close. I'd known Steve a short while and some of my earlier assertions about him were spot-on. He could be gruff and short. Irascible at times (but aren't we all). How that translated in the 'real' world was embedded in the wrinkles in his face.

"Hey Jason," Steve went on, "if your wife's looking for a bike I can help you out."

"Oh really," I said, quickly discarding whatever skepticism remained in my head. The scent of a 'deal' was in the air and any previous conclusions were wiped from the slate.

"Yeah, I've got a nice mountain bike she can have if she wants…."

"Sure," I said without thinking, "I'll take a look at it."

The new thinking that has crept up in recent years, inspired by the book 'The Secret' and other media related to the 'Law of Attraction' suggests that when you want something if you 'put it out there' it will come back to you. In the overarching realm of the 'universe' that works on those thoughts your request will be answered. To those whose lives evolve organically and seem to only have opportunities magically appear before them so crystal clear as to practically be carted off on a chariot into their kingdom, this might be the case. Who could argue? For those of us who want to believe but have to somehow make the 'results' shoehorn into the dream, there is not the wholehearted embrace of this phenomenon. In fact, in the fine print of that law what form that request takes is often open to interpretation.

I could sense I'd made a mistake long before we got into my truck and drove over to his place. However, being a terrible liar and even poorer at theatrics to cover up a bad lie, having said yes there was no way I could back out of the arrangement. Out of sheer purpose of wanting to do one human being a favor Steve offered his help to secure my wife a bike. Only in hammering out the logistics of what time and where did I even begin to fathom the scope of what I'd set in motion.

"Okay Steve," I said, "what time should we rendezvous over this bike?"

"We're finishing at the same time, why don't you give me a ride back to my place and we can get the bike there…"

The fact he himself trusted public transit over this very fine work of self-generated commuting should have been yet another alarm bell to find any means necessary to abort the mission. But having put this moment into gear to follow its logical, tragic, conclusion, like most racing fans who are really only in it for the crashes, I too was quite curious as to how the scenario was going to play itself out.

On the way over was the time to turn into an informed consumer and quiz him about the merchandise.

"Where do you live Steve?"

Oh, I live right beside Regent Park"

I cringed. Regent Park was the brainchild of some astute urban planners whose inspiration was an experiment in social housing. On the downtown east side of Toronto, sixty-nine acres of slum living were turned over to community housing for redevelopment in 1949.

Perhaps in anticipation of the collective consciousness of 60s thinking, the patterned grid-work of streets and arterial roads was removed and replaced somewhat haphazardly by large communal structures that isolated itself from the rest of the city. From the large streets that border it on the north and south, Regent Park looks like a fortress against intrusion. Perhaps the thinking was that by forcing the poor to live in close proximity to one another without the annoyance of a world beyond their homestead, a 'back to the land' mentality might evolve in the heart of the city. Instead, the lack of passageway through the project created a haven for drug dealers and gangs. The result of the experiment was worse conditions and more crime than before the redevelopment.

Steve sensed my apprehension and assuaged my fears.

"Oh, don't worry about it. It's really not as bad as everyone makes it out to be."

"You haven't seen any problems, stabbings, shootings, etcetera…"

"Probably no more than occurs in any other part of Toronto."

"Yeah, I suppose you're right. We've had our own problems…"

"It's a city, it doesn't matter where you live."

"Maybe, but some areas are more susceptible than others."

"Yeah, but these drug dealers in the Park are fucking pussies."

"Oh."

"Well that's how I got your wife's bike."

"Come again?"

"I get a different bike pretty much every week."

"How is this now?"

"Well I can watch them from my window, y'see…"

Steve looked to see if I was still following along. I nodded my head, the apprehension replaced with a bewildered confusion one might show someone who confidently held a gas can just before opening the spout and spewing the liquid onto a roaring bonfire.

"And what I like to do is wait until I see them pull up on their bikes and drop them on the yard. I'll watch them with their little grocery bags looking here and there as they walk up the steps to the row house apartments."

"Uh huh."

"And I know they're doing a deal. That's how they get around Regent Park. A car won't get you anywhere. Y'see only the dealers ride bikes."

"Alright," I was aware of where this story was headed, but not quite sure if I wanted my suspicions confirmed.

"So when they're inside doing their deal I'll stroll on over and help myself to their bike.…"

I gulped.

"I mean, hell, it's no big deal because they're fucking stolen anyway."

And Steve let out a curdled laughter that was arrested by a rasp, a grimace and then a heavy smoker's cough. As he was already gambling with his health with his smoking habit, I didn't see the need to point out to him it wasn't the legality of what he was doing that was worrying me.

"And they never come back for them because they just assume another dealer took it so they go and steal another one."

"The cycle of life as it were."

Concluding the product description with the salesman, I was now more eager than ever to get my hot product into my truck as quickly as possible and beat a hasty retreat home. I didn't really care what the bike ended up looking like. Once Sylvie heard the whole story she'd be terrified of being spotted on a desolate trail deep in the heart of Rosedale by a vengeful Regent Park drug dealer and have to flee for her life. She had that way about her. That way of taking a perfectly innocent tale of a noble Robin Hood striking a blow for the common man against the lawlessness of the Regent Park drug trade by interrupting their drug transportation system and returning the bikes to law-abiding citizens too cash-strapped to be able to afford to buy their own and making it up into something else.

When I lifted the bike out of the back of my truck her words said it all:

"You'd better have gotten it for free!"

A dark, shadowy thing whose original color had been camouflaged in several layers of black paint, its time of service was evident in the dents, scratches, scrapes and unkempt appearance of the whole machine.

As I leaned it against the wood retaining wall at the front of our house, Sylvie retreated two steps backward as if it were about to lash out at her.

"It's in pretty good shape. I could paint it. I could replace the seat," I offered, plucking at the seat that vomited stuffing every which way.

"Look, Jase, I know you meant well and I know we don't have a lot of extra money right now, but when I say I want a bike, I mean something with bright colors, no grime or soot or whatever else is living on this thing. And a seat that won't spear my ass! Y'know, something pretty 'cuz I'm pretty."

I nodded.

"Okay, fair enough."

"Where on earth did you get this!?"

"A guy I work with gave it to me."

"Gave it to you?"

I recounted the story as accurately as I could, hoping the spirited nobility of the perpetrator might make her see this acquisition in something of a new light.

"He lives near Regent Park and when he sees drug dealers drop them down to go and do their business he scoops in and steals them back. Pretty noble don't you th...."

"You got me a CRACK WHORE BIKE!!!"

And that blunder has been on my resume ever since. So much so that, of course, Sylvie told her mom who told her dad and the original, noble deed being done by my co-worker was completely lost in translation. It might be an Acadian thing, it might be an Irish thing, whatever cultural tree branch she was hanging her hat on at that moment a little exaggeration was in her make-up.

What it meant was that as we set out to make our plans to construct our vision, I couldn't always be trusted to make clear and rational decisions on certain matters.

In my mind, we had an abundance of time and I deemed it worthwhile to commit some effort to ideas that might save us some money in the long run. And in the early planning stages we were also unsure as to what our overall budget was going to look like. In theory the money we were going to use to build the yurt was going to come from the sale of our Toronto home.

I say theory because: a) until the house was sold we had no real idea of how much equity was available: b) we had already borrowed against some of that equity on home improvements to get the house ready for the market and: x) the real estate market south of the border in America had tanked and it was still too early into the bursting of the bubble to determine whether or not our little semi-detached home on the main street of a dodgy neighborhood was still worth the price we paid for it.

Hence the idea of tearing down my brothers dilapidated barn, pilfering whatever useful material I could out if it, strapping it to a trailer and shipping it out to New Brunswick had some merit. At least it did in my eyes.

"You think you're gonna save some money shipping out used materials to build your yurt?"

"Look Dad, you're not hearing me. Listen for a change. I don't KNOW if it's cheaper. I have absolutely no idea. It could be more expensive. Let's just say, hypothetically, what do you think it would cost to say, rent a trailer from Dobson's and have you haul the material out for us?"

He squirmed a bit in his chair, perhaps he anticipated the request perhaps he didn't. Logistically it would be trouble for him. A full-time truck driver who finally found a posting close to home without extended trips to faraway places. He was just now beginning to reap the benefits: holidays, home for supper and weekends off. That extra time lent itself well to his never-ending roll call of moonlighting businesses: firewood cutting, lawn rolling, snow blowing, and, in recent years (mirroring my own hobby) carpentry. I think he even managed to find a few precious minutes in the week to spend with my mother.

Though I (fond as I was of leisure and relaxation) could not quite comprehend his litany of hobbies, I respected his time and the scope of his commitments would not allow him to easily schedule a few weeks to chase off into the wilds of New Brunswick to help his son build a yurt. (Incidentally, when he did take holidays it was mostly to pursue other work opportunities. Oh bliss!)

And yet, because my brother had inherited my aunt's farm a few years prior and my dad had been heavily involved during the renovations, he couldn't easily say 'no.' It was still an option, but I could read his face and knew he was calculating the checks and balances of being a fair parent. My brother Jeff had three kids and lived close to home. He repaired cars for a living and had the same deep obsession with money that ran throughout the Hamilton bloodline. Jeff was easy, the kids were close and their values, beliefs, hobbies, dreams and community all matched his own.

Had I been closer he undoubtedly would have helped me the same. But because I lived in the big city, worked a strange job and dreamed of penning novels and traveling the world…we didn't quite match. (Or so it appeared on the surface.) But none of that mattered. As he sat there pondering my request for some assistance though his immediate reaction was "this idea is insane it's like the gas cap debacle all over again" he managed to suppress his gut reaction.

It was quite impressive.

Imagine a sixty-year old man, (still in pretty good shape for his age) stepping out of his favorite comfortable chair and spontaneously contorting in the living room like he was trying out for 'Cirque du Soleil'….with his face. Jim Carrey could not reproduce such brilliance!

And then the rubber snapped back to formation, his eyes and mind returned from the far-off place from whence they'd traveled, and he managed to walk that delicate tight-rope of being as supportive as possible while allowing himself his own thoughts: my son is f#*!@g nuts!

"I tell you what, I'll look that up for ya," he said cheerfully before surprising both of us and continuing, "what you might find more economical, instead of Dobson's or hiring a trucking company, is maybe look up U-Haul and see if they're cheaper."

"U-Haul?"

Now it was my turn to be dubious. The whole point was to engage someone else to haul this material out to the coast, not yours truly.

"Don't they have a spotty safety record or something?"

"Trust me, so does Dobson's. You should see some of the shit they get me to haul around."

As we chuckled my dad moved into overtime. He was on a roll.

"Surely you could find a barn out there?"

"Yeah, I'd like to, I just don't know anyone that's the problem."

"Mmm."

Thoughtful. Pointed. The tables were turned and now I was scared. When he had focus of this magnitude it was usually because he had another inspiration that generally required a bucket of perspiration: Mine. Be it stacking, chopping or hauling wood, building fence posts, forking manure, or chucking hay, I could thank him for the perfectly strong back I now possessed.

As Sylvie and my mom turned the corner and saw us deep in deliberation Sylvie stopped dead in her tracks.

"Whoa, whoa, whoa, I don't like the look of this. Jerry, if you come out to help us there will be no, I repeat NO chainsaws within, around or anywhere near the vicinity of the yurt!"

(In addition to being something of a lumberjack in his spare time my dad has been known to do home renovations that feature the chainsaw as his tool of choice. Again, hard to shake off the resume.)

"Hey, wait a minute, I haven't done any renovating with the saw in this house," he defended.

With perfect timing my mother chimed, "YET!"

3

The Two Ministries

"I don't want to hear anymore about money!" Sylvie declared.

As I looked up her eyes hadn't left the screen. I stood up, stretching my back and neck.

"I know you want to say something, but why don't you just let it go for now," she continued not shooting me a sideways glance.

"Look, I'm trying to share my plans with you so you know what it is I'm doing. Don't you want to know what I'm doing?"

The long pause gave it away. She said nothing.

"Sorry hun, I'm trying to do my own thing here."

"Wait, what thing here!?!"

I hadn't taken the time to notice, but if I had, I would have seen by the scatters of paperwork strewn around the dining room table. The large flat surface, twenty-four square feet of it in the centre of our home, had become the nerve centre, the office and the general receiving area of any and all things yurt related.

Though we were trying our best to keep the area as tidy as possible, the paperwork was overwhelming.

"What is all this shit?" I asked and crumpled up a seemingly random pile of torn magazine pages in my hand.

I grabbed her attention.

"This SHIT is the vision for the yurt!" she bellowed.

"A goddamn pair of jeans draped over an old couch is your vision for the yurt. Hallelujah!"

"No, not the jeans." She snatched the page out of my hand.

"Well what then!?! I'm over here calling every goddamn dispatcher from here to Timbuktu trying to figure out WHAT we're going to put this thing on and all you're concerned with are the colors. I'm more concerned about actually, y'know, building it. Who gives a fuck what it's going to look like. How is it going to function? How is it going to be plumbed, wired? Are we going to have a bathroom, a kitchen? Have you thought about any of those things because it seems like there's a hell of a lot going on on my plate and all you have is a freakin' color wheel?"

"Okay Jase, you want me to care about how it's going to be built, fine. Call the stupid lumber place and just order the wood. Don't make it any harder than it has to be."

"But I don't know what's going to make the most sense. I just got a quote back from Kent Building Supply in Bouctouche and between the deck and the platform it's going to cost us almost $10,000 in just wood. Ten Grand. Don't you think it might make just a little bit of sense to see if we can get the wood for free and ship it out. Maybe we can save, I don't know, three or four grand."

"Okay, well what do you want me to do then 'cuz I don't know. All I know is if you're going to drive me nuts trying to figure it out then it just makes sense to buy the freakin' wood out there doesn't it? How are we going to save when it's probably cost you about a thousand dollars in long distance charges just to play with a bunch of numbers in your head?"

I hated it when she was right. I hated it when she could see through to a logic that was somehow blind to me.

"Look Jase, you know that that side of things is not my expertise. I don't know anything about shipping and systems and crap like that. You know me, build it so I can decorate it. I'll do the interior...."

I nodded.

"Speaking of, before we get any further, maybe we should think about the layout. I was thinking of the inside being like the spoke of a bicycle wheel. What do you think?"

"I like it," I said stiffly.

"Come over here," she curled her finger towards me.

The pages of things that had been strewn about the table suddenly came alive. The tear outs of seemingly random images were given a story and a context. With the visual aides woven together an emerging whole was constructed.

"What's this?" I said and picked up a tiny scrap of magazine.

"Oooh, I found that in the Costco catalogue. Don't you think a claw-foot bathtub would look amazing in the bathroom?"

She turned to look up at me and caught that faraway blank state that indicated my brain was taking her divine vision and complicating it…slightly.

"Geez, y'know my Dad just came across a couple of those at an auction sale. We don't need to get it from Costco, I can just tell him to keep his eyes out for something…."

"Uh, no."

Before my lower lip even had a chance to curl into a pout, she pressed her advantage.

"We're getting the one from Costco. I do share your passion for trying to use recycled material, but knowing your Dad he'll probably get a bathtub they use to clean goats or something. I know you both mean well, but I've already looked into it and you get the tub, the taps and they'll ship it anywhere free of charge. I'll get it shipped to Mom and Dad's in Bathurst..ha ha, Bath-hurst, get it?"

"But wouldn't it be great to have the real deal?"

"Yes it would, but it won't come with the taps, you'll have to glaze it to make it look new not to mention the cost of shipping something that weighs a ton all the way from Ontario to New Brunswick."

She had me, again.

"Y'know what," Sylvie continued, "I've got an idea."

From her stacks of scrap paper she reached under a pile. Shuffling around for a moment, careful not to disturb the contents or spill the pages she found what she was looking for.

"Here's what we're gonna do."

She folded the page in half before tearing the seam. She pulled out a Sharpie and wrote on each piece of paper before handing it to me. It read:

"Minister of Finance"

I chuckled, "Clever. What's your title?"

She flipped her page around: "Minister of Design"

"And," she continued to hold my attention, "all of the yurt stuff goes in here. We'll make separate folders for all of the information so we know what gets crossed off the list and what doesn't. This way we can both keep on track, not completely take over the living room and not drive each other insane while we plan this thing."

"Okay, that makes sense. Look, I've gathered a whole bunch of flyers and things over the years from those Green Living shows that maybe we can use too."

"I don't care what you use, understand, but the first thing you've got to do is actually, y'know go through those forests of information and do some editing. Make up your mind, pick something and go with it."

Though my portfolio was larger and with greater responsibility I was raked across the coals by the Minister of Design.

I stole off to the far reaches of some corner of the house on the hunt for a folder. Everything became a folder. Compartmentalized. I graduated from stacks of paper and inspirations randomly placed throughout my life to the old shoebox method to finally the folder.

When recall of a concept was needed I could almost instantly remember where the file was located and within that edited folder the ideas were available and user friendly.

In true government fashion, I accepted the challenge to claim space on the dining room table for my own ministry. Though the contents were modest, I plopped the paperwork down and spread things out to appear bigger than I was. Her portfolio may have a higher profile and involve more detail, but I would be damned if my less glamorous work would in any way be compromised.

"Hey, look at this," I said and unfurled a large brochure.

"What's that?"

"It's the brochure I got on composting toilets. I'd love to do a composting toilet."

"Uh, are they a lot of work?"

"I don't think so. In fact, I've asked around a little bit and apparently when you install one all you need to have is a grey water system."

"Okay, first you're talking about shipping, now you're talking about toilets and systems. Do we even know what the first step in the building process is?"

"Uh, yeah," I said with less than utmost confidence.

"Well, where do we start?"

"We ordered the yurt, that's a start."

"Yes, but beyond that."

"It starts with the septic system. After you get that figured out then you can get your building permit."

"Well, call me crazy, and I don't want to be the ministry that goes around and starts stepping on others' toes, but shouldn't you start with that?"

"Well, I have. I'm researching that."

"Research. Why does it always involve research? At the rate you're going you'll be able to build the yurt out of all these pamphlets and shit."

"Hey, hey, easy now, as Minister of Finance it's my job to maximize this budget…whatever it's going to be."

"Yeah, but my parents are going to be in town for Christmas and when we start talking about this they're gonna want to know what you're doing and how you're doing it. They don't want their daughter…no wait, they don't give a fuck about what happens to us tee hee…they don't want their GRANDSON stuck out in the woods somewhere with his ass swaying in the breeze."

****

THE TWO MINISTRIES

As though preparing for interrogation, Sylvie and I, in our capacity as Ministers, went over the paperwork we assembled to paint as clear a picture as possible of what it was we were going to build. She looked like an eager law student ready to graduate magna cum laude. Her attention to detail was immaculate, her recall exceptional. In the other corner, the Minister of Finance fell under the weight of his portfolio. Instead of delegating which task was most important and tackling it first, I chose to dabble in several areas and had yet to make determinations on anything. As usual, instead of following the linear path that was quite simple to follow in the construction of a dwelling, I veered in my own direction, much to the dismay of my partner.

As the arrival of Sylvie's parents for Christmas loomed on the horizon, it was evident our efforts to plan this endeavor would be closely scrutinized. Sylvie accepted the challenge of persuading her family with thorough preparation. Her tactic was to woo the jury with a simple, yet solid portfolio with great attention to detail. Window selection, kitchen inspirations, floor layout, appliance coordination, color choices, style scheme and the like.

As she adjusted her collar, closed her eyes and visualized the final deliberation, she was as confident as ever that her parents would be utterly transfixed by her work and forget everything she was doing would be housed in a giant tent. As the visualization ended, she took a sideways glance over in my direction. I inhabited the opposite end of the spectrum: The disheveled genius at work.

No focus, no attention to detail and seemingly no game plan. In short, it looked bleak. I didn't even have the confidence of my own partner, let alone feel certain I could sway the tough crowd that was about to come our way. But unbeknownst to her, I had a tactic up my sleeve that even she wasn't aware of. At the very least, because of the way our ministries had been dissected, I would not come under the careful microscope of Flo, Sylvie's mother. Instead, as we covered the grounds of our case, I would be assigned the task of convincing Fern, Sylvie's Dad, of the building process.

As the executives stepped through the door to examine the progress on the ground, they had their own ideas of what should be done and why. However, in a bit of strategic genius, they chose a battle plan that we were in no way prepared for.

****

The Appalachian range or 'uplift' stretches from the south of Georgia through the rest of the thirteen colonies and Maine before getting obscured in the neighbouring province of New Brunswick. Although this geography, which dips below the ocean in the Gulf of St. Lawrence before resurfacing on the western edge of the island of Newfoundland, is still sparsely populated, it was one of the first regions to be colonized by Europeans in North America. Principally, the French first settled the Canadian Maritime provinces to take advantage of the abundant marine life. (Legend has it the fish were so thick you could walk on them.)

However, in the years after its discovery in the early seventeenth century to the rise of a new country called 'Acadia' in the eighteenth, the population remained relatively small compared to the massive migration to the thirteen colonies directly south. With more favorable growing conditions and an eagerness to expand westward over the mountains, the thirteen colonies expanded rapidly until the French and English inevitably came into conflict over ownership of the New World.

That rivalry reached a boiling point in the mid seventeen hundred's before England gained the upper hand. Before winning the Seven Years War in 1759, that sparse Acadian rural population came under direct fire from the British who doubted their ability to remain neutral. In 1755, since the Acadians were in possession of the territory that led directly to the mouth of the St. Lawrence River and the greater French colony beyond in Quebec, the English forcibly expelled much of the population and dispersed its peoples throughout the thirteen colonies.

Some of the expelled perished, some traveled hundreds of miles from wherever they were deposited back to their homeland and others adopted their new homes. And some assimilated: This history still lives on in the rich Cajun dialect of the continued ancestry that inhabits Louisiana.

Back in New Brunswick, though the English triumphed in the war, the riches of that victory meant an increasing settlement into former Acadian territory. There was a catch: it was a tough sell to get Scottish, Irish and English settlers to till the modestly productive soil (with vast mosquito producing bogs) with the extremely long and harsh winters. (Especially when more productive soil and a better climate existed further south and west.)

Twenty or so years later, when war broke out again, this time between the independent thirteen states and the mother country, New Brunswick became a haven for those who wished to remain loyal to the crown. Those English speakers claimed the southwestern portion of the province for themselves while the French retained the north and east. Those two ancestries live on to this day with the ensuing two hundred and fifty-odd years of friction still a topical subject.

The population and immigration explosion that dominated the rest of North America was, more or less, lost on New Brunswick. Today it contains barely 700 000 souls spread out over 27 500 square miles in a land that's 80% covered by forest. A density of twenty seven people for every square mile. It's a fairly isolated outpost and most people live there for that very reason.

****

Sylvie's lineage is borne of that original French Acadian colony. Her family cluster is fixated at the Mid-Eastern edge of the province. The mighty Miramichi River, world renowned as having some of the best salmon fishing in North America, almost splits the province in half at latitude. The Mazerolle's live at the very eastern reach of the river where it meets the ocean. The port of call: Baie St. Anne also happens to be one of those places where the wayward Acadians found route after their long journey home from expulsion.

In the times I've visited, about the only serious industry outside of fishing and peat moss that I could discern was drinking and hunting. It's about a forty-five minute drive out of the bush to a smattering of towns that encompass Miramichi City where the hobbies extend to anything you can do with an engine, wheels and more drinking.

Before Dustin, when Sylvie's parents arrived from Bathurst (a town in the northern reaches of New Brunswick) for a spell of time, they had an agenda: spend some time with their daughter, take in a few sights and activities, and most importantly, SHOP. When you lived in a town of perhaps fifteen thousand souls in a province that wasn't much bigger, the pickings weren't that great. Options did not abound.

With Sylvie in Toronto the chance to go even further, to a much larger metropolis, with the spoils of selection, price and quantity, they seized the opportunity.

I thought (naively) with our son Dustin in the mix, that that might change. Alas, the only change was that it took a little longer to gather him up and his accoutrements to come along with us. And so for almost two full weeks at Christmas, there was hardly mention of the yurt and our plans for it.

Sylvie and I were dumbfounded. All the planning, all the preparation and it seemed as though they were hardly interested in the progress of the yurt. We were like a heavyweight boxer eager to get at his opponent only to have the delay tactic foisted upon us.

"What gives?" I said to her as we nestled in for the evening.

"I don't get it. Usually when it comes to decorating Flo's all over it. She hasn't said a peep."

"Fern's been quiet, no questions, no 'I wonder how dey do dat now?' no nothing. I think it's actually starting to tick me off a little bit."

"Hey, whoa, take it easy. I've told her on the phone. Don't worry, they're interested. I think maybe they're just afraid."

"Huh, afraid of what?"

Sylvie squirmed, "uh, afraid of you a little bit. They know how sensitive you can be and maybe they don't want to step on your toes…'

"Hold on there. I've been pretty good. I haven't lost my temper. I've been pretty calm."

"Yeah, but you haven't got anything done and I think it's starting to worry them."

"What do you mean I haven't gotten anything done? More importantly how would they know? That's a breach of Ministerial uh protocol…?

Sylvie rolled her eyes.

"Uh, I told them. They're my parents and their son-in-law is about to build a giant tent for his family to live in and he hasn't got fuck all sorted out yet."

"Well, doesn't that just go to show, the Minister of Design is showing up the Minister of Finance."

"Alright, enough of the constant 'Minister this' nonsense. Get your shit together and be prepared for when they DO grill us."

The gamesmanship of Fern and Flo's seeming disinterest lasted until the last evening of their stay. With the wine flowing, the lips loosened and the thoughts frank, Sylvie and I bonded together to give a progress report on the planning of the construction of the yurt.

Sylvie led the way with a surprise caveat that immediately caught their attention and put us on firm footing immediately.

"Ooooh," Flo said as the first tagged piece of evidence (the bathtub) was laid out, "where did you get that? Did you find it online?"

Softening up her audience, Sylvie moved in for the kill as two more pages of details followed the first.

"These are the official architectural drawings of the yurt."

Before them, drawn sight specific, the inside renderings, outside cross-section and profile of the yurt were accompanied with the land layout all neatly crafted.

An 'ahhh' escaped our captivated jury.

"Where did you get those?"

"I posted an ad on Craigslist with the promise of a free two week vacation at the yurt after it's constructed and this guy Mauro responded."

"Muh, muh, muh" I mumbled under my breath, "I got a big fat architect to do my work."

"Really, you found this guy on Craigslist?"

"Yup, and he said he was so excited about it, he pushed his other work aside to do this. He's absolutely thrilled about the idea."

The rest of the presentation was seamless. Building from a solid platform, it wasn't long before she had all of us charmed and convinced that we would have the most luxurious yurt ever designed.

We were just about to leave the situation at that when Fern, snapping out of his trance, managed to utter a few words in my direction. It was as though the dean realized that the entire group enterprise had been undertaken and directed by one student and glossed over the shortcomings of everyone else. I squirmed.

"Oh," Sylvie squawked and trained her ears upstairs, "I think I hear Dustin."

And with that she bolted out of her chair, slammed down the laptop and left me twisting under the weight of their gaze. I was exposed, vulnerable. There was no way of hiding the fact I'd spent most of my allotted time squabbling with my father about the nobility, yes of using recycled material, but also the pain and suffering it would cause. Not only were the materials I wished to use still presently assigned tasks holding up structures, but they were also scattered around the province. There were the barn beams at my brother's farm that could only be acquired if we took the time to pull it down, disassemble it, pack it, and ship it two provinces away. Or there were the engineered floor joists I could have for a very reasonable price from a co-worker who acquired them from a film set and had them stored at his farm in Belleville on the exact opposite side of Toronto from my brother. Logistically it was insane, economically it was tantalizing.

And perhaps because the other steps were so straightforward, I felt I had the luxury of setting them aside in order to indulge this other whim of fancy.

Like a stern judge annoyed with being lectured on the finer points of the law from an upstart student, Fern poked through my posturing with a pointed question that hit at the heart of the matter:

"Do you know what you're going to build it on?" he said point blank.

"Uh, well, from the pictures I've seen most people just put them on deck blocks."

It was like watching an amateur poker player at a table full of professionals. He couldn't have had a more profound 'tell' if he'd turned his cards over and let his opponents look at them. When something disagrees with Fern he folds his arms across his chest, scrunches up his nose and furrows his brow. And then to punctuate the pose comes the short syllabic word that sums up everything that's going on in his mind: "Enh"

Like peering into the mind of a sage, I could easily read the thought bubbles forming just above his head as though he was a character in a comic book:

"Are you fuckin' nuts! What the hell are you going to do with my grandson, building a tent, sinking a lot of money into a nice new building only to fuck it up by putting it on deck blocks."

Instead, not wanting to provoke me, Fern curdled his thoughts and chose his words carefully: "Are you fuckin' nuts, what the hell are you going to do with my grandson, building a tent, sinking a lot of money into a nice new building only to fuck it up by putting it on deck blocks."

"Excuse me?"

Sensing a growing animosity, Flo's attention was averted away from Sylvie's carefully crafted case and into a mediating position between Fern and I.

"Jase," she purred, "do you not remember what the floor's like on our cottage?"

"Yeah," I said and floated my arm up and down, "it's like a wave."

"Exactly," Fern piped back in, "de t'ing is up and down like a yo-yo. It's because it's on deck blocks and when de frost goes in and out so does de res' of de building."

Sylvie, reappearing in the room, hung her head. We'd blown the examination. I saw the disgust in her eyes and realized our failed presentation rested completely on my shoulders. However, digging deep into my bag of tricks, I hunted for an improvisation that might get us a passing grade.

Though it pained her that I devoted so much time and effort into research, what I'd done was to shoulder the load of ideas. Though I could be stubborn in my approach and emotional in my sensitivity, when those forces were cured and directed properly the results were amazing. Instead of asserting that I am in the sole possession of all ideas great and small, I allow that when I don't have an answer to a problem to share that lack of insight with any and all who might. The result sometimes is a lot of dead ends and the occasional assault of the egotistical. If there's one thing I've learned is that, without fail, EVERY man I've approached with a challenge or problem has always opined first about how THEY would do my project before allowing me the useful information on that particular objective.

To his credit, Fern was not exactly like most men, instead of wading in with his opinion before asked, he allowed me to stumble in my own stupidity and then ask for help before offering insight. It was a rare quality.

"In all honesty, I haven't really spent much time on how I was going to secure it to the ground. What do you think I should do?"

Whereas Sylvie dazzled with the scope of her work, my secret tactic was to gain the confidence of our quarry by including them in the process. If I didn't have the answer, then perhaps they might.

"Well, whatever you do your going to have to get below de frost line."

"Yeah Jase, hello, you want the yurt to be secure. You're going to have a full kitchen there, a washroom. I mean, look at the bathtub Sylvie is gonna get, you don't want that to lift up and break any of the plumbing. No, no, no, no, you've gotta do it right."

The haunting legacy of the crack whore bike incident (and other moments of frugal decisions being wrought with disaster) exposed the hidden meaning behind Flo's words. What she said was "do it right" but what she meant was "don't do it CHEAP!"

As the summation of our progress drew to a close, Sylvie stole a sideways glance in my direction. We survived this checkpoint in the planning process, but in no way had we inspired unflappable confidence in those who would monitor us closely. For as much as they weren't the authors of this venture, our family and friends would be a part of it in various capacities. In the direct form, we would need to call on Fern and Flo to watch our son while we dealt with logistics or other issues. In an indirect way, we extended our ideas and asked for input on their viability.

Though they grilled us hard, Fern and Flo demonstrated an outward enthusiasm for our project and vocalized their full support to our cause.

My family was decidedly mute.

That's not to say they weren't just as excited about what it was we were trying to accomplish. Far from it. They just weren't the kind of people to blurt it out, jump up and down and sing the epic from the mountaintops. It wasn't their way.

The very reserved, very repressed emotional displays were saved for only a few special occasions: play-off hockey games. In this environment even the most refined individual has been known to lose their minds, remove the blanket that is keeping their seventy-year old posterior warm in the cold building and drape it over the head of the referee. The reasoning: "He wasn't seeing anything anyway!"

On the one hand, hailing from New Brunswick with deep French-Acadian roots, Sylvie's family was all things continental European: emotional, demonstrative, expressive, artistic, flamboyant, proud (to a fault), vain, and in those rare individuals: arrogant.

My Southern Ontario farm family background with deep historical roots in Germanic and Anglo-Saxon traditions was decidedly different: reserved, quiet, conservative (emotionally and financially), strong willed, humble, and very pragmatic.

The kind of culture that places a great deal more value in deeds rather than words. It's the kind of place so rooted in attitudes that a racial slur can be used to name a dog, but the person who did the naming would aid absolutely anyone regardless of race, color or creed if they were in distress.

I have often been confounded by this paradox. It's kept me on my toes for the simple reason it requires far too much interpretation of the true feelings and motivations of the individual involved. However, as the exposure to those layers of understanding are revealed, the scope of depth in the people involved has left me astounded in our capacity to be complex.

The folders packed, the boardroom closed for the evening and the deliberations concluded, the wine was poured in celebration of our adventure. Whether love or conflict, the French fondness for wine knows no bounds. Just as the second cork was popped the phone rang and the distinct cadence of a long distance ring hung in the air.

"Must be Jerry," Sylvie said. It being Sunday night, it was only natural my family would call for our weekly chitchat.

"Bob!?!" I said into the receiver.

Sylvie's ears perked. Flo and Fern, curious as always, quizzed Sylvie once more.

"It's Jason's Uncle."

"His Uncle, I've never heard him mention anyone other than Elgin."

"Yeah, he has an Uncle in Winnipeg I think."

Not hearing her interpretation of our conversation, I brushed Sylvie aside and turned to the computer.

"Wow, that sounds like a fantastic idea for the yurt! Hold on, I'm just going to do a search and see if I can find something…"

Hearing "yurt" the wine was abandoned momentarily. We all leaned into the laptop.

"And they just screw into the ground? You don't' have to dig holes and you don't have to pour cement. Wow, thanks Bob, I really appreciate that. And you say the ground doesn't stick to the metal? Ahh right, I see, because it's galvanized steel. Perfect. Hey thanks a lot. How did you know I was building this? My mom, okay, well, Merry Christmas to you too."

"What, what?" Sylvie says.

"Here you go Fern, this is what we're going to do. Auger Piles."

"Auger Piles?"

As we pulled up the screen, the surprise inspiration from my truck-driving uncle in Winnipeg left me stunned. Not the idea, timely though it was, but the source. It seemed the Hamilton's, while not appearing to be demonstrative, had eschewed traditional, normal patterns of communication for the quantum, butterfly-like path to demonstrate their emotions. The interjection of my Winnipeg uncle told me they were talking about the yurt. The rest of the picture, selling the house in Toronto and moving to New Brunswick, was still fuzzy. Even how they felt about building a round canvas structure was unclear. Should it matter? Should what we were doing be necessary to have the 'rah-rah' encouragement of family?

****

My feet sloshed through that insufferable mixture of snow and warm that is the tantalizing stage of late winter. Cresting a non-descript building in the east end of Toronto, the setting sun snuck below the horizon. We were beginning the ascent into afternoon though the deception of the winter hours gave the feeling it was almost midnight. It didn't matter. Behind me, past the concrete walls and tall ceiling, the crafted lighting and uninterrupted supply of electricity meant we could film for as long as humanly possible.

Our cause, the cause of all crew from the moment I first started in the movie business, was to hold our collective breath and pray to the film gods to be kind to us and send us home in less than twelve hours. It rarely happened. I might as well be pleading my case right before the door of the star of our show. For as much as we can craft a set for an infinite amount of time, the duration of its life is entirely dependant on the people who perform in front of it.

On this, the set of *Red* that person had a great reputation with the crew but wasn't always so kind to production. He was that Hollywood star who very much flexed the muscles given to his exalted status.

Knowing that in just a few months time I would be leaving this delusional world to create my own (delusion that is), I took advantage of the long pauses in our shooting day caused by "BWT" or Bruce Willis Time. In some respects, the freedom in downtime was productive. I was able to wade right into the first stage of the building process: the septic system. On the other hand, the elongated work day, poor sleep habits and strain on family life caused by the long hours wreaked havoc on my intestinal system. I suffered from Irritable Bowel Syndrome and through ten years of searching, testing, poking and prodding, I was nowhere near finding a coping mechanism than I was after my first attack. The wisdom recommended by medical professionals was universal: get out of film!

Alternating between work on set and work away from it, keeping my intestinal floral system in delicate balance was a constant challenge. The longest I'd been able to stave off the excessive abdominal gas, constipation, stomach bloating and dull ache (symptoms that lasted about three days) had been four months. As the clock ticked on and the catered lunch settled into the second stage of digestion, being able to step away and wade into my own shit (literally) was keeping my mind away from the low throb that was just getting underway in my abdomen.

"Hey Lee," I called into the headset, "Anything happening?"

"Uh, well, as opposed to five minutes ago?"

"As opposed to half an hour ago."

"Then, no, nothing's happening. I think Chris has moved closer to finding religion, Vince is chanting to return to Malta and Danny and Franco are about to start an argument in Italian so they're clearing some space on the floor. Other than that, sigh, we're lit, we're set, we're waiting on Bruce."

"Perfect, then I've got time to make a phone call."

"Hey hey, no fair, you've got something to keep you sane. Give to me.."

"If you like dealing with shit then you can go right ahead."

"Hmm, maybe I'll take a pass."

The infernal wait. The never-ending pause while someone else makes up his mind to do something that has such a massive effect on your own. I've been stopped and interrogated many times about my work in film. Quizzed about who I worked with, what movies, what were they like. In some cases I could fire back with some comical anecdotes about intricate moments or crazy antics. But in most cases being on set and being around famous people was tedious. Most of the antics and comic relief was in trying to find ways to deal with the crippling and colossal waste of time that, if thought about seriously, would only cause you to go mental.

With an eager and willing assemblage of people there have been a few individuals on the crew capable of exploiting this pent up energy with gags and other physical comedy. The transient nature of the business and the short-term work ensures a constant turn-over of those whacky nuts who, while, on the one hand aren't always eager (or capable) to hoist a mammoth 18 Kilo-watt light that weighs a hundred and fifty pounds onto an elevated platform, but are sure able to make you laugh while the rest of the four people grit the beast into position.

Then there are those times when hanging around set for thirteen or fourteen hours a day would make you want to eat glass…or interpret the antiquated plumbing philosophies of my soon to be homeland.

It all starts with a little imagination.

Spinning the foundation into the ground.

Running out of things to do before the yurt arrives.

Low flying aircraft be warned. The burning sensation on your retina may be the surface temperature of the sun.

What the!?! Doors First?

Taking shape.

When all the material arrives, the structure is assembled in a day.

Success is likely to increase with proper direction of material.

A little rest and relaxation at the edge of the coast.

"Ask him. He's the guy in charge!"

The flooring team finds its groove.

An interior world of limitless possibility.

Finally, the room has a view.

Raising a child in a construction zone.

Motorcycle adventure to the East Coast: $2,500. Saving a yurt in a hurricane: $50. Waltzing back into class two days late to start the school year with a motorcycle helmet under your arm: Priceless!

Rescue Team!

Kayaking off into the sunset.

Is it a yurt or is it a Smurf house?

4

A Backed Up System

Depending on the philosophy of the reigning government the amount of land needed to build a home on the water in the province of New Brunswick could be one acre one year and almost three acres the next. Sharing decisions regarding such matters were buried deep in the bowels of local news. Out of sight and out of mind from the swirl that was the centre of the universe.

At the time we purchased our property in ought three it came with a pre-approval for a septic system. Our sole responsibility was to renew the approval on a yearly basis. As film tanked one month then swelled another, the documentation was lost in the shuffle. Forgotten actually. After all, firmly committed (at the time) to a childless life it was with retirement in mind the investment was made. Who cared enough about the future to commit a hundred bucks a year to renew a septic license?

As long as the rain barrel fed the toilet for our business while we visited for a week every couple of years, what else did it matter? It never occurred to us, after the fact, to investigate the scope of what had been approved previously, or what had already been constructed. There was also the matter of the dosage of eco building literature I'd accumulated that could help me out when the need arose.

Amongst my film colleagues (who also had ample time on occasion) I witnessed the many different pursuits it was possible to have while working in film: stock day trader, alternative energy entrepreneur, model ship maker, driftwood artist, etc. From that roster of interests was someone who valued the eco values I did as I was constructing the yurt. Someone who knew something that would tell me my idea could work. What I failed to take into consideration was having those discussions was one thing, having a track record of success with it was another.

"Sure Jason, I know about a Grey Water system," Bruce Crysler said when he overheard an idea I was floating. He was a big man, sturdy stock, very capable of the hoisting and lifting requirements of a film lighting technician. He also had an appropriate nick name: DFB – Dog Food Breakfast. As in, "Damn Bruce, we've gotta lug that eighteen kilowatt, two hundred pound monster to the top of the CN Tower, strap it to the outside and not die in the process. Bruce's disarming reply: sounds awesome. How soon can we start?"

He was a painfully optimistic man who was never perturbed by the brutally tedious or the physically demanding aspects of the job. He always seemed to tackle everything with aplomb and very little grumbling. Even the complaining and whining of his peers were no deterrent. Feed him dog food and he'd convince himself it was caviar: hence, the nickname.

Not a bad quality to have, mind you, it just stood contrary to the usual cynical, jaded film dialect. I discovered that underneath the Lennie Small exterior there was a curious mind of great depth similarly interested in my pursuits.

"You do?"

"Oh yeah, they're very easy to do. Pretty cheap too."

(If you haven't been paying attention by now, those are about my two favourite words in the English language. Easy and cheap!)

"Right, well, I think I want to do something like that at the yurt. I'm pretty sure I'm going to have to come up with something different because we haven't got the right soil for a proper septic system."

"Oh yeah, well, you don't need a full system because you just separate your black water from your grey water and the ground just filters it through easy."

"Oh, whew, thanks a bunch. When I need to come up with something I'll pick your brain alright."

"Hey, no problem. I was almost an engineer you know. I can design it for you.."

There's about nothing in my repertoire that makes me feel good about myself more than feeling like I have THE answer. THE one amongst many. THE right response. THE right knowledge. The one that reinforces that I have solutions, great, small and well, correct. It's a bit of a character flaw. DFB was speaking my language and arming me for the first phase of the building process. Arming me with the knowledge I felt could conquer any rationale of the building inspector. It was with the confidence of that knowledge I allowed myself to be insulated from any potential objection.

There is an inherent flaw, in any way of thinking, when it hasn't been exposed to anything other than the values of its own source. It doesn't always hold up under scrutiny. What I had yet to appreciate was a good idea becomes better when it's allowed a little turbulence to test its mettle. I was about to find out how difficult my life was going to be by not appreciating such a shortcoming.

Whatever concept I had for how to deal with our shit the first step to securing a septic system was to have our soil tested.

Sand would have been acceptable. Gravel would have been ideal. Anything to arrest the effluent after it's sifted through the pipes and mechanically starts to pull apart the molecules before it reaches the water table. The earth eventually purifies the excrement, breaks it down and absorbs it. It takes a great deal of real estate to lay out the pipes in direct correlation to the number of people living at the dwelling. It's a pretty simple equation owing to land size and number of bedrooms.

But what if the yurt wasn't going to be a permanent dwelling? Our foundation was going to be screwed into the ground. To me, that lent us the technicality of non-permanence: more ammunition for my cunning.

I was also of the belief that if the grey water from the sinks, bathtub and washing machine was separated from the black water of the toilet, the necessity of a full septic system was nullified. I was, in the words of Monty Python, about to pay for an argument.

My native province of Ontario with its challenges in the northern portions of the territory of the some of the oldest, hardest rock on the planet that's completely impervious to effluent absorption, had to adapt to that reality. Nestled amongst that rock, in every crevasse and cranny, are deep lakes that hold 20% of the world's freshwater stock. It presents something of an engineering challenge to convince the well heeled of Toronto to brave two hours of traffic to nestle amongst the rocks, water and lakes during the summer months if those septic issues haven't been solved or addressed.

In Ontario cottage country, the outhouse is still an acceptable part of the tradition of squatting in the woods. Literally. By extension, a composting toilet has been accommodated to bring the latrine experience into the heated comfort of the rest of the cottage. Other parts of the world (such as Australia) because of a lack of abundant water stock, encourages rain water collection and the use of grey water throughout the life of the plumbing. The codes and regulations reflect that necessity.

Water used in washing and cleaning is diverted back into the toilet for black water before the well-utilized aqua is exhausted and given a rest in the septic system. Most of Canada, save the rain shadow of the interior plateau region of the Yukon and British Columbia, is abundant in both water stock and water supply.

Why would anyone even bother to investigate a composting toilet when it wasn't necessary? Partially out of my environmental conscience, and partially believing a specified system would also be a little cheaper to install.

From deep in the bowels of Showline Studios on Lakeshore Boulevard, while Mr. Willis was acting out a character contemplating his life as a retired secret service agent, I was contemplating the very deep shit I was about to walk into.

"It didn't drain very fast," Mike Vautour said. "I'm no expert, but I'm pretty sure the officer from the Ministry will say the same thing."

"I see," I said, feeling confident my idea, superior in every way, would be approved without hassle.

"What would that mean?" I decided to ask.

"Well, if you want to have a septic system then you'll have to build up a septic bed. That means, uh, I don't how much, but A LOT of fill. You'll probably have to build it up about three or four feet...."

"Yikes," I said aloud. I trusted Mike was coming from a place of genuine knowledge of such things. He'd never met me, had been called from Toronto to dig a hole for a soil test before re-filling it a day later without any confidence I would pay him besides my word on the phone. He wasn't fucking around.

"How much would something like that run me?" I asked.

"Between the soil and the septic system, oh, something in the neighbourhood of ten to fifteen grand," Mike replied.

I gulped. "Alright then, I'll keep you posted," I said, confidence fleeting. My mind leapt back to the holding tank. The pre-approval that was once impossible to maintain now seemed incredulous to have let slip.

As these thoughts began to swirl through my head, I lurched back to set. The walkie-talkie was quiet, the pandemonium had subsided. I turned a corner and leaned against a lighting cart. Pulling a bag from a light, I flipped through the quiver of gels hanging from it. A coworker, Stephen Myers, rounded the corner. I pulled out a square and unfurled it for careful inspection. It wrinkled and crinkled with each fold. I held it up to the light. The colour correction it was supposed to be rated for had been burned through. The deep hue of blue on the outside edge of the gel was bleached away. In the middle, a perfect white circle, burned through from hours of use, was left in its wake.

Stephen and I looked at one another, shrugged our shoulders, rolled the offending gel back into a tight roll and jammed it back into the quiver. I sighed.

"Problems in yurt planning?" Stephen asked.

"Do you know anything about grey water systems?" I continued.

We were about to continue our discussion when out of the labyrinth of sets, carts and lights, Bruce Willis shuffled between us.

"Hey fellas, how's it going?" he asked.

"Good Bruce, how you?" I stammered.

"Good great, hey which way is set?"

Stephen and I looked at one another. I'd been fumbling around so long away from set I had no idea what scene we were doing or where we were shooting.

"Uh, I think it's that way Bruce," Stephen rescued us quickly.

"Thanks," Bruce said, "here, for your troubles,"

He handed us each a rudimentary gumball Green Lantern gift ring. One red. One green.

With the distraction, Bruce took one look toward set and retreated the other way. I was too overcome to notice: a gift from Bruce friggin' Willis!

Stephen and I looked at one another, trying our hardest to keep a straight face, and quickly donned our jewelry.

"Heh," I said, "that was pretty cool. I take away all the bad things I said about him."

"Oh," Stephen said.

"Not really. How can you say anything bad about Bruce Willis? The longer he takes the more money I make!"

Stephen and I both laughed. A call came over the headset.

"Hey guys," came the familiar voice of our Gaffer, "they're asking if anyone has seen Bruce?"

I looked at Stephen, who was about the take the reins again. As he sighed before responding, I took my cue to bolt and dive back into the folds of the studio.

****

I could offer some sort of long, drawn out introspection about my personality type as to why I'm hesitant to accept the front door method for tackling and subsequently dealing with issues and problems. The truth is I'm quite swift when the answer is obvious (to me). The pain and suffering is inflicted when I cling to a dying thought despite the heaps of evidence against it. I'm a sucker for a lost cause.

Or perhaps it's just the fear of what the reality is going to entail.

With Bruce finally doing his thing on set I had enough time on my schedule cleared to finish circling the wagons and get right into the thick of things.

"Allo, Napoleon Basque," I said, "greetings from Toronto."

"Oh, Mister 'amilton, I was wondering 'ow long it was going to take for you to get back to me…."

"Well, even before the soil was tested I had a pretty good idea what the prognosis was going to be," I said.

"So you're aware you 'ave lots of clay."

"Boy, am I ever…"

"Yeah, you'll come to find that it's pretty common around 'ere. Do you know what you're going to do nex'?"

"Hmmm, I sort'a thought you might be able to answer that question."

"Hokay. 'ere's 'ow it works in dis province. Because you have a smaller lot, less dan one acre, and you fail your soil test you're going to 'ave to get a spacific, uh, specificalluu, spcial. Uh an engineered system to your specific-ations."

I could hear him breath a sigh of relief. I speak the language and that many specialties in one sentence would be hard for me!

"Okay, hmm, well, here's what I was thinking," I retorted.

"Alright," Napoleon said, anticipating not a conflict with a builder, but a genuine interest in what I was going to suggest.

I was still feeling confident in my idea and how could I not. If the mandate of the province were to develop in a way that was responsible to the integrity of the land then surely a system that didn't allow any effluent into the ground water would be applauded.

"I was going to install a composting toilet with a grey water system.."
There was a pause on the other end.
"Dat's a very good idea and I wish I could say okay, but the government won't allow it."
Ouch.
"What you have to unnerstan' is we work wi' de Ministry of de Environment when we make dese decision. And when we make dese choices it is from de guidelines we've been given. I know dat dese systems are in use in udder parts of de world but we have to plan for resale. We have to make allowances for expansion..."
It was sound reasoning. Had I been pleading my case before anyone other than a representative of the government in this matter I might have had a chance. Napoleon could have left everything well enough alone, told me, politely, to fuck off and get with the program. But from probably engaging in one conversation too many with someone like myself, he decided to do us both a service and elaborate on the no.
"And dese are de guidelines we've been using since 1978."
"Uh, whu?" I said, dumbfounded.
"Dey are in de process of making some changes but dese are de guidelines we've been using 'ere since de seventies."
"Wow. The seventies. Y'know, you wouldn't think the way to deal with shit has changed much in the last three thousand years let alone the last three decades, but there's been a lot of new ideas emerge since then."
"I know Jason, it's not my fault. Dis isn't my decision."
"I know Napoleon. I understand. I will take it up with the province..."
"Please do!" he offered, "in de meantime, can you tell me what you are building so we can speed dat process up for when you get your septic..."
"Uh, well, it's a yurt."
"Excuse me?"
"A yurt. It's a round, canvas structure. Do you have a computer? Just search for 'yurts' and you'll see what I'm building. I've got engineering

specs. Snow load rating."

"Hmm, dat's okay. Are you building in town?"

I had to think about this query for a minute. My concept of a town is well defined. It's boundaries distinguishable. From the road, amongst the cleared fields and flat land, you see the town as you approach. The houses scatter off in either direction from the main street through a fairly simple grid layout. You know where the town is before you get there, the closeness of the homes within the boundaries reinforces that idea, and the return to flat arable pastures upon exiting bookends the concept.

I have absolutely no idea where a town begins and ends in New Brunswick. Homes clog themselves along roads and string out in either direction. Before long, after fifteen minutes of driving you've somehow passed through five different communities. Communities that, to the outsider are indistinguishable, but to the locals might be five different countries—with dialects to match!

"Uh, well," I started slowly, making sure not to offend, "we're building in Upper Rexton…"

"Oh no, dat's not in town. You can do whaddever you wan' den. Call me when you 'ave your septic figured out and den I can give you your building permit."

As the day drew to a close and the call time on the following day pushed us into the afternoon, I would have ample time in the morning to begin the investigation.

The question was where to begin? How do you start to track down the nature of the problem and who was responsible for it? Was it the MinistRY of the Environment? Was it public works? Was it the MinistER of the Environment?

I started with the Ministry of the Environment. I explained the situation carefully, telling the listener what a yurt was, why we were having difficulty getting a septic system approved and then left my audience hanging on the dilemma of who might answer to the antiquated laws.

"Have you spoken with Napoleon Basque?"

The next inquisition I worded my monologue slightly different:

"I'm building a cottage in Kent County on the water and I have less than one acre. I'd like my cottage to be as environmentally friendly as possible. In order to achieve that I did some research and discovered that if the grey water and black water are separated with the black going into a composting toilet that that is the best possible system. I'm made to understand you don't have anything in the books to accommodate that....?

"Uh, well sir, you're probably right. I don't have your information right in front of me. You said you're building in Kent County?"

"That's correct."

"Well, the one to talk to would be Napoleon Basque. He's the one who issues permits and the like..."

I danced around the Ministry for several hours. Five times I was told that Napoleon Basque was the one to contact. I wanted to be angry, frustrated, but they were all very polite and helpful and not deserving of such treatment. Perhaps my investigation needed a new angle. Instead of contacting the MinistRY of the Environment I decided to move up the government food chain somewhat and contact the MinistER of the Environment.

The immediate results were not initially encouraging:

"I'm really sorry sir, I'm just a receptionist and I only started working here this week...."

My head hung, she continued with some determination.

"But I'll ask around the office, I'm sure somebody must know something. I mean hey, it makes sense doesn't it, surely the office of the Minister of the Environment must know something about these things...."

And before long I was engaged with the right person who had full knowledge and the liberty to speak about the subject.

"..1978 that's how long these rules and regulations have been in place. We're in the process of updating them right now. For example, the one thing we're going to be doing is giving the installers the ability to put these systems into the ground without needing the stamp of an engineer. That is, provided the design has been used before. So you don't have to approve the same thing over and over again."

"Well, that's great, how long before that happens?"

"Those new regulations should be in place by the fall."

"The fall."

I always tell myself the information gathered is worth the effort despite what the results might be. A tangent can lead to unexpected avenues of wisdom. Unfortunately, in this case, I was no further ahead. I managed to tie up several weeks worth of planning in shit and material whose value most thought was shit. The real crime was that my normal experience with bureaucracy was usually one of escalating arrogance. I could feel righteously enraged based on the comeuppance of the person on the other end of the line. This experience was completely the opposite: super nice and overly helpful. It was impossible to channel my inner Hulk, no matter my frustrations.

"Oh, you're calling from Ontario aren't you? Why don't we call you back on our long distance plan and save you some money."

And they would. Without delay. Far beyond the bounds of customer service I'd experienced.

But regulations are regulations. No amount of pleading and begging was going to change that. The jig was up. To build a yurt I would need to have my septic system designed by an engineer. The Ministry could do one thing for me however, and that was to provide a list of those registered septic engineers (think Ed Norton of the Honeymooners. A little better educated and minus the chubby combative neighbour.)

The first call I made was to 'Fisher Engineering'. He was a small firm. Small. Just him. Mike Fisher. We talked over the situation: The location, the structure, the number of bedrooms. (The amount of shit we might produce.) How complicated could it be? Sewage is sewage. It needs a rocky terrain to bust up the stool. My only request was for the weeping bed to not look like a giant tortoise had buried himself in the yard. Sadly, none of his initial suggestions sounded pleasing. We could backfill behind the yurt or we could backfill in front of the yurt.

Options did not abound.

"If I build closer to the road then I'll have to pump the sewage up to the weeping bed."

"Hmm, well why didn't you mention that before."

"Uh, sorry. I don't know how you mean."

"Do you have a grade of about 3%?"

"Come again?"

"Is there a slope?"

"Yeah, a little one. Nothing major."

"If your grade is 3% or higher than I can do a contoured system and we won't have to truck in a mountain of gravel."

"Wow, really," I responded. I liked what I was hearing: no septic mountain, a small (individual) company, and someone who listened to my meanderings.

"Uh, how much?"

"About 12. That's everything installed and my fees. Final sticker price."

"Grand. Alright then, I'll be in touch, I'm just gathering quotes right now but we're building in just a few months. I'll talk to you soon."

Moving down the list I explained my situation to the next engineer. End result:

"Fifteen to twenty grand."

"I see."

"Did you say you were from Ontario?"

"Yes, why"

"I have a business partner you should speak with. Krista Fleiger. She wants to build these green friendly homes and she's run into all sorts of problems in trying to get them approved. As a matter of fact she had me design a system for her that was also supposed to have composting toilets."

Now, despite the hefty price tag he was quoting my interest in what he had to say suddenly returned. By now I was back on Bruce's dime (who I'm told can spare a few here and there) and the walkie was in no way beckoning me back to any pressing concern (my job). I decided to continue my conversation.

"So what did the Ministry have to say?"

"She wasn't having any problems with the Ministry of the Environment."

"Oh, what was the issue?"

"The problem was with the plumbing code."

By necessity and by default there comes a point in time when the vision of what you're trying to build inevitably bumps up against the actuality of the situation. In no way did I expect, with my limited knowledge, to find a way to circumvent building codes, plumbing codes or environmental laws to build the yurt. I did not have the wherewithal, the fortitude or the expensive lawyers on retainer.

I was beginning to face the necessity of making challenging decisions against the march of time and the restraints of finances. I was stepping out of the long shadow of film where the vision on the storyboards wasn't necessarily going to make it onto the screen.

However, approaching something so archaic, the need to point out and tackle such blind silliness is wound deeply in the fabric of my character. I would be kicking myself if a little exploratory work might save a few thousand bucks WASN'T explored.

With a potential ally who might be able to help my cause, or at least shed some insight, I called Krista eager to hear her challenges.

"Hi Krista, my name is Jason Hamilton and I'm about to build a yurt in rural New Brunswick. I'm having some issues with my septic and I spoke to your friend Eric about it. He said you've come up against the exact same thing."

"How much did he tell you?"

"He just said you were having trouble getting a few things approved."

"Yeah, you might say that. I'm designing a home that has a grey water pond on the outside of the home that feeds an ecosystem. The ecosystem will be filled with plants that will get rid of any toxins in the water. The rest of the home will feature two composting toilets. Or so I hope. I also have to install a regular flush toilet in order to comply with the plumbing code," Krista went on.

"The plumbing code? So far my battle has been to get approval for a septic system so I can get my building permit," I countered.

"No, I've got Eric to put his stamp of approval on the system. He's my partner. I was like you, from what I heard about building these homes the biggest obstacle would be the ministry of environment but so long as the system is done by an engineer then they sign off," Krista said.

"Alrighty then, so how are you having such problems with the plumbing code," I asked.

"I thought you'd never ask. According to the plumbing inspector, and he's the guy who interprets the plumbing code remember….every home must have a flush toilet. End of story," Krista stated.

"Okay, is there any reason why? Did he give a rationalization?"

"As a matter of fact yes there is. He's worried about gas."

"Gas as in methane?"

"Yup, he's afraid that with a composting toilet there will be a build-up of methane gas in the home that in a sufficient quantity will cause an explosion or toxic circumstances to the inhabitants."

"Really!"

Just as I thundered that response the door to the studio broke my concentration. Lunch had been called and the crew was making their way past me. I waved at my succession of bosses, DOP, Gaffer and Best Boy as they, embroiled in their own conversation, were to busy to notice me embroiled in mine.

"That's the reason and I've had absolutely no luck changing his mind. I know him very well and that's what he's decided," Krista continued matter-of-factly.

I was dumbfounded. Krista heard my silence as opportunity.

"You said you were from Toronto right?"

"Yeah."

"And you're building in New Brunswick?"

"Yeah, we're looking to build the yurt to get established and have our son closer to my wife's extended family…"

"Y'know, since I have so much experience dealing with the province, and I am a licensed architect with building experience, I could supervise the construction of your yurt while you're still in Toronto," she offered.

"Oh, really. Well, we do have a limited budget. We need to sell our house here before we know what our real budget is going to be…."

"Okay, well, I could either charge you a flat rate, which usually works out much better in your favour or do it as a percentage of your overall budget…"

"Thanks Krista, I appreciate that. Let me think it over and I'll get back to you. The information you've shared has been great. I'll be in touch."

I finally hung up.

The Minister of Finance was not pleased. The Minister of Interior Design would no doubt jump for joy. Now instead of continuing to talk around the issue I was forced to make a decision. Krista's offer was not in the budget (fictional though it remained). Eric's quote was out of the question.

"Hi Mike. How soon can you go up to the property and take a look? I know there's about three feet of snow covering the land but that shouldn't make much of a difference for you to be able to tell if you have enough slope to install the contoured system you're talking about."

The first, most critical obstacle was out of my hair. There was no shame in admitting I didn't have the wherewithal to tackle a province operating under legislation that was thirty years old. But as I was come to discover, as the project became more concrete with each passing day, the interpretation of our intentions and the expectations of our family and friends in regard to such matters was giving our round, vinyl tent a lot more dialogue than we expected.

5

To Sell Or Not To Sell

The phone calls, the long musings about whether it was in any way somehow cheaper to ship reclaimed building material brought me no closer to a resolution. The cost of shipping was fairly reasonable. Getting barn lumber to the dock, in a way that could be moved on and off of a truck easily and efficiently, was another matter.

Being fair, offering input even after I'd given up on the notion, my Dad kept offering suggestions though we both knew the story. Our best chance to make it work was to buy a trailer, have my father drive it out with the material, and sell the trailer when we were finished.

"We could do it Jake," he said, "but I don't know what kind of hassle you'd run into in Que Bec. If you did it with a U-Haul you still might run into the same troubles. Regulations. Tariffs. You just don't know over there."

He'd had his fair share of hassles in his transportation career over the distinctiveness that was "La Belle Province". The eighties saw him trucking potato chips and French fries outside of Quebec City on an almost regular basis.

Politically the eighties were the height of the Quebecois sovereignty movement (with intermittent rumblings after the fact) and the realization of francophone rights within Canada. Feeling a sense of self-determination and power that was historically English, they chose to flex that right.

Initially the goal was a referendum. Sovereignty association. Another country within Canada perhaps. The loose definition was deliberate. And annoying. Like a whiny kid brother who wants to stand proud and be independent, yet have the luxury of his mother's skirt whenever that challenge proved difficult.

What the separatist movement did manage to implement successfully were harsh language laws: Gestapo-type regulations requiring French prominence in business signage and other such inanities. It was revenge politics for years of being made to feel inferior at the hands of the English. The threat of separation and the heavy handed language laws caused the English business population to migrate out in droves. It has since been a steady alteration of the Quebec mindset to make distinct, in any way possible, that which is possible.

For a small-town Ontario trucker who's more swayed to Dixie the French assertion was a good enough reason to stay as far away from Que Bec as possible. Throw up the barbed wire, roll in the tanks, Gerald Hamilton wanted no part of that quagmire. But still he tried to help.

I allowed myself to indulge those shipping theories, content to be occupied in negotiations about tariffs, shipping costs and packing. In my own way, I'd decided that since there was no concrete budget then there was no need for concrete decisions. In my estimation the world would hold perfectly still while we took a few months off to build the yurt.

"Jase, I don't mean to pry, but have you booked anything yet?" I could hear the nerves in Sylvie's voice.

"Uh, well, I've got a few quote's on shipping material. It's not cheap."

"What, shipping?"

I turned to study the floor.

"You've looked at septic and shipping. I don't know much about building but I'm sure there's more to putting up a yurt than that."

I considered her words for a moment.

"I just wish I knew what we were working with you know."

"What do you mean?"

"How much money do we have to spend? We don't have a budget. I've got costs and quotes but I have NO idea what we can do and what we can't. I don't know how much money we're going to make this summer. How much we're going to get for the house…."

"This summer?"

"Yeah, this summer."

"Wait, you mean work. What do you expect to do?"

"We'll head out, build the yurt. That should take maybe a couple of months. That's July. Come back, work our asses off during the busy season. Put a few more grand in our pocket. Sell the house and rest easy while we look for careers in Moncton."

"That's your plan?"

She had that look in her eye and the matching fire in her nostrils. If these were my plans they most definitely were NOT hers.

"That's what I was thinking. I didn't write it in stone."

"Do you think the summer is the best time to sell the house?"

"Yeah."

"When kid's are going back to school?"

"Sure, why not."

"Okay Jerry," she pounced like a cobra. It was her lightning strike. Her secret finishing manoeuvre. Reserved for special occasions when my intentions and know-it-all gene had kicked into hyper-drive.

I returned fire.

"So you're the real estate expert then? Tell me oh master, when is the best time to sell our house?" I parried the attack with a counter-strike of my own.

"I don't know."

Uh. Excuse me, we were having an argument here…

"You. Don't. Know?"

"No, I don't know. And neither do you. That's why we're going to call Margaret. She's the agent, she knows what she's doing.

****

"Are you ready to do this?"

Sylvie and I looked at one another.

"Because once you sell your home you won't be able to get back into the market here. Once you leave you won't be able to get back into the Toronto market."

We both gulped. The finality of it stared us in the face, but there was no hesitation.

"Yes, we're going to do this."

Whether we were ready was another matter.

"I'm gonna miss you guys!"

"We'll miss you too Margaret."

"Okay, well then, enough of the mushy stuff. So what do you need me to do?"

"Sylvie and I have been arguing about when is the best time to sell the house."

"For you guys, to get the possible price. The end of March."

Forget the blubbering sentimentality, the slap in the face wiped those emotions into the closet.

"Uh, March. That's six weeks away…"

"If you want to get the best possible price. We both knew you'd be arriving at this point. This was the reason you got yourselves into the market in the first place."

"But wait a minute. We're hoping to be able to go out, build the yurt, come back for the summer, make some more money and then sell the house in the fall. Can that work?" I interjected.

My mind was racing. Why did I waste so much time!?!

"Sure, you can do whatever you want. It's your house and I'm your agent. I'm merely suggesting the best possible time to sell your home will be this spring. The earlier you get your house on the market, the earlier you will be able to differentiate yourself from the other houses out there."

Sylvie and I looked at one another again.

"I just don't have the time to get it fixed up and ready…"

Sylvie and Margaret turned squarely against me.

"No, you don't and no you won't!" they both exclaimed.

"What, hey!" I responded.

"From this point on you can't think of this as 'your house' anymore. If you're going to profit from this investment, then you have to think about what it's going to take to sell. Look, I've got this guy who's very good who can do everything. His name is Tom."

"Really!" Sylvie responded with enthusiasm.

I had been so accustomed to being the one to get my hands dirty on the house the thought of another man violating my space and touching her walls wasn't appealing. Sylvie was excited at the prospect.

"You mean old Jerry here isn't going to be the one to take the chainsaw to the house?" Sylvie said.

"Excuse me?" Margaret chuckled.

"Oh, go on!" I said, defending the family honour.

"It's Jason's Dad. He used to do renovations with a chainsaw. Taking walls down, building cupboards. He'd fix it on the kitchen table...."

Margaret held her head in shame. I beamed proudly.

"Not the house they have now! Just all the other ones," I interjected before I continued, "Margaret, I accept that this is no longer going to be our home. I will do what is necessary to put it on the market and get the best possible price for the return on our investment."

"Right on, that's the best attitude to have."

Sylvie's surprise spread all over her face.

****

I anticipated Tom arriving in a massive beast of a truck that dwarfed our house but whose sole function was a traveling office. As the doorbell rang I looked out the front window to make sure the van wouldn't be crushed. Most contractors arrive ego first. Not caring a whit for pedestrians and neighbours (gnats) and the like. No truck, no small earth moving machine. There was nothing hogging the sidewalk at all. I was sure I heard the doorbell ring. Someone was on the porch.

I opened the door and peered past him for a moment. There, chained to the railing, was his ride. It looked somehow familiar. A straight black frame, the seat partially torn. A heavy chain anchored it to my home. Could it be the crack whore bike!?! I thought.

"Oh, hi Tom, say where did you get…" and my words were interrupted by the less burly, but equally invasive Margaret in her compact SUV as it rolled onto the sidewalk.

"Nice to meet you," came the voice about four octaves lower than James Earl Jones.

"I see you've met Tom," Margaret called as she stampeded past me.

"Don't worry, Dustin is sleeping," Sylvie called as she walked down the stairs.

"Okay, we'll try and be quiet. First thing we're going to do is a walk around and figure out all the major work that needs to be done. We'll make a list and sort out everything in order of priority. Then we'll talk colour and paint. Jason, Tom doesn't have a car so you will have to coordinate with him things he'll need etcetera. After he's done that he'll give you an estimate of how much time it will take and we can come up with a budget for his work. Once we finish that we'll sit down with our list of comparables and start talking price point," Margaret paused.

Reactively, I took a breath on her behalf.

"We've got four weeks Hamilton. Four weeks to get this place onto the market," Sylvie busted into my dementia.

"Uh, er, do I have to do anything? I'm only, uh, planning a build in another province. Nothing big y'know…"

"All the more reason to just sign the cheques," Sylvie blurted. This was the breaking point. All the momentum could be put to a halt if I wanted. I just had to balk, stumble, flinch, anything to put our enormous ambition at rest. It was all or nothing.

"Hun, up until now you've done a great job on the house. Really. It looks good for the little you've had to work with. But now is the time to trust that we know what we're doing. Think you can do that?"

"I promise you, everything you spend on the house will come back to you ten-fold. We're not talking about a major overhaul. That's not what this is about. But if we spend 5 to ten thousand dollars now I can assure you that money will triple," Margaret measured.

"Yeah," I brightened, "but what about the new furnace, new roof and all the basement waterproofing we've done already? There's twenty grand and no one notices that."

I wanted to storm off like a kid and pout. I couldn't. What was the point? Yes, after five years of home ownership the balance owing on the mortgage was the exact as when we'd started. We'd already spent almost twenty thousand that would have little impact on the market value of the house. Sure, all of those things were true. But all of it meant nothing. Now was the time to cash in. Now was the time when, if we just gave our home that last little cosmetic lift would make all of those earlier changes have a liquid value.

As much as part of me wanted to jam on the brakes and take a time-out, the momentum had already started. It started in America when the overblown real estate market imploded. It started in the oil fields around the world where the amount of easy oil still to be extracted was suspected to have peaked. It was in energy, resources and the pillage necessary to keep our numbers. It was all of those things and more, whittling away in the back of our mind, that had us realizing the choice to cash out was in our hands, our fate. Whether that moment was at its apex was irrelevant. Real estate in Toronto could still very well go up. The film industry could have a banner year. But the change we decided to make left all those other factors as set dressing. We could in no way impact those greater forces. We were making out choice clearly and consciously. An eye to the greater good of our son being closer to extended family. The first grandson closer to his MeMere and Pepere.

"Okay Margaret. I will keep my mouth shut and sign the cheques. I accept that which is beyond my control and I trust you have our best interests at heart," I let out a sigh of relief.

"Come on over Jason, this is great. And this is where we need your input," Margaret said and invited me to sit.

"I've got a list of comparables. These are homes in the neighbourhood that have sold within the last year," Margaret continued.

I shuffled to the spread of paperwork now taking over our kitchen. Sylvie and I immersed ourselves in the information as Tom and Margaret slipped away to scout the house.

"Wow, $349,000. $365,000."

"Those are big numbers," I said.

"What do you think hun, think we might be able to get that much?"

"I hope so."

I poured through the descriptions: Semi-detached homes in the up and coming neighbourhood of the old East York borough of Toronto. Dwellings whose original function was to house the working class people that once toiled in the factories east of downtown. Homes approaching a century old. What would they think now? There were a few differences between the east end and the west end of the city, one of them being a somewhat (by city standards) more sizeable lot size.

Our front yard was large enough to gouge out a parking space. The back yard had a modest garage, parking space, a patio and a about 50 x 20 feet of fenced in green space. Except for some of the shortcomings from the surrounding environs (which wasn't about to appear in the literature) it was a very desirable home.

"These are the comparables for your neighbourhood and this is what we're going to base the price point into the market. After we get this place into shape then we're going to blow the rest of those homes out of the water," Margaret reassured.

The transformation was underway.

It's very easy to lend your home over to the idea that when you are going to sell it it's no longer yours. That's the easy part. The hard part is the actual transition until the transaction is completed. You still have to live, you still have to work and you don't have enough money in the budget to hole up in a hotel until all the work is finished.

My time with Bruce Willis was over and for the rest of our stay in Toronto I would be prepping the sets for *The Thing* both in the studio and in a quarry north of the city. The rigging world is substantially different than being on set at the beck and call of the talented and powerful of Hollywood. It was almost like having a regular life. Up at six, cleaned, showered and out the door to be at work for seven. I was also fortunate to have my boss, Larry Smith, as my tenant.

"You just let me know when I have to vacate when you go to show the house, alright," Larry offered.

"Thanks Larry," I said, "I appreciate it. You don't mind if Tom is working away in the basement while you're not there?"

"Not at all," he said, "so long as he doesn't touch my fuckin' stuff we'll get along alright."

"He's honest, he's from Saint John," I said.

"That doesn't mean a god damn thing Jason," Larry said and laughed.

We were on our way north of the city. Past halted traffic, chuffing along the DVP southbound into the city, past former pristine farmland that was once the great breadbasket of Ontario. We crossed that threshold, still farther north where the idea of development was still that, and descended into a massive gravel quarry. There, in the cement process for the growth of the city south of us, was Antarctica.

The truck descended down a sloping hill. Each foot seemed a degree cooler. The pit hindered atmosphere. The sun did not yet crest the ridge. Reaching the bottom, the appearance of snow blankets draped hundreds of feet up the ridge brought Antarctica a lifelike quality. It was all I could do to duck into a Quonset hut and wait out the winter. I was just about to mention this, and take note of the time of day on my cell phone, when my phone short-circuited.

"Are we below sea level or something?" I asked Larry.

"Cell phone reception is shitty here," he commented.

"Oh fuck. I've got contractors. Material I need to order," I lamented, "a house to fix up and sell. Oh crap!"

I've told myself I have come to accept the amount of technology that has invaded our lives. Did Marshall McLuhan see this moment? His line, 'the medium is the message' was delivered at a time when television, and by extension the Vietnam War, was invading households on a nightly basis. Andy Warhol also very famously opined, "every one will be famous for fifteen minutes". Could he have had the same crystal ball?

I've reached the saturation point. I find myself sucked into the abyss of my computer in every room of my home, including the backyard. Perhaps I could justify such connection for networking purposes. But am I always forwarding my career? When I set aside the time to write I interrupt my progress first with a few hockey highlights. I get back to work for a while, perhaps as much as an hour or two, and then read an article about hockey. Once I'm reading, I want to keep reading. The articles are short, I tell myself, and I'm not wasting too much time.

Before long I've glanced at all the newspaper websites, gleaned a few articles to see what the National Post is pissed off about and half an hour has whistled past. Angry, ashamed at my lack of discipline, the waste of time (when I should be working) I shake my head and dive back into my idea. And this was BEFORE the worlds of Facebook, Twitter and Wordpress crept into the vernacular.

I had to draw the line. I had to draw the line because of how easy it is to assume a minute piece of knowledge about a friend is worth a slice of my present moment. That present moment to use the perfectly good senses I've been granted through evolution to interact with the world around me: sight, sound, smell, touch, ESP, what have you. I see those senses being robbed of their ability to be trusted to provide the proper information to the person who owns them. GPS systems leading rational individuals to drive into hazards that their own deduction skills would have told them was a bad idea. All because a little screen with a nattering voice insisted "make a left". (I, of course can lose myself on such roads WITHOUT the aid of a GPS!)

But more importantly, what I've seen these virtual worlds do is rob people of the ability to interact in person. Walk into a coffee shop or a restaurant where a small gathering of women is sitting at the same table and I guarantee more interaction is done between individual and smart phone than between individual.

The smart phone was once the realm of the businessman who was more concerned with how his BlackBerry made him LOOK important than whether any message actually conveyed such material. It has given a completely different sense of ourselves: Once only Doctor's carried the pager. Now: we are constantly on alert for a message, a tweet, a status update to ensure we are in constant contact with one another.

Being a freelance technician I could justify with myself the necessity of first owning a pager and then a cell phone as to why I needed to be available. But ever so slowly, when I was away and deliberately taking time off the need to be reached was still activated. Something important might happen. A gig might present itself. Even with just a damn pager I had to tell myself to turn the fucking thing off and leave it at home. The same with my cell phone. At first it was liberating. Like a tick had been removed. But then….try it. Tell yourself as you go about your day that you will not bring your personal communication device along for company.

How does it feel initially? Liberating? Relaxing? Satisfying? How long do those feelings last? Half an hour. An hour. How long before those happy endorphins start to dissipate. How long before a small bead of anxiety starts to curl onto your upper lip. How long before you think, hmmm, something's missing. I'm feeling exposed. Is my underwear showing? Is my zipper down? Do I have a food stain somewhere? No, seems to be a bit more revealing than that. Something a little more noticeable. Am I fucking naked? Seriously, am I fucking bare ass naked standing in this busy mall? Seriously. I'm missing an appendage. I've actually lost a piece of my body and no one seems to notice.

As I dug my hands into the sand of the gravel pit north of Toronto to dig out buried cable, that was the anxiety that was starting to creep into my head. All the time I would be in the quarry I could in no way communicate to anyone but my co-workers. No contact with Sylvie or Margaret about the goings on at the house. No contact with the progress on the yurt.

It was disconcerting initially. To know, unequivocally, that an entire world was spinning about that I wasn't allowed to participate in. But then, after a few days away from all the hustle and bustle, those anxieties started to disappear. You allow yourself the liberty of realization that if there isn't anything you can do about cell phone reception then why lose sleep over it? Or, in my case, allow that worry to build up in my stomach and cause a bout of Irritable Bowel Syndrome?

At any rate, the minute our day was finished and Larry and I were driving in the truck back to town, I was more than happy to dig my phone out of my pocket and make up for lost time. Larry in no way minded that as the road changed from sand to asphalt I was glued to my phone. In fact, ever since we announced our intention to sell our home, he was completely supportive of our idea to repatriate ourselves to New Brunswick.

"You can't fuckin' raise a kid in downtown Toronto!" he would exclaim, "not with the nuts running around your neighbourhood."

"For sure Larry, but there's more to the story than just that," I said.

"Yeah, like are you gonna be bumming a ride from me every time I drive up here to work?" Larry asked point blank.

"I hope to hell not," I said.

"Well, good luck trying to find something out there that pays as good as this," Larry declared.

"Yes, but Larry, you complain every time you come up here about how much you hate coming up here," I retorted.

"You're right dear boy," Larry agreed.

"With what we're hoping to get for the house, and for what we can buy one out there for, I'm hoping we won't NEED to make a lot of money in order to survive," I stated.

Larry considered this for a while as I married myself to the phone once again. I pulled my note pad out of my pocket. It was my building bible. Jammed into traffic, Larry cursed under his breath before stealing a glance my way. For as much as he hated any interruption to his best-laid plans, the slow traffic was a bonus for me.

"Great, this saves me from having to do this when I get home. Though with the extra hour to New Brunswick I can make calls a lot longer," I said.

"Jason, what the fuck are you talking about?" Larry hammered, obviously annoyed at the slow pace of the Don Valley Parkway.

"Hi Mike, yeah, Jason Hamilton here. Just checking to make sure you got the deposit. Perfect, so you'll file with the building inspector? Good, the sooner I get that the sooner I can get in touch with NB Power. Oh. So you mean I need the building permit first. Oh, okay, thanks for telling me, I didn't know that," I took a breath.

"Man, thanks for the ride Larry, I just needed to get this building permit. Now everything else will just fall into place" I sighed.

"Well that's just great Jason, but I don't really give a shit unless you can do something about this traffic right now. I mean really, how can anyone do this every day? I think I'd shoot myself in the face!" Larry said.

"You do it all the time when you come up here for work," I noted.

"Yes, but at least I'm getting paid to do it. Usually," he responded.

"I guess you get used to it. This is nothing compared to Bangkok."

Larry looked at me and shuddered. I let Larry stew until, either reaching his breaking point or sensing we were closer to home, he exited the slowly moving road and snaked his way through the backstreets. He screamed down Coxwell before rolling the truck onto the sidewalk. Tumbling quickly, I spilled myself out of the passenger side before Larry roared off again.

Before taking two steps toward the house I cringed about what might be taking place inside. Tom had been a fixture for several days. The front door was wide open. With some apprehension, I eased my way up the stairs before poking my head through the front door.

"Hmm," I said initially, "it's awfully quiet…"

I hadn't taken notice of the car. I stuck my head back out the door.

No car. Nobody. Just the dark bike of Hades gripped to the front porch with a chain so thick Alexander himself couldn't break it. I pulled my shoes off as quietly as I could before closing the door behind me to investigate further. What the hell was going on?

The farther I stepped into the house, the deeper the silence gripped me like a spell. Where was the clatter? The whizzing power tools? The superlative vocabulary of a tradesman? I was almost disappointed. I wanted to learn some new swear words! I was met with a wall of nothing.

"Alright then Margaret, everything seems to be fine here, let's just slap a for sale sign on the front, hoard some wannabe homeowners into the joint and start counting the money" I thought to myself. Only, I didn't. I didn't want to start thinking too far ahead about the money. Margaret was right, once we cashed out they'd banish us from the casino. We would never be able to afford another piece of Toronto real estate. Once we were out, we were out. There was no way was I going to jinx it by talking about it.

I was about to heave those thoughts out with a deep sigh when the silence was broken by 'The Swirl'...times two.

"Jason, great, glad you're back. Go on out to the car and help Sylvie in with the bags. When you get back you can meet us downstairs. Tom and I made a list of some things he's going to need you to get. Sylvie and I picked out some paint that's being mixed. You can get that the same time you get Tom's things. Sylvie and I are right on schedule with planning. You know she has a very good eye. It's too bad you're leaving because I think she has a future as an interior decorator. She should really think about it. Okay then…" Margaret continued into her Bluetooth. It was a little unnerving, as though she'd been arrested to another dimension.

"Uh, I booked the electrician and carpenter," I stammered.

"That's great," she responded to me.

"How the fuck does she do that? Wasn't she just talking to someone else," I babbled, looking around.

"Sylvie told me everything already. Says he put it up already. Great, talk to you soon hun," now really focusing on me, "we need to talk price point."

"Did the other person hear that whole conversation? Are they still there?"

Margaret ignored my desperation and ploughed along, "Now, we know what the market is capable of and we don't want to abuse that knowledge."

"Is it the talk?" Sylvie said from the doorway. I nodded. She dropped her bags and walked slowly to the kitchen

"Houses have sold for between $315K and $375K. Last year was lower. This year, the market is dictating the price. I have to prepare you for this situation as best I can. We could get into multiples but there are absolutely no guarantees. I won't make you any false promises. When we set our price we have to be comfortable with what is our absolute bottom. We don't list that, but that's what we tell ourselves. And then we enter the market with an educated price based on what's occurred before. Again, it could go into multiples but I can't promise you that will be the case. Now, having said all of that, do you have a number in mind?"

Sylvie and I looked at one another.

"I say we're not going to go through this mess if we're not going to make at least a little bit of money. Our absolute bottom is $375,000."

"Okay."

"And our list price is $389,900."

"That's very fair. It's not deliberately too low like all those other twit real estate agents' like to do; it's fair for what the other houses have sold recently. Very good."

"Now, can you be available for Tom to get him the things he needs?"

It wasn't what I had in mind. It was one thing for another man to waltz into my house to fix it and I had to pay him. That I could tolerate. But to have to miss work to be his errand boy?

"I know this is rough," Margaret responded.

What App did she have on that cell phone? How could she know what I was thinking?

"But Tom's work is of quality and reasonably priced. You don't want a contractor to do this as the cost would be astronomical."

"I understand that this is no longer my home.."

"Very good. Trust me Jason," Margaret said and bolted out of the house.

It wasn't much of a fight. Besides, I could use the time to confirm a few things for the yurt. Sylvie had other plans.

"Wow," she said, "that woman is insane."

"Oh?"

"I thought I was busy behind the wheel. I'm...no, forget it," she said before stopping her train of thought, "Uh, there's stuff in the car. I got a new lamp for the living room. We picked up a few things. Not a lot, really. Margaret said the house is actually in pretty good shape, plus we've already done a lot of purging. The big thing is going to be painting, patching, sanding, trim. So, since most of my work is done and I don't want Dustin to be exposed to all of this dust we're going to head home for a week," Sylvie declared.

How did I let myself get talked into this?

"And I talked to Rick and Marsha and they said that for the week-end we're showing the house we can stay with them," she continued.

I stood, pivoted for a moment in Margaret's direction and pointed. I waved my hands all around in the air then pointed my finger back at myself. I pointed my finger at Sylvie, made airplane arms and then swirled around in the living room.

"Yes, that's right, we're flying away while you stay and make sure Tom has everything he needs to get the house on the market. You know we really should play charades more often," Sylvie said before spinning around at the door.

And then all I remember before the blackout was Margaret shoving a list in my hands while Sylvie and Dustin were boarding a plane for New Brunswick.

****

As a story-telling device in the entertainment world, a concrete deadline creates the heightened suspense for drama to play itself out. It's why action films work so well: a countdown until the bomb or explosion or whatever detonation concludes the story. Will the good guys get to it in time?

The concept has carried over very well into the realm of reality television: renovation team (despite ample opportunity to somehow stop and share wit with the hunky host) has imposed deadline to finish renovation before the family living in said home returns. Miraculously, the tension builds as the team is putting on the finishing touches just before the stunned family walks in the door.

Never mind that the family would have been ecstatic for a fresh coat of paint, they now have the latest home style trends, a HUGE renovation, colours and appliances to ever want for a different house.

For the first time in my life, despite being part of many a film crew that was arriving to work just as the paint on the set was still drying, I actually felt like I was living in my own filmed reality: Sylvie and Dustin returned to Toronto without all of the work being completed on the house.

As they stepped inside a wispy cloud of drywall dust greeted them at the door. She handed Dustin to me, marched up the stairs, packed up some new clothes and got right back on the road to take up our friends' offer of a place to stay.

It wasn't until after the house was on the market that we ourselves would get a chance if the results were worth it.

6

SOLD!

It was the normal things I was trying to remember. How the streetcar snaked along College Street at Grace. What the patio at 'The Dip' looked like in the summer when the season was in full bloom. The first beer I ever had at Sneaky Dee's: Ground zero for an expatriate from a small town.

"Despite all the computations you can just dance to the rock and roll station...."

I wanted to bottle Toronto up and take a part of it with me. Why? What is it about a city that's almost impossible to imagine it won't be a part of your life any longer? Sure, you can transport people, put them into a different setting and they'll still behave the same, but what is it about a place that seems to stick under your skin with a smell that will never leave your nose?

Alone with my notepad, I couldn't begin to fill the pages fast enough with all the memories, the sensations, the latent desire to hold onto everything I'd been and everything I'd endured to reach the point we were about to reach. Gradually, like all the other rides I've had on the streetcar, I turned my attention to something else. Away from all the crazy people I swore I'd never forget the first time I ever rode public transit to the moments yet to come. I lost myself in my own thoughts once again.

I moved to Toronto in the spring of 1997, fresh out of university, armed with a Bachelor of Arts degree in English and Film Studies. My goal: to get an entry-level position in the film industry, gain enough knowledge and confidence to be able to make my own short film. I achieved my goal. That was 2001. A lot of life happened after I made those plans.

My beliefs changed as they do when so much of who you are is evaporated after so much effort and toil results in exactly one screening at one film festival. You start to turn your attention over to those things where you have a tangible representation of your hard work.

But, when you've owned your home for a period of time you learn its idiosyncrasies and shortcomings as much as you would a spouse. When you're exposing your home to scrutiny from would-be homebuyers, somehow a part of you is up for auction as well: your tastes, choices in decoration and home fashion.

A film or creative endeavour has similar misgivings. An audience will only ever witness the finished product and pass their judgment based on what they see. In a few instances though, the ordeal of getting to the finished product far outweighs the achievement of the original idea. Think *Lost in La Mancha* or *Hearts of Darkness: A Filmmaker's Apocalypse*.

Thankfully, as is the custom in the Toronto real estate market, we would never have to hear what was to be said about our house. We were snug as bugs, deep in the heart of North Whitby, waiting out the ordeal. After the last of the touch ups were done, we turned the enterprise over to our real estate agent. The first open house was reserved for her fellow agents. They were the first to scrutinize 410 Coxwell. Take their discerning tastes back to their wide and varied house hunters and make their decision as to who might fit where and under what budget.

Judging from the responses of the other seasoned realtors, they could determine if our asking price of $389,900 was reasonable, too low or too high. Depending on the market, (those tens of twenties of people who were serious about attaching their lifestyle to their biggest investment) and whether her hand might be robust or apprehensive, the clients would ultimately decide how the pride of home ownership would be allowed to impact their lives.

The initial number is the scariest concept. Though a city dweller for over a decade it has taken me considerable time to wrap my heard around the staggering numbers that are coughed up in real estate.

"A mortgage that big," I could hear my Dad cringe, "they'll never be able to pay it off."

"But a mortgage that big no one has the INTENTION of paying it off," I retorted, "It's an investment."

"Yeah, but as soon as you attach the word investment you attach the word risk!" he said cryptically when we purchased five years before.

There was no arguing with him then and how could I? In many respects he was right. It was just no one had informed him the rules of the game had changed. In the boomer dialect you bought a home and that was where you were going to stay until you were too feeble to care. Pensions were secure, so was retirement income.

How can you reconcile that with the fact in thirty-odd years where once an executive made ten times that of an average worker he (or she) now made over 400? And yet that status was no way directly tied to the performance of the company even AFTER they went to the government for billions of dollars in bail out money?

To which, in order to save the workers from potential lost wages those governments capitulated to stave off perhaps a greater harm.

The resulting roller coaster of wealth and distribution: people turned to the one thing they knew had some value, their homes. And when you have an over-inflated sense that home will always be worth something?

Joe Kennedy once said, "When I heard the shoe shine boy talk about getting into the stock market I knew it was my time to get out!"

We would have to remain confident that the price we chose to list was a reasonable representation of the value of our kind of home in our section of the city.

Staying in constant contact with our real estate agent, it was also her commitment to us to read and interpret her fellow agents and report those findings.

"It's looking good guys. You've got a very good house. It shows very well. Parking. The backyard. A basement apartment. Those are all very good qualities. There's not anything you don't already know. The feedback has been great. We're looking promising for the open house this week-end," and with that report, the communication was once again silent.

The temptation to take a drive into the city and rub shoulders with the people who were interested in purchasing our home was extremely tempting. To want to know what they think it might be worth. And then, when the numbers begin to dazzle before your eyes, you start to fantasize about the things you can do. The things that money can do for you. Maybe we could travel again. Maybe it would be easy to find good jobs out east. The possibilities were intoxicating.

I'd sat tight on the yurt front. The two most important hurdles had been dealt with. The septic system that begat the building permit. The cheque was in the mail. Anything beyond that could be shelved until a later date, or so I thought. If worst came to worst, I told myself, I could scramble up the pole and tap into the grid for power. I'd done it before.

****

If we really knew how much our children were paying attention to our conversations it's doubtful they would ever be allowed to share our table. Within each and every household there lies a Watergate scandal that could easily be prevented if a small rule that designated our kids to the shitty card table until adulthood. They are a sponge for every word, every syllable and every phrase. But what they don't always translate is the context, or the body language or the hidden meaning that is evident in everything we say. There is an entirely more astute dimension to how we communicate: it isn't always what we say. It's how we say it.

Rick and Marsha have a son Griffin, who is a month and a half younger than our son Dustin. Rick and I grew up in the same country neighbourhood where our parents were friends. Being both blonde haired and blue eyed, pale complexion gave us the nickname "albino twins". Our house was a converted one-room schoolhouse on the eighth concession just outside of Palmerston. Rick's family owned a farm around the corner. The house was a massive two story, red brick, three-bedroom behemoth who's every nook and cranny was necessary for the four children raised in its confines. Not to mention the two, my brother and I, who were constantly present to add to the energy that whirled around the place. Of Rick's three siblings he had a younger brother, Scott, and two older sisters, Tammy and Laura. Rick and I would maintain our friendship despite attending different elementary schools and the usual distance that two years difference in age and high school inevitably imposes.

The tight bond between the Hamilton's and the Noble's would be snapped through time but rekindle once again in the next generation: my brother Jeff and Rick's sister Laura would elope to Niagara Falls in the summer of 1999. I was best man at my brothers wedding. Their first daughter, Bethany, would be born two years later in 2001. I was in Saint John, on the set of *Vendetta: No Conscience, Nor Mercy* starting my romance with Sylvie when Bethany was born.

To say it was inevitable that Sylvie's emergence on the family stage would ruffle definitions, positions and other sensibilities would be a gross understatement. Stubborn, smart-mouthed, sarcastic and fearless, Sylvie was, and is, the perfect foil for the patriarch dominated Hamilton clan. The challenge for all of us is sometimes muting the urge to say what we really think for fear of offence or misinterpretation. The result, sometimes the necessity of speaking our minds, saying how we feel and dealing with the fall-out is constantly shelved for some more or less opportune moment. Instead of a more contained family explosion, the tension can and does mount to the point at the time of ignition the emotion is tantamount to a nuclear detonation.

It was closing in on the last moments of our stay with Rick and Marsha as we patiently waited for the presentation of our house that the beginning rumblings of a family showdown started showing evidence.

We were settling in to our evening meal, enjoying some wine, when the inevitable lubrication of ideas started to tumble down past our teeth. While in the one corner Sylvie is opinionated, feisty and unafraid to ruffle feathers, Rick's wife Marsha is more reserved, political and able to diffuse potentially dramatic situations. She is the ultimate referee.

The conversation turned to our plans after we would arrive in New Brunswick.

"Jason doesn't speak French, so I'm a little worried that he won't be able to find a job right away," Sylvie said.

"Worry pas," I responded, "I know that if worst comes to worst I can either always commute back to Toronto and work in film or I can go into the trades. I'm just worried about you."

"It's not easy changing careers," Rick said as Marsha took a sideways glance, "look at me. I'm volunteering right now. I went back to school, got a job out west where the commitment to the environment is abysmal at best and I can't even get a temp job in my field here in Ontario."

"Ouch," I said, "but at least one of you has a steady job."

"Yeah, for now," Marsha piped up at last.

"Oh?" I queried.

"Well, there's always change going on in my field. The Team Leader who brought me in might be leaving and I'd have to report to someone else..." Marsha drifted off.

"At least we have some control of our change," I said with confidence.

"So what kind of job are you going to get in, where is it, Richibucto?" Rick asked.

"Well, we're not going to be living in Richibucto," Sylvie and I both responded.

He was leading up to something. Something was on his mind. Something he wanted to share and reveal.

"Yeah, don't you remember Rick, I told you we're going to build the yurt and then live in it until we got jobs in Moncton," I said before turning to Sylvie and continuing, "y'know, we really should have had a press conference to declare this information…"

We all laughed. Rick continued to smirk.

"Well that's not how Bethany tells it," Rick revealed. The sentence hung in the air for a moment before Sylvie interjected.

"More wine!" she declared and hopped up from her seat to pour another round. The woman lives for spice.

"I think the bottle is empty, maybe I should go and get more?" Marsha said diplomatically, trying to eradicate herself from responsibility.

"Yup, I've got some right here," Sylvie said and plunked a bottle onto the table.

Marsha squirmed for a moment until another sharp thought escaped.

"Oh, let me get the corker," she said and tried to get up. She was just about to push away from the table when the familiar 'pop' from the cork arrested her efforts. She was trapped.

"Okay Rick, what's this now?" I asked. Marsha was keen to let the conflict rest. Her tactics were highly subtle and difficult to detect.

Rick's mom, taking some minor offence at the minimal clutter of their home, imported many boxes of Christmas 'knick knacks' for decoration. Marsha, wise to not broach the gulf between husband and mother-in-law, did not immediately object or raise commotion. Instead, over the course of time, some of those 'knick-knacks' started to disappear. A few choice pieces were allowed to remain and not arouse suspicion. But most were put out in bulk. Rick noticed the hint of change, asked a question or two, then, satisfied with the response let the matter rest. It was genius. I only wish my own wife could be so savvy.

"A few weeks ago we invited Bethany to stay with us for March break. We thought it would be nice to have a little extra company for Griffin. We were having dinner one night and we started to talk about the yurt," Rick began.

"Oh, I'm sure they've been talking about us," Sylvie said, a little offended.

"And Bethany said, 'yurt'. No Uncle Rick, Uncle Jake and Aunt Sylvie are going to live in a silo," Rick said.

"A Silo!?!" Sylvie said incredulously. I laughed, knowing the reasoning of an innocent child.

"Yeah, don't you remember the email my Uncle Bob sent me?" I responded.

"No."

"Well, after Uncle Bob heard what we were going to do I guess he either got interested in the idea or somebody sent him something through his email. Apparently someone got the idea of taking an old grain silo and converting it into a home. It was a really good idea. The space was small, just a one bedroom home. It has two stories with the bedroom on top and a spiral staircase in the middle. It's quite amazing."

"And that has what to do with a yurt exactly?" she continued.

"It's round," Rick chimed.

"Bingo. I guess they were just sharing the idea…" I said in defence of my family.

"What else did Bethany say?" Sylvie quizzed.

Rick turned to Marsha. Now the comedy was over. The conspiracy among family had been revealed. Marsha shrugged toward her husband and absolved herself of responsibility. She quickly spun into damage control.

"Well she only said what you probably already know they're talking about," Marsha said, hoping the redirection would work.

"Oh, I'm sure they're talking about us," Sylvie said indignantly and continued on her tangent, "I'm sure they're saying 'they'll never be able to cope with that small town. They'll never be able slow down after living in Toronto. They'll come crawling back. They'll freak out because there's nothing to do. It's not the big city. There isn't enough stimulation….'" Sylvie went on.

"And don't forget 'high falutin' lifestyle. Money on trees. Cash to burn. Easy life and all the rest of it," I interjected, "did Bethany say something like that?"

Now Rick started to squirm. Though he wasn't the one who said it the guilt of feeling he'd spilled the beans shifted to his body language.

"Don't worry Rick. We've heard it before, and believe you me, we've been thinking the same things. It's scary and we know that. I think we're walking into this with our eyes wide open. At least I like to think so," I said.

Rick breathed a modest smile of relief.

"But if I listened to half of the things my family advised me to do I wouldn't have done a fraction of the things I've done in my life," I said with conviction.

"Yeah, I know they're probably just scared for us, but don't worry, we're probably more terrified of this than they are," Sylvie said.

"And we're not going to live in Richibucto forever," I said.

Rick and Marsha both let out a sigh of relief.

"Yeah, we'll buy a house in Moncton. The yurt is just going to be our cottage," Sylvie said.

"Why does everyone think that just because we're moving to New Brunswick we're going to be living off the land? Where the hell does that idea come from?" I said.

"I guess it's because that when you say yurt and then start to explain what a yurt is that people start to think a certain way," Marsha opined, "I mean once you say it's still used by nomadic herders in Eastern Asia it's hard not to get the picture out of your head that that's what you're going to do."

Her words hung in the air for a moment.

"I wonder if it would just be easier to do what everyone expects us to do and live 'off the land' for awhile?" I mused aloud.

"Uh, what?" Rick interceded.

"Fuck it, why not? Grow our own food. Tend to a flock. Make our own bread. Blankets…" I continued.

"Jason, do you not remember what it was like at Chez Noble?" Rick thwarted, "Paul was the only farmer who wasn't a Mennonite that wanted to farm with horses. He wanted to do things by hand. If there was a hard way of doing things….then Mr. Noble was well schooled in the methods necessary for making his children complete the task! Do you not remember? Why else do you think you and Jeff were invited over to the farm so often….CHEAP LABOUR!"

We roared.

"Look, the point is, we know your family is going to think you're crazy. You know they're going to be talking about you because small town folk don't always have a lot to talk about," Rick was on a roll, "but what they say and what they do will probably always be two different things. As much as they might not always come off as though they don't support you, the truth is they have absolute respect for you because you DO have the balls to have a dream and carry it through."

"Yeah, I guess you're right. It's just that as the house goes on the market it's fuckin' terrifying to think we're actually going through with this thing and the last thing we need to be doing is wasting time fighting with family," I said cryptically.

"Yeah, well, they said the same thing when you bought the house didn't they?" Rick said.

"True. But with the market south of the border taking a shit, I'm a little worried they might have been right!"

****

A mixture of excited nervousness and fearful dread accompanied us in the car as we drove back into the city on Monday. If she'd known how, I've not doubt Sylvie would have put the house under surveillance for the duration of the showing. Not for monetary purposes: she wanted to know how well her decorating was received. Our Mommy friends, Amie and Sarah, saddened at the prospect of losing one from the flock, both offered to covertly survey the clientele.

"I was talking the place up," Amie said as we gathered with them again, "I was saying how much promise the neighbourhood had. How the school had been approved for the 'whole child' program. How close it was to downtown. Sarah on the other hand…"

"Oh, I was just casually interjecting if anyone could tell if the smell had finally left," Sarah said.

"Excuse me?" I said.

"Y'know, from where we'd stored those dead bodies," Sarah deadpanned before continuing, "Amie is trying to get rid of you guys and I was trying to sabotage the whole thing."

"I love you guys. We're really going to miss you," Sylvie said, teary-eyed.

"I tried my best, but I don't think I was very successful. If there isn't a dead body in your backyard, maybe I can, I don't know, install one," Sarah mused.

"Just make sure the cheque clears first, we can buy it back later at a discount," I offered.

"Hey, great idea, we should try that," Sarah said enthusiastically.

"So," Amie interjected, "tonight's the big night."

"Yeah, we have no idea how this works. I had a dream last night about a number that I'm not going to tell you because I'm still scared we're going to jinx this," Sylvie said.

"At least for the meantime we can move back into our house," I sighed, "and we can get back into a routine."

"You'll be back at our Wednesday night supper?" Sarah wondered hopefully.

"For sure. I don't care if we have to offer a friggin' Halal meat or a vegan voodoo dance before we eat. It's back on until you won't have us any more," I suggested.

"Perfect. Well, good luck. If you move, Audrey and Ruby won't be the same," Amie said.

It wouldn't have mattered if we were twenty-one or fifty-one, there would always be a special bond with our first-time Mommy friends. I've always found it gratifying and simultaneously humbling when being a parent obliterates careers, status, money, wealth and power like a cyclone through a tarpaper shack. You either bow down and submit yourself to that reality: you will be overwhelmed on occasion, you will lose your composure, you will make mistakes both colossal and benign: or you resist and alienate yourself from the community of people and ideas it will take to see you through that challenging period.

Admittedly, some parents handle their circumstance with a grace and calm that seems to shower the rest of us with the impression they were born to raise children. Those people are few and far between. Perhaps after a brood of several kids where mistakes and accidents in parenting style have been smoothed over does that state of enlightened parenting occur. I would wager that that never happens with the first-born.

Without a close network of family to lean on for back up we drifted around the corner to the Roden family drop-in centre. Almost immediately, I was introduced to Sarah and Amie. Like ourselves, they were also in their thirties and figuring out this parenting thing. Sarah, a whimsical, devilish redhead, and Amie, curly long blond with the presence and personality to match were not even aware of one another's existence until the onset of parenthood: despite living just six doors away from one another!

As the idea of getting out from being stuck in the house day after day became more comfortable, the drop-in centre became our home away from home. Except it was closed on Friday's. The more we got to know one another, the more comfortable the idea became to have someone open up their doors for our own impromptu mommy group.

The more the idea evolved, the more the thought of rotating homes became part of the vernacular.

"Okay, sounds like a great idea," I said initially to Sarah, "do I need to bring anything?"

"Well, we usually keep it fairly simple. Biscuits, coffee, cookies, that sort of thing," Sarah responded.

"Okay, great, I'll tell Sylvie about it and hopefully we can both make it," I offered before going home for the day.

Hesitant at first, was how Sylvie first reacted to the drop-in centre. Like me, she was raised in a small community where drop-in was across the street to an aunts or grandparents house. My formative years were spent similarly at friends and family going from farm to farm. Drop in, we both opined, sure, we used to do that all the time.

(One of the challenges of parenting. You can draw on some of your own experiences when raising your children, but there is absolutely no way you'll ever replicate it.)

Hence, it was I who first went to break the ice and extol its virtues. It wasn't long before Sylvie got on the bandwagon and crashed the Friday drop-in with her own east coast flavour.

"Coffee, cookies?" she said incredulously, "frig that, I'm bringing wine and cheese. If we're not going to be doing this at an institution, then I think we should make it a little more social."

The idea was a smashing success. Breaking down that little unwritten rule of responsible parenting we imbibed in a little of the nectar of the gods. Not a party, but as a means to remind ourselves we were adults first before becoming parents and there was no reason we shouldn't continue to behave so.

As maternity and paternity leaves ended and children were shunted off to jockey for position in the most desirable of daycares, the Friday afternoon tradition needed rescheduling. It became a Wednesday night supper. Now the wine could really flow with the knowledge it was a great crutch to escape the drudgery of full-time employment.

But as our friends integrated back into the working world and feeling the pull of achievement and team bonding, our film lifestyle was starting to feel more isolating. Try finding a day care that can take your child at the last minute on a Friday afternoon and watch him until the next morning. 'When are you going to pick up your kid again?' they might ask. 'Hold on, I'll get the director and maybe he can answer that question.'

Because I was the breadwinner and that was my work situation, Sylvie's career options were severely limited. Being the last of the moms who wasn't able to get back to her career furthered her desperation. Stepping up to the porch and turning the key, the relief to get our new life unfurled was measurable.

"Wow," Sylvie said, "it's beautiful!"

"Yeah, don't get too attached to it," I said before hauling the car seat into the kitchen. The house was the best it was ever going to look. Tastefully decorated for staging and immaculately cleaned. As I looked over at my wife I thought she might need a moment for herself.

"I need to go pee!' she declared before charging into the bathroom, blubbering with every step. Just as I exhaled a deep breath, the doorbell thundered off the walls. Margaret waited outside. Sylvie dabbed at her eyes as she emerged.

"Hello Margaret," I said as I opened the door.

"He-lo," she said before stepping forward to give Sylvie a warm hug, "it's going to be okay. Look, I know this is a big moment but you've got nothing to worry about."

"Y'know, I really thought I was the one who was going to be a basket case..." I said.

"It isn't easy, this is your first house and you're not upgrading or moving to something different in the same neighbourhood," Margaret understated.

"I'm good. I'm good," Sylvie said as she too took a quick breath, "I'm just going to take Dustin upstairs."

The mood became quiet as we sat down at the dining room table.

"Okay, you've received six offers on the house," Margaret began. I haven't looked at them. The agents are outside. They will present their offer on behalf of their client. We will take everything in, closing dates, home inspection, financing and of course, purchase price."

"They're outside?" we asked before Sylvie stood up and walked to the window. Lined along the street, a horde of expensive vehicles hugged the curb. Agents either lingered along the sidewalk and paced in nervousness or clutched their mobile device of choice like the warmth of a lover's body.

"Wow, this was a different kind of pressure than I was expecting," I said.

As the door opened and the first agent presented their client I was feeling less and less like a homeowner and more and more like a privileged father as prospective grooms approached with cap in hand to make their best case for my 'baby'. Now my eyes were beginning to light up as I began to imagine the numbers dancing and bouncing higher into the stratosphere. The sweet smell of greed was tempting me with her bounty. How could we exploit this moment for all it was worth? Maybe we could reject all of the offers and tell everyone to try again. Highest bid wins. Brow furrowing, grin aching, I started to smack my lips in anticipation.

"My client was very impressed with your house. It shows well. They like the basement apartment that gives them options to help with the mortgage...."

I was already salivating. I could feel myself lift out of the chair, casting the door as wide as possible, letting the flock gather before my feet before telling them to collect every single penny they could rub together before I decided who should have my beloved home.

"My client is offering $405,000 with no conditions on home inspection or closing date. Thank you."

As the door closed before the next invitation was extended my beaming smile muted somewhat: 405, who is he kidding: To the gallows with you and your low-ball offer!

And the procession began, with varying degrees on the same theme: the clients making a bid for our home were made aware of the other interested parties. Each presentation not only included the purchase package, they also included a little back-story about the individuals looking for a home. Now our mood started to turn. Sylvie and I looked at one another for a moment and realized the gravity of our situation. Here was our opportunity to not just pocket some hard-earned cash and run like mad to the East Coast, it was a chance to leave our neighbourhood in a little better place than when we arrived. Thinking of Sarah and Amie and all the other young families we'd gotten to know did we really want to sell our home to someone who was going to throw up walls, divide the place into more apartments and rake in their own cash all while living comfortably far away from the situation?

It was the last presentation of the day: A young agent who'd been working extremely hard for his client who'd been through the disappointment of bidding on several homes only to lose out. His client was young (late twenties) in a relationship, professional, originally from a small town who could one day see her life transforming as ours had by starting a family. We were blubbering before the number was revealed.

"My client has no conditions on financing, home inspection or closing date. She's making, what I think is a very fair offer: $435,000."

"Thank you very much," Margaret said courteously. Sylv and I tried desperately to suppress our delight at such an easy decision.

Margaret lined up the offers on the dining room table.

"Now, we're going to look at all the offers one by one before determining..." and she didn't finish her sentence.

"The last one," Sylvie and I both nodded.

"Yeah?" Margaret concluded.

"We could go back to these offers, we could get greedy and turn this into a bidding war and get maximum dollar," I began.

"But they've all made a fair offer. I like the girl, we know how hard it is to get into the market and we think she'll be a good fit for the neighbourhood," Sylvie opined.

"Okay, I'm relieved. You had other people interested in your home and you could have increased the price for it, but you also risk not selling your house at all if you do that. I think you've made a smart choice. Congratulations, you've sold your home. Now Jason..." Margaret continued.

I slumped back in my chair. One hurdle had been cleared, but Margaret wasn't going to let me off the hook.

"Did I not say that whatever money you put into your house would come back to you ten-fold?" Margaret said and crossed her arms.

"Yes, Margaret. Forty-five over asking. You were right!" I agreed.

"Alright then, congratulations, you've sold your home!"

When he walked back into the house, the agent representing the buyer was elated to the point of tears.

"Oh my gawd guys," he said, "we've probably been in on half a dozen houses that turned into a bidding war and Alison just couldn't afford what was happening. She's going to be extremely happy. If you don't mind I'm going to call her right now and deliver the good news. And for me, well, this is my first house…"

For them, it was their first house. For us, the clock was beginning to tick. Certainties had been achieved. The certainty of the budget we could work with. The certainty of when we would have to move. The certainty of change. There was still some time until the official closing in the middle of June. But that time would not stand still. Materials needed to be finalized. Contractors hired and the yurt livable.

While everyone was celebrating what was a significant milestone, the sands of time meant that that celebration would change quickly.

7

Setting Out

"I taught you were a telemarketer," the grizzled voice intoned. I harrumphed to myself. I'd been at the phone for two days. Two days to find a company that would drill the water well. The first attempt was unsuccessful. I left a voicemail.

"Hi Roger, my name is Jason Hamilton and I would like to inquire as to your availability to drill a well. I can be reached at the following numbers…"

No hidden agenda, no promise of the need to purchase goods. As his business number it made sense that he would thereafter check his voicemail and return the call. A few hours passed. Being the persistent sort, I tried again. Who knows, I said to myself, maybe something wasn't working and he didn't get the message.

I tried again and again it went to voicemail. Rather than repeating my earlier script, I decided to hang up. Lacking true patience, I gave it five more minutes before calling again. This time, someone answered:

"Hello. Hello. Hello!" I called into the phone. No voice, no breath, no scent or psychic resonance that another human being was on the other end. Instead the phone died.

Gritting my teeth, I punched the numbers. After just one ring the phone went to voice mail.

"Alright," I thought to myself, "we have an interesting phenomenon. He obviously has call display and doesn't bother to check his voice mail. He's seen the number appear several times and reached a critical decision. That decision is this: I would rather maintain all discretion and distance from a potentially annoying telemarketer than risk picking up the phone to entertain legitimate business. What has the world come to?"

More importantly, what had I come to? Why didn't I take my business elsewhere? He was the only local. The rest were farther away. The farther away, the higher the cost.

To break the luck I called Roger from our home phone number to try and throw him off the scent.

This time: Success!

His reaction, "I taught you were a telemarketer…."

"Uh, no Roger, I'm not a telemarketer," I defended.

"Well, we 'ave de call display," Roger continued.

"Yes, and you must have been quite surprised when a Toronto area code flashed across your screen…" I commented.

"Uh, yes. Soo I taught you were a telemarketer…and didn' answer de phone. It's jus' so, time consuming to 'ave to listen…" and on he went. The most notable element of our exchange was his cadence. In university I took a linguistics course and felt quite confident in the quality of my ear. Judging by his voice, the high rasp and throaty delivery, I pegged my man Roger to have lived in a very small place in a very remote area for a very long time. The kind of place where change is a modest guest who doesn't regularly schedule meetings.

"Well, I'm not a telemarketer. In fact I have legitimate business concerns. I'm shopping around for a price," I said.

"Where you property?" Roger asked.

"Do you know where Upper Rexton is?" I asked.

"I know dat place. I tink we do one or two well dere…:" Roger continued. It was the pause in his voice that had me wondering if he should really be doing this line of work much longer. (Or, if he actually COULD do this line of work much longer.) Rather than abandoning the line and calling 911 to make sure someone could verify animation during these momentous breaks in his dialogue I made a conscious effort to be patient. I would be dealing with local people. Local people who, while on the surface seemed as though some remedial education about the particulars of the modern world might be necessary, had vast reserves of information. A rural life continually takes in information about the world around them. They knew more about the ins and outs of the local soils and rock formations than could be gleaned from the best topographical map.

"Is good soil dere. Lots of clay. Good for bes' water," Roger continued along. I was getting impatient. Impatient to speed the conversation along. Impatient to interject my own thoughts, my own questions about what was involved and who was responsible for getting the water into the yurt. And then what becomes of it after the whole thing is hooked up.

"I know you place. I tink we get water dere 'bout twenty feet," Roger said.

I remembered the words of my neighbours. How they'd struck water at just twenty feet. Plentiful but undrinkable. Rogers recall was remarkable.

Before I mentioned those concerns, the slow diatribe and heavily accented English covered all the bases and answered all of my questions.

"You wan' we can do everything. Run you line into you plumbing. Make sure you can drain for de summer," Roger said and continued right along, "we use a plastic hose now. Easy to drain. No problems for you when you shut off for de winter…"

"Okay Roger," I said, not to remind him that I was still on the other end, but to accept his services.

"Alright," he seemed to hear, "when you come out we can wait for de road to dry, you know, and den we star' a' mebbe seven or so and we finish aroun' 1."

"Great," I said, "I'll contact you when I get in town and we'll take it from there.."

****

I need no full explanation of how the big, wide wonderful universe works. I know with absolute clarity that I am just a small, infinitesimal speck on the ass of the whole thing as it tumbles around the cosmos. However, in these, and other instances when I have endeavoured to reach beyond my knowledge to pursue a project or creation, it is astounding to me how many helpful hands there are to guide me along the way.

Stuck was a film adaptation of a real-life event. A nurse in Texas hit a homeless man who became lodged in her windshield. Where care would have helped him live she callously let him die before disposing of the remains.

The filmic version, where Saint John New Brunswick stood in for 'somewhere in America', the homeless man (Stephen Rea) frees himself and kills his assailants (Mena Suvari and Russell Hornsby). While the film was a bit of a flop at the box office (it cost 5 million to make and grossed $67,000 in theatrical revenue's) it was a boon to Sylvie and I. The replica garage that was erected in the studio for filming was dismantled and the material free to any who wanted it. We hoarded a bunch up to our property for future use. But the real bonus was in the crew list.

Richard LeBlanc was the construction coordinator for that little show back in 2006 and he happened to live in the area where we were going to build.

When the time came to assemble my building team Richard was the first person I called.

"I'm sorry Jason, I'm teaching, but I will help you out anyway I can. Do you remember Chris Hudson from the show?" Richard responded.

"Unless he was at the wrap party," I said.

"No, I think he went home. He's a great carpenter. Anyway, I have his number," Richard continued.

"Thanks Richard, that's awesome. I'll get in touch right aw...."

"Do you have an electrician?" he asked.

"Uh, no, don't have that yet either," I said. This had turned into one stop shopping. Keep it coming Richard, I thought to myself, I haven't got a plumber lined up either.

"I don't know a plumber, Jason, sorry," Richard apologized.

"Don't worry, you've already put me farther ahead than I was hoping. I'm gonna get in touch with Chris and call the electrician. Thanks so much," I hung up enthusiastically.

"Hello, Chris Hudson," I hesitated into the phone.

"Yeeaaa," Chris said on the other end.

"Hi Chris, my name is Jason Hamilton, I got your name from Richard LeBlanc. We worked together on Stuck," I blurted.

"Uh, okay. Sorry if I don't recognize you," Chris said.

"No worries. I didn't do the whole show, plus I was on set and it was four years ago. You were in sets or something weren't you?" I asked.

"Sets, construction, props, you name it," Chris said.

"Anyway, I was wondering what your availability is for the end of May?" I said.

"Oh, well, I'm waiting to hear about a show but I should be finished by about that time," Chris said.

"You don't know for sure?" I said.

"Well, it's supposed to go soon and they haven't told us whether they're pushing it or not. If that's the case then we should be finished in time for me to help you out. And what would I be doing?" he queried.

"Well, I'm going to build a yurt," I said.

"Okay," he said, unfazed.

"It's a round canvas structure. The walls are made of lattice," I went on.

"Okay. Uh, what are you building it on?" he continued.

I explained, and as I did, I looked for the signs. Signs that I might be losing him, signs that what I was proposing might be out of his range of skills and abilities. He remained as calm and cool as though I was proposing to trundle out to sea and dredge up the Titanic.

"Okay, so, pully and winch it is then," I could already hear him put the pieces of the puzzle together.

Anytime I've been in a similar position I've poured over copious amounts of information to get to a point where I absolutely KNOW a project, and its demands, inside and out before I start. And then, by the sheer volume of evidence I've managed to compile, the simple understanding of what needs to be accomplished and why is lost under a mountain of information. And then I panic, stutter and stew and throw as much energy at the situation as I can muster until it somehow rights itself.

Only now can I appreciate how I operate. Then I think I was secretly gauging my hires ability to steer clear of such a swirl and maintain buoyancy during the inevitable patches when answers weren't immediately visible. He passed with flying colours, and so I put his status on 'Hold' until I landed in New Brunswick and construction was to begin.

With such a tiny project, outside of traditional building sensibilities, and with a project manager, me, at the helm, it became abundantly clear that having like-minded individuals involved with construction was my best option at success.

I pressed Richard for further names and possibilities.

"Bill is my electrician," Richard continued.

"Would he be okay to entertain a project like this?" I asked.

"I don' tink electricity cares WHAT kind of structure you build," Richard responded.

On the other end of the phone, Bill had that familiar slow cadence to his voice that I was to discover was symptomatic of others from the area. Their thoughts and words representing a deliberate need to say only what needs to be said.

"I'm building a yurt," I declared and went along on the same preamble I'd executed for countless others. Cutting through the banter and getting to the point, Bill had some pointed questions.

"So, you want me to install the temporary then?" Bill inquired.

This moment gave me pause. A temporary?

"Uh, excuse me?" I asked again.

"Are their power lines?" he asked, "You are going to be hooking up to permanent power aren't you?"

"Well, yes, of course," I stammered.

"Then I'll just set up a temporary pole and you can use it to build," he continued.

"Ah right," I said stalling as it took a moment for his suggestion to trigger a place of recognition in my mind.

"Y'know, from my days in the construction industry I was always accustomed to working alongside an electrical generator. I just assumed that that was how you built things. Right, get a temporary panel hooked up and that way we can have as much power as we need without having to hear the grinding noise of a small motor all day. Thanks Bill," I responded.

"Just give me the coordinates and I'll go and set it up for you," Bill said.

Here was my first opportunity to assert and address one of those small little footnotes of communication. That small moment when the issue of trust for the professional and the willingness to reveal my lack of knowledge (and loss of face) is delivered a glancing blow instead of opened up for complete transparency of function.

"Hmm, install," I should have asked, "does that mean complete where all I have to do is plug in my extension chord and away I go, or does the utility (NB Power) have to come along and connect the temporary power pole to the grid?"

But I failed to make that positive affirmation. Partly attributable, no doubt, to my previous experience working as an electrical apprentice. In that role temporary service work was performed by the electrical contractor. The utility completed the permanent hook-up at a sometimes much later date. Those temporary connections were performed by yours truly on a couple of occasions.

It wasn't with career intentions in mind that I once upon a time I sought work in the electrical trade. I'd seen enough fire and electrical shock to appreciate the fine line the protective rubber insulation kept me from oblivion. I'd even stood on one of those 400 amp rated cables at full capacity and felt my shoes buzz beneath me to realize the scope of electrical influence wasn't completely measurable.

But, when the necessity to work is great, it made sense that I would find work in the trade when film was slow. And find work I did.

****

As I crawled up the aluminum ladder that was propped against the outside wall, the nervous shaking in my legs was evident.

"This thing's a little wobbly," I called down to the audience of two (my boss and his assistant) that were standing in the driveway.

They snickered to themselves as I reached the point where I could perform my duties.

"So just reach up there with your pliers and cut the service. Start with the black first," Andrew called, "make sure you hold onto the other end, we don't want the live end to whip back and strike the house…"

I took a deep breath, remembering as much Zen as I could. "This day will pass. This day will pass."

I reached up with my gloved hand and gripped the black wire. Fumbling in my pocket with my free hand, I pulled out my pliers. I was in position. I took another breath. I'd always wondered how much rubber insulation was necessary to prevent the transfer of electricity from the tool to the person holding the tool. I was about to find out.

I spread the pliers apart and arched my hand toward the insulation. Sweat dripped from my brow. My legs quivered beneath me. The jaw of the pliers opened up around the wire. I checked once again to make sure I was holding the right part of the cable. All good. I shuffled my feet, feeling the presence of a long drop to the pavement below. Oh god, I thought to myself as my chest hugged the outside wall, hoping against hope that that proximity might give me some suction quality should the ladder slip out from underneath me.

I couldn't stall any longer. Without taking a backward glance, I closed my eyes, gritted my teeth and tensed the muscles in my hand.

Just as I was about to carry through my action: "BANG!"

Carlos yelled from the ground. The two giggled like school kids. If

I had the leverage I'd have hurtled the pliers in their direction. With spite and anger, I fulfilled my obligations before returning to safety. I wanted to spew profanity and stomp off never to return. But that day I had the first taste of having to learn to arrest my emotions and my fragile being for the greater necessity of being a provider. I was not amused, but I was also unable to retaliate in any way. I needed the job, and no matter of damaged ego could change that situation.

It was with that previous experience I assumed he would be the one to connect the temporary pole to the grid. I let the matter in Bill's hands and moved on to other objectives.

****

The quotes were starting to return for the materials we would need to build the yurt. The platform, the beams, the joists and the plywood were going to account for close to seven thousand dollars. It was necessary. Without the wood there would be no yurt. I chose the granddaddy of all wood supply shops: Kent Building Supply. Kent was a subsidiary of JD Irving Limited. JD Irving was the largest owner of real estate in the province of New Brunswick. New Brunswick just happened to be covered in 80% forest. I could never purchase building material any cheaper than from the mother ship Irving (aside from tearing down my aunt's barn, packing up the lumber and getting it hauled out, but even that was debatable).

Even with the hard numbers of the sale of the house, the building costs of the yurt were starting to add up quickly. Well: 5 grand, septic: 10 grand, yurt: 30 grand, material: 7 grand, auger piles: 8 grand. We were almost sixty grand deep with only a shell to show for our efforts. And as all the DIY and Decorator and Mike Holme's shows will tell you, it's in the finishing efforts, the kitchen and the bathroom, where the real money is spent. I hadn't even tracked down a plumber to know how much that was going to cost. This cheap little yurt was slowly and steadily climbing close to being a hundred thousand dollar investment.

"What about labour, what about lodging?" I said aloud to Sylvie.

"Don't forget moving expenses," she chimed in.

I could see our tidy little score whittling away like sand in an hourglass. The hundred and fifty thousand-dollar profit was quickly vanishing. And for what? I started to ask myself. A tent. A fucking tent. I was beginning to wander off by myself, mumbling and scratching my head: what were we getting ourselves into?

Sylvie herself was a little less reassuring.

"Hun, don't worry about it. It's going to be the most elaborate tent New Brunswick has ever seen," she boasted with a hollow tinge to her voice.

I couldn't eek out a response. All I could fixate on were the tallies and summaries of our dream.

"And besides, the house is sold, we can't pull the plug on this now. We've got nowhere else to go," she continued.

"Well, since you put it like that…" I chided, a little edge beginning to grow in my voice.

"You worry too much. Look, we've got a roof over our heads, you've made some good money, we made a good profit on the house, we'll build the yurt, find a house in Moncton, get jobs. You watch, it's all going to work out great," she finally said.

Perhaps it was that I found myself mired too much in the significance of the big picture to lend my attention to the present situation. Our child was healthy and happy. The troubles of the neighbourhood had subsided. And as news of our imminent departure started to spread, old Shaky himself made it a point to amble across the highway and offer his support. He was even sober.

I was beginning to entertain the thought that half liquored and swaying like a loon every May Two-Four week-end maybe wasn't such a bad way to be. This was going to be the first year in five that I wouldn't be greeted by Shakey's shenanigans as the summer season unleashed itself. I would be in my new province, deep in construction.

As it was, the time for departure was quickly approaching. The septic system was going to be installed on May 18th and I promised the septic engineer I would make a token appearance. The plan, like the giant boulder that careens down the mine toward our hero Indiana Jones, was starting to gain momentum. I was starting to make the more acute, immediate decisions about the build. Namely, what equipment, tools, personal items and the like I would need to bring with me on the drive. Not to mention, increasingly paranoid as I was about the budget, I decided that that long trip would be best to be maximized.

I marched out to my shed and started to take an inventory. The garage door open, I was going through my options of what was important and what wasn't, when the footfall of Larry Smith echoed behind me.

"Hello Jason," he said.

"Hello Lawrence. Another fine day on *The Thing*," I said.

"Are you sure you don't want to come back. It's picking up again and we could really use a hand. One more week of work before you leave…" Larry offered.

"Thanks Larry, but I'm finished. Retired. I should have had a press conference," I lamented.

"Well, don't say I didn't try," Larry responded.

"I mean, it is after all, the whole point of the move. Y'know, to actually get out of film. And I'm not gonna be like you there, I'm not going to be commuting back and forth," I retorted and continued, "because if I have to, I'll be grumbling louder than you will."

"Fair enough. I hate coming up here. I curse myself the minute I arrive almost until the minute I point the Ford to head home," Larry said.

"I know, I was working with you remember, I got to hear it every day."

"Yes, dear boy," Larry said, "you did. But say listen, thanks for letting me stay for free since you guys cashed in on the sale of the house. I appreciate it."

"You're very welcome," I said.

"You didn't have to do that. I mean, the damage to your plumbing alone…" Larry went on.

"Not to mention the aroma from the maple flavoured bacon," I continued his thought.

"Not fair, Sylvie loves my maple flavoured bacon!"

"True. So do I."

As the exchange subsided, I focused again on the modest hobby shop that had grown in my garage. Lumber donated, given, salvaged and purchased over a period of time. Tools accumulated through Craigslist including a behemoth of a table saw with its cast steel tabletop. I was sizing up the van.

"Hmm, what do you think Larry, how much weight do you think I can carry in the Mazda 5? Six seats, average weight of occupant: two hundred pounds. Theoretically I should be able to take about a thousand pounds with me."

"Sure, but have you ever carried that much weight for fifteen hundred kilometre's on New Brunswick roads?" Larry retorted.

How much would it cost to ship all of our worldly possessions across the country? More importantly, how much was a thousand pounds going to save us versus the wear and tear on the van?

Larry finally relented.

"Y'know, I've got a whole empty truck I'm going to be taking with me."

Ah, guilt, that great harbinger and equalizer of action. I'm sure as soon as he offered the compensation in lieu of rent he was starting to regret his decision. My eyes lit wide with anticipation. Seeing my reaction, Larry tried, in earnest, to add as many footnotes, appendages and fine print as he possibly could to the offer.

"Now, be forewarned, dear boy, the old Ford is starting to show her age. The transmission is slipping and I don't know if she'll make it all the way back to the East Coast," Larry corrected.

"Are you saying you can't take anything?" I asked.

"No, I'm not saying that," Larry continued, "I'm saying if you want to send anything with me you'd better make sure it isn't anything of value. If this wreck falls in a heap halfway through Quebec I'm leaving it at the side of the road and find another way to get home."

Tools were scratched off the itinerary.

"Well, I'm planning on having a yard sale to get rid of some excess. See anything you like?" I offered, trying to sweeten the deal.

"The same rules apply. If you're sending it with me you've gotta be willing to part with it."

"How do you feel about this lumber?"

"Not a problem, so long as it all fits in the box of the truck."

The lumber, itself, was nothing very special. Old barn floor joists and a few nice pieces of black walnut. Whatever was too big would be cut to fit.

What really concerned me was a rather large piece that I had yet to bestow a purpose. It came from my Gooderham and Worts collection: an 8x8 thick beam that was over six feet long. I'd damn near busted my gut lugging it out of the construction site when no one was looking.

I stole away to make a measurement of first the beam and then the box (said the actress to the bishop.) It would fit, with room to spare.

"Perfect," I said, "when I fly back from New Brunswick to close out the house we'll load you up for your drive. Sound good?"

Larry took a second look at my stock. I could see the inner turmoil. Outwardly a curmudgeon, his reputation was mostly a facade, but would rear its colours on near-perfect occasion.

He grimaced a sigh: "Jason, what in the fuck are you going to use this shit for?"

****

While we had an account our upcoming adventure was discussed in the family circle, pulling that dialogue into public consumption was not on the agenda of our last family gathering. At least not intentionally.

"I hate the posey posey pictures," I heard Sylvie grumble.

"Yes hun, I'm aware of that. But, y'know, it's nice to indulge someone else's wishes don't you think," I said, trying to coax cooperation.

"Fine," she huffed.

"Look, I'm not a fan of them either. But it's better than nothing at all. Not to mention, my family can't afford to hire a photographer for a day to catch the natural stuff that you like," I countered.

"I know, one day I'd like to. I offered to go halves on the idea with your brother. Where did that idea go?" she said.

Sometimes you just learn to edit some ideas before they're proposed.

"I can't remember if I floated the idea past them or not… Regardless," I continued, "we've got two days there before I head out on Monday. Let's just try to get through this week-end with our skins intact."

An hour later, at a rendez-vous in Waterloo, we were seated at the Wal-Mart for our family photos. Dustin was in a state, fidgeting and fussing as my mother tried to anchor him to her knee. Beth slipped into a comfortable photogenic pose that wasn't in the script.

"Bethany," her mother pleaded, "can you sit up like the rest of us please."

Sylvie leaned into my ear, wanting to make a comment, I held firm. Better not to give any fuel to this dangerous ship that was teetering on the red zone. Kids, four in total, all under ten, being made to sit for what seemed like an eternity, for the satisfaction of the six adults who were just as equally out of their element.

With deliberate patience, the first series of photos managed to be captured. Breathing a little easier, the kids too starting to relax a little, the itinerary changed to the couples. As my mom and dad sat facing one another, the young attendant switched their hands to reflect some kind of affection. First high, then mid, then low. She peered through the monitor at what would be the final capture.

Sylvie moved to make a suggestion. I gripped her wrist, a little tighter than normal, but enough to arrest her words.

Settling on a pose, the attendant quickly snapped a picture. Sylvie's lip tightened, the artist in her wanting to break in on the dance, draw on her considerable experience, and create something more. For her it must have been like watching a hack amateur invade her kitchen, make a huge mess of every cooking utensil she possessed only to turn out something as simple as Kraft Dinner. The frustration was digging into her core.

Dustin seized on her attention during the solo session with all the grandkids. His tantrum was starting to fizzle. Hungry and impatient, the armchair parents all started to weigh in.

"He's probably just hungry," Laura opined.

"Not enough sleep maybe," my Dad wondered.

The intentions are generally good, we all do it even when we know what we're saying is probably more hindrance than help. In men it is the 'there's a problem that needs attending to, and I can't rest until I've done whatever is in my power to try to fix that problem'. It explains why we'll opine, aloud, about any and all things we truthfully know nothing about simply because we're hard-wired to seek solutions.

The opposite sex (wired modestly on the problem-solving front) is more unnerved by incessant children. It is their worthiness as a caregiver they feel is under scrutiny. Every whisper, every gesture toward a flailing parent is somehow heard despite the piercing wails of a screaming child. Our self-esteem in our own parenting abilities locks on, with deadly accuracy, any peripheral behaviour that might reinforce that fragile self-esteem. We're hard on ourselves and seek the fuel to corroborate.

The challenge in parenting is to subdue reaction to such stimuli. This is much harder to do when, before child, you yourself were just as guilty of being in possession of all knowledge parenting.

Sylvie and I clashed many times in our young parenting lives over one subject: sleep. We never seemed to be getting enough and couldn't agree on what was adequate for our boy. No matter the bedtime he greeted the sun as it rose. We argued incessantly about the subject and came away with no conclusions and a deadly case of amnesia. Destined to be repeated ad nauseam. Nothing was resolved.

We could agree on one thing, however: once he was asleep, he was asleep. Getting him to that state was another matter. Like his Grandfather Hamilton and his Great Grandmother Dodette: if there was a party going on he most certainly wanted to be a part of it.

The scene shifted to the cavern of the small bungalow. The afternoon light faded behind the drawn curtains. The scene at Wal-Mart passed into oblivion. I don't know who needed the nap more urgently, us or our son.

It is with great envy that I've seen children who can crash at will despite bedlam and hoopla all around them. Out on the couch, faces pressed into the cushions, bums stuck in the air. The party careening around them. Nary a hint of wakefulness. Such children are an anomaly. Or so we'd become accustomed to believe.

His snack complete, his pajamas, after much struggle and the indication the change was a wish to invite slumber, he began to relent. His restless form started to show signs he might find the calm to be able to pass into unconsciousness. With a nod and a wink over to Sylvie, we too bedded down. The fast twitches and spasmodic muscles told us he reached the initial state of slumber. When his brain neurons finally aligned, he would be in such a deep state it would take a nuclear blast to rouse him. But the stage prior was critical. The initial stages of sleep most closely resemble the waking stages in brain wave pattern. The neurons not quite in unison.

If either of us were to so much as switch a sleeping position, the commotion would interrupt his rested state and we would be forced to start over again.

In that moment I realized my thoughts didn't concern Dustin the restless devil, but were free from that fixation. They'd had time to stray. Did that mean he was, finally, painfully, asleep? I lifted my head from the pillow and glanced to my side. In silence, Sylvie shook her head 'no'. Frustrated, my head rested back onto the pillow. "Go the fuck to sleep," I thought to myself.

Just as I settled back, the side door to the house opened and a burst of commotion was ushered inside. In synchronous motion, Sylvie and I bolted upright. "Shit!" we whispered aloud.

I leapt over my family, gathered clothes, and charged up the stairs to try and quell the disturbance.

I couldn't explain how difficult it'd been; in the year and a half we'd been parents, of the lengthy struggle to establish a solid sleep pattern. I couldn't explain the worry that not enough rest might be hindering his mental development. I couldn't explain how stressful it'd been for the relationship between Sylvie and I. I couldn't explain any of it. I couldn't because I was trying to get all of that across to two women who'd raised five children (and several adults).

The words that I formed, in hapless sleep-speak, were far from their intention. It came off as a command. A command to three equally precocious children who, unless they were obedient pets couldn't remain noiseless, no matter how hard they tried. It was preposterous to think so.

Instead of trying quell the commotion, I inadvertently tripped with my can of gasoline. The smouldering ember (one that, unbeknownst to me had been simmering for a time) immediately ignited. I was engulfed before I knew how to react.

****

"Cheerios. Fucking cheerios!" I said to Sylvie. "She's been holding onto that since Easter."

Arguments are never what they seem are they? Of course it wasn't about Cheerios. It was about what cheerios represent. (Incidentally, the circle metaphor, as it pertains to the yurt, isn't intentional. We really did have a fight over Cheerios.)

It was about respect. Or lack thereof. Cognizant of the sugar content in most cereals we asked for a chocolate reduction for Easter just a few months prior. My mother complied with the Cheerios suggestion and diligently sorted to accommodate our wishes.

After the hunt was finished, Sylvie callously chucked the excess into the garbage.

"She didn't even wait!" my mother barked, "I don't care if you get home and throw them out there. That really pissed me off. I did what you asked, I didn't say boo and she just, pfft, chucked them in the garbage. And now. You want us to tip-toe around you again!" I flinched, waiting for the big F. U.

"No. I'm not going to pussy foot around you two, three, anymore!"

"Cheerios!?!" I said incredulously, "I'm about to take my family out to the East Coast where you'll probably only see us once every few years and you want to give me grief over goddamn Cheerios!!"

"It's not about Cheerios!"

And these things never are, are they? The cheerios are a decision. A decision on taste, on values on belief. We made a decision for an exception on the amount of sugar intake our son would be allowed during Easter. With a culture that worships at the altar of sugar (and whose population is 50% obese) for every special occasion we asserted our wish to tone the consumption. It is a fine line between asserting your authority as parents and offending others who don't see the danger in the indulgence.

In another's eyes, the point of being a grandparent and enjoying certain holidays is watching the expression of children as they take absolute delight in devouring copious amounts of chocolate. It is those special occasions that are unique to the position. Whereas parenting is front line vigilance on diet, exercise, media consumption, pollution, bacteria, clothing, sleep, mental stimulation and everything in between, the grandparent gets the opportunity to exact a little revenge on their children by not being so vigilant. By allowing all those things that they once had to make special care of for their own children.

Their children who might (and still are) be a little spirited and determined about where they place in the general order of things.

That general order of things that always seemed to infringe on the balance that existed in the homestead. At the Easter holiday we had overstepped that balance and deliberately exercised our authority as caregivers to tone the feast of chocolate. Nothing out of the ordinary. We requested raisins and cheerios instead of nuggets of gooey chocolate goodness and the like. After the bits were collected up and Dustin had had enough Sylvie disposed of the rest in the garbage. Not bothering to hide her transgression.

The golden rule was broken: the less you know the better! Had we not been present during the Easter holiday and chocolate was indulged without our knowledge that would have been part of the special bond that exists between grandparent and child. A shared secret "Screw those tightwads that don't want the kids to have too much fun," they would have shared. Subsequently, had the discarded Cheerios been trekked back to Toronto and dumped in a homeless man's lap then no disrespect would have been witnessed.

So a fight that originates over cheerios, or who doesn't put clothes away, or who does most of the work around the house or who snores or whose shit doesn't stink go much deeper than a surface discussion.

That small, round cereal was all about respect. It was about my mom stepping out of her comfort zone to respect our wishes and we stepped on those efforts by very indiscreetly throwing the offending breakfast cereal into the garbage where she could see it. She was displeased and she was going to let me/us know about it.

"Mama." I could hear faintly from downstairs, "are my cousins here."

And the beast was awake.

8

Getting To Know The Locals

It wasn't the send off we were expecting. No ribbons, sparklers or pomp and circumstance. Just cinders and ashes in the wake of the fury. Was the matter tabled for further discussion or soothed emotions? No, it was as if the moment was erased from time. Citing the need to return to Toronto and continue our packing arrangements, we dashed away from Harriston with little fanfare. We arrived Saturday morning and left just as abruptly on Sunday.

"Well," Sylvie offered as the van sped away, "I wonder if they're still planning on coming out to see us this summer?"

I harrumphed, still simmering, "I don't know if I want them to come see us this summer."

Very little was added to our dialogue the rest of the way. No point lingering on the confrontation. We needed to return to Toronto and pack the van. The septic installers would arrive Tuesday. I had 1600 kilometres to cover between now and then.

"Are you going to stay in Bathurst with my parents on Monday night?" Sylvie asked.

"Nah, the septic installers are going to be there on Tuesday. I'd like to get in as soon as I can," I replied.

"Jase, you've hired them. They're doing the job for you and it's a job you know they've done a gazillion times before. You'll probably just be in the way," Sylvie retorted.

"You're probably right, but I should at least put in an appearance," I remained steadfast.

Sunday was quiet. Dustin careened about the backyard. I started the slow, methodical packing process. I would be in the province from now until a brief sojourn back to Toronto to close out the house. I would be building the yurt, staying at a rented cottage a few kilometres away. I would need clothes (both work and play) tools and other essentials that Sylvie would not be able to take on the plane.

Judging all of those considerations, the last, most important factor was weight. The formula germinated in my head.

"This isn't a little two hour joy ride, dear boy," I could hear Larry caution, "you'll be driving on New Brunswick roads. They're great if you're on the highway," he informed me cryptically.

As the afternoon sun wore on, I slugged first one, and then the other kayak onto the roof rack.

"Those aren't going in the moving van. Better to get the heavier items out of the way first," I declared.

The next heaviest item was the table saw: an older Delta whose body was solid steel. But the real heft was in the tabletop. I carefully took apart two of the panels. I huffed heavily as I wrestled one leaflet into the back of the van. It settled onto the floor and the van shrugged noticeably.

"Those have got to be about seventy-five pounds a piece!" I said initially with pride. Proud that we wouldn't be paying the freight to ship these items across the country. I was saving some money already. (Blatantly forgetting, of course, that moving expenses incurred in the pursuit of a new job is a massive tax deduction.)

With just two items loaded I'd already reached half my travel weight. Or so I thought. After all, how could I know for sure? It was a complete guessing game. With each piece that was added I judged the weight according to my own lifting capabilities and spread the items across the chassis. It was the best I could do.

I thought about taking the load down to the recycling centre and testing it there, but as the wheels almost kissed the housing all I wished to bring wasn't possible.

I opened the back of the van and ventured a gander inside. There was volume to spare, but how could I know for sure if the car could handle this much weight?

****

I have had occasion when leaving an item to chance has worked out in my favour. The year we purchased our home was the year the councilor in our ward championed a movement to do away with front pad parking. I hurried to get our application in on time. Several months later I received a notice rejecting my application: the reason? A four-inch diameter tree that reproduced via its root system could not be in any way altered, transferred or harmed in the construction process.

Taking the dimensions used to explain their reasoning I appealed with the assertion an angled parking space could be achieved. Several months passed before a city inspector arrived to perform his own tests. I just happened to be home when he was conducting his investigation.

Yes, he agreed, an angled parking space could be achieved and yes he would file just such a motion.

More months passed. And more. I filed my application in March of ought five and appealed in August. No decision was forthcoming. I followed up in November.

"Sorry sir, but (given the acceptance of the new legislation to ban front pad parking) you shouldn't have even been ALLOWED to apply for front pad parking."

A fairly definitive claim one would think. And so I thought. I abandoned the matter. After all, you can't fight city hall can you?

We adjusted to that lack of an extra parking space. Because of city boundaries for street parking zones the side street directly in front of us was off limits. In our dodgy neighbourhood we had to park the car down the street, around the corner and in a bit. A half a kilometer walk is a bit much after you've worked a sixteen-hour day.

We worked. We traveled. Viet Nam and Thailand for six weeks in winter of ought six. My nephew was born in February of that year. My aunt passed away.

Fully fifteen months after our original application a rather large dossier arrived in the mail. "You have been approved by the city to install front pad parking." The documents therein contained detailed specifications of where we could put our parking, the dimensions of the space and how it pertained to the rest of the configuration of the house. It also came with two little caveats as addendums: 1. Perform the work in six months time or the approval is null and void. 2. Upon completion submit that the work has been performed in order to receive a license subject to yearly renewal.

But the city wasn't completely accommodating to such alterations. The curbside, where the driveway met the road, wasn't formed in the cement. After the inspection of the parking space was completed a road crew came to build a ramp. A lump of pavement was slapped onto the edge of the curb. Not wanting the pavement to jut out into traffic, the slope was quite large.

****

I would know, in the moment I eased the weighted van down the slope and into traffic, whether or not I would need to shed weight. I got in the van, turned the key, eased off the parking break and slowly inched down the drive between our house and our neighbours. Ever so gently, I slowed the car down until I could survey the traffic on the road. This was to be no rush job. I needed time and space to test the load. I waited patiently until the perfect opportunity presented itself.

Gritting my teeth, the van rolled ever so gently ahead. The front tires started to dip over the edge. I released the break a little more and let gravity take over. Before the tires even touched the road an unmistakable scrape echoed loudly. I pounced on the break. Firing the transmission into reverse, I touched the gas in the hopes of preventing any serious damage. The last thing I wanted as I eased the car out of the driveway with a thousand pounds of weight rigged to it was to leave the oil pan on the sidewalk.

Scraping more, but saving any further damage, I backed the car to the front of the garage. Some weight would need to be jettisoned.

By the time the car eased its way into traffic early the next morning I still hadn't been able to weigh my load properly. At least I'd managed to learn something from my test the day before. Instead of taking the ramp direct, I aimed the wheels toward the right. One tire contacted the street before the other joined it. As the car touched down onto Coxwell our two bikes swung on the rack that hung from the roof. The rubber grip on the handle bumped noticeably against the back window. As the last of the back wheels met the pavement I clasped my teeth. No scrape and no shattered glass. It took me a moment to realize the car was still propelling forward as I fixated on the rear-view mirror. I spun around, astonished: I was lurched perpendicular to the road, listing. I backed across the four lanes until I was safely on the side street

With a break in traffic, I wheeled the van around ever so gently until I was piloted northbound on Coxwell. My only concern left was navigating the heave's and to's of traffic lights and potholes until the sweet smooth surface of the major highways was under my wheels. Fortunately, I had five years of knowing where exactly the major disasters lay in wait. Cognizant of what a too fast corner or sudden break might do to the poor Mazda 5, I commandeered the slow lane all the way out of town.

Feeling brave that I managed to avoid any major catastrophe's on the way to the Don Valley Parkway, I let the car loose a little on the on-ramp. A test. Just to see.

I'm lucky I didn't end up in the rhubarb.

With the extra weight, the car whipped down the hill at breakneck speed. I failed to accommodate for the extra breaking pressure necessary to arrest my trajectory. With all the weight the wheels were clinging to the road but the upper body was pulled wherever the momentum would take her. I pressed on the breaks for emphasis, but the ride down was met with another dip uphill and brought my suddenly out of control car onto the happy side of gravity. The momentum slowed substantially and I was able to bring the skiff into traffic without catastrophe.

I pitched the autopilot to never leave sight of the slow lane and maintained vigilance until the eastward bound lane of the 401 beckoned me. The good ship Mazda 5 was well on her way to New Brunswick.

Except for a minor exchange with a convoy of dump trucks halfway toward Belleville, the drive to my soon to be new province was largely uneventful. Largely.

Having fixated on the intricate details of shipping materials, packing the house, building the yurt, and then loading the van for the drive east, I neglected a very critical detail: Nutrition. When I become so absorbed and fixated on a certain task, it's almost as if my mind tells myself that in order for it to proceed properly, I need to torture myself as best I can. I throw all my energy into what I'm doing and neglect to replenish where that source of fuel is originating. This is especially true during a road trip. By the time I got in the car, my only sources of fuel were two bags of snacks: one of trail mix and one of prunes.

I was closing in on Bathurst when the familiar twinges of discomfort were starting to percolate in my stomach. The one companion I'd forgotten to make room for had had plenty of time and energy to snack on a heady diet of stress and fatigue. The only question that remained to be answered was the length and severity of my attack of Irritable Bowel Syndrome (IBS).

Stopping in for the evening at Bathurst and the inevitable slow, steady onslaught of symptoms, I resigned myself to what the doctors have continued to inform me. The disease is difficult to control. It can be done so by altering diet, maintaining a regular schedule, getting proper rest and reducing stress. 'Great,' I would often hear myself agree with my doctor, noting the obvious, 'tell me something I don't know.' It wasn't necessarily what to do about the prevention, but what do you do once the symptoms are starting.

I'd had varying degrees of luck with a whole host of different elixirs and mixes. While in Squamish BC working on a movie of the week, the symptoms flared up after a few weeks away from home and working all hours. I'd heard that perhaps Olive Oil could help relieve the bloating and discomfort. I poured drops of olive oil into cup after cup of water and quaffed the remedy with such regularity I spent half the night in the washroom either pissing or stooped over the toilet hoping for a puke that wouldn't come.

As much for psychological reasons as scientific ones, the concoction worked. For a time. And they often would. For a time. Aspirin. Ibuprofen. Gazol. Tums. Pepto Bismol. All brought marginal temporary relief until eventually my body adapted to the interference and the IBS returned with a vengeance. I'd resigned myself to two things: it appeared that nothing I did from a diet perspective was ever going to change things so why not just live as I live.

And so, after flopping out of the car from fifteen hours stuck behind the wheel, I clamoured up the stairs to Fern and Flo's and socked back a few beers to quell my nerves.

Setting out the next day, intent on meeting the septic system installation team I was besot with an onslaught of symptoms. Imagine wanting to vomit, belch, fart and defecate simultaneously. My eyes, red from fatigue, started to water as I grimaced to hold in the pain. I might arrive in one piece, but there was no way I would be able to hang around and supervise. No matter, before I was to even set foot on our property, a lingering problem that I forgot to deal with was suddenly presenting itself. My phone rang with a twinge that I could already sense was urgent. I hadn't spoken to Mike since the time I hired him to design the system. I knew what the problem was, I only hoped it wasn't catastrophic.

"Yeah, hi Jason," Mike said.

"It's the holding tank isn't it?"

The holding tank mystery. Its presence was known. We'd let the approval of its usage lapse through the course of time attrition: out of sight out of mind. What was its size? Its location? The previous owner told us it had been approved but there was no supporting documentation of any kind. At least not from him. And now its existence was impacting the current construction. Why, or why hadn't I dealt with it before?!?

"Uh, yup, we just came across it."

A grimace, a pause.

"It's not that bad. But what we don't know how big it is, how much is in it."

"Well Mike, (brrp) I'd tell you if I could, but honestly, I haven't got the foggiest idea how big it is. When we bought the place the previous owner had a toilet in a little shed that was fed with rainwater. I thought he said he was approved for a septic system, but anyhow, I can't say how big the holding tank is…"

"Hmm, alright. Well, we'll have to get it pumped out first and then Pat says we can probably just crush it."

"Okay, great (another pause. I swallowed air to force up some gas.) Sorry, excuse me."

"Do you want to make the call to get someone here to come and pump it out?"

"Well, (errfff) I'm not really capable of making that call right now. I'm in the car and I was hoping to be there already. I'm just outside Miramichi…."

"Well, we can take care of it for you. I'll just add it onto the invoice and that way we can get this taken care of right away and finish getting the system installed…"

"Perfect, I trust your judgment. Thanks Mike and I'll see you in a little bit."

As I hung up the phone and the miles ticked away on the odometer, a familiar refrain was starting to warm up in my consciousness. Depending on the severity and where it falls during the session it can be either a very long, protracted monologue, or it can be short and sweet. It is the angst-ridden guilt of an alcoholic either suffering through a severe hangover or desperately intoxicated. That was the place where my own desperate pleas began as I struggled to cope with the effects of IBS.

"Auugghhh, why me? Why is this fair? (Fart, burp, belch, sneeze cough.) I'm doing everything I'm supposed to do, I'm eating right, and I don't drink much. I exercise. Why? Why? Why? Why? Fucking' Why!!??!!"

And then come the screams, the howls of protest and exoneration. It is the pain that takes over. The nerve centre in the middle of your gut that's spitting out the words and somehow not you. It's another version of yourself that's taken over, putting the conscious part of your personality in suspended animation. You hear it, know it, are fully aware how sad, pathetic and futile every word, expression and utterance is, and yet, you're also helpless in being able to stop yourself from making the expression.

I loathed myself for the better part of an hour until I grimaced through enough of a recovery to be presentable for the crew.

When I finally arrived at midday and spilled out of the front seat the septic truck was busy drinking the sludge out of the holding tank. The installation process was on hold until the truck was to be loaded, packed up and out of the way. (From the cozy confines of my sleep induced healing coma, I would witness none of this.)

I shuffled up the driveway and into the action. As I was one of perhaps two cars that would be on the road that day, it wasn't long before Mike spotted me and walked over for salutations.

"Hi Jason," he said in his Nova Scotia accent.

"Hi Mike, how's it going (suppressed, under the collar burp)"

He had a grin he couldn't suppress. The kind that says, very deliberately, there's something I want to tell you and you're going to be quite astonished when you hear it.

"Guess what?"

"What?"

"How big do you think your holding tank was?"

"No clue."

"A thousand gallons!"

We both stood and stared at one another.

"A thousand gallons!" I repeated.

"Yup. If we'd known that before, we could have just hooked the weeping bed up to that."

"Honestly, I knew it was there, but I had no idea how big it was. A thousand gallons eh?"

"So, you're pretty lucky really," Mike continued. My stomach was bursting like I'd been sprayed with a shotgun blast and my thoughts were fixated on sinking eleven thousand dollars, literally, into the ground when it wasn't necessary, I was having difficulty agreeing with his viewpoint.

"It's not going to be in the way of the rest of the septic," Mike declared.

"Okay, so you're going to dig it up then?" I asked.

"Not unless you want us to."

"What's the best option?" I said.

"Crush it and then fill it back in," Mike said.

"Alright, well that should make it easy then," I said.

"Okay, we'll go ahead and do that. And it looks like your shed isn't going to be in the way after all," he said with continued cheer.

He could have told me I won the jackpot and it's doubtful I would've reacted any different. I took a short stroll around the property. About the same one I always take when I'm renewing my acquaintance. Down along the side of pines that separate's our space from that of our neighbour and along to a small little cut in the scrub bushes that announce the edge of the bluff. It's a small incline that drops off about eight to ten feet in total before a very modest beach in advance of the tidal river. When the tide is low, the sand gives way to muddy clay that seems to be home to every kind of seaweed and sea sludge I've ever known.

Long and out about half a kilometer of shallow tidal river flats the water intertwines with mud, foliage and the creatures favourable to that ecosystem. It is the primary reason we managed to purchase our property for such a modest sum some seven years ago: it is not so suitable for boating or motor-powered pleasure craft. For kayaking, it's ideal. A tidy slip to shrug into the boat and push away without having to step down from a dock.

I stood at the river's edge, looking back up through the bluff toward the mini hi-hoe that ambled back and forth a hundred and fifty feet away. The sour stench of the low-lying sea sneaked into my nostrils and gurgled my abdomen once again. Swiftly breaching the bluff, I powered past my contractors, mumbling something about needing to get unpacked, spilled myself into the car and headed away.

Some twenty minute's later I was at another precipice: on top of a cliff overlooking the Atlantic Ocean. With the smattering of dwellings that were very sparsely sprinkled around the area, the precipice might very well have been the edge of humanity itself. The van pulled up in front of the middle cottage. Desolate. Remote. The closest life across the straight on Prince Edward Island. The season was very much low and the swarms of camper trailers that would give her life had not yet arrived.

I fumbled at the door, unlocked, before bulling myself in with the only bag of importance for this crucial time: my mini-pharmacy kit. I opened a cupboard door in the kitchen, filled the first glass I could with water and powered back three or four painkillers. I doffed my shoes, stripped my pants and flopped onto the bed before rolling into the fetal position begging for a healing coma that would make all the pain go away.

****

Appearing the next day, this time with a stomach that was showing the beginning signs that the symptoms had subsided and would eventually pass; I backed the still loaded van onto the property. There was work to do. The van had been made to suffer almost as much as I did and it was time to lighten her load.

I opened every door, somehow with the vain hope that the ship might unload herself. As I puzzled over where to begin unpacking, I loaded my arms with the first thing I could scoop up and headed over to the shed. I set the tool bag down, rifled through my pants pockets for a key and inserted it into the lock. It gave way with a quick click as the doorknob turned with the key. First with my forearm, followed by my elbow, shoulder and finally, head, all of my forward momentum was halted by a door that begrudgingly didn't move. Cocking my head to the side, I was about to rear back and thunder a body check at the door when the access to a memory file had suddenly been accessed. Instead of plastering the physical expression of my faulty testosterone all over the barricade I took and step back and reconsidered.

"Oh fuck," I said finally to no one in particular, "all the wood from *Stuck*."

Remembering what I was up against, I marched to the back of the van and pulled out a long kayak paddle. I sauntered up to the two large doors at the back before letting out another sigh of frustration. The crack between the large double doors was covered with siding. I was about to hurl off a string of expletives when the tool bag caught my attention. From it a screw gun with a Robertson bit was put to work undoing the siding. In short order a small slit between the double doors presented itself. I slipped the narrow blade of the kayak paddle up between the two before it rested on the underside of a two by four.

With a little "Kiya!" I popped the wood out of the sleeves and one of the doors sprung open with a blurt of arrested energy. Jumping back quickly, the stored wood settled a little into the new breathing space.

"Ugggllyyy," I muttered. Before I could even begin to unload the van I would have to march the several hundred pounds of used lumber that was now calling the shed home. I took a moment to size up the situation. How best would my efforts be served? Traversing the shed, I had absolutely no choice. I stood in front and gazed ahead. The front of the structure was sitting almost on top of the septic system. As I looked first one way and then the other, I was really left with no choice. The shed would have to move. Already my brain was beginning to process the best way I could serve the situation. 'Sure,' I thought out loud, 'I'll have to unload all of my other stuff again, but I absolutely can't take any more weight over that gravel road in the poor van. Okay, good thinking Hamilton, you're making for an excellent project manager already. One decision in the books.'

I looked around again, and this time finally took notice over a few new developments I failed to grasp the day before. A large pile of rocks was humped up beside the shed. 'Hmm,' I thought again, 'does that mean the septic installers are finished?' And then more details caught my eye.

"Okay, the temporary power has been stabbed into the ground. No hook up just yet, but I'm sure that's in the works. The grass had been cut, wow, we're doing well."

I was beginning to rest easy. I would unload the contents of the shed onto the grass close to the property line. With the shed empty, I would deposit the tools and other working necessities for building the yurt into the space. When I wrangled a local to come with a tractor to haul the shed to another location, I would empty out the truly heavy contents (my table saw) to aid the transition. The temporary electrical mast was in place and only needed connection to the grid.

More relieved, the items I'd left to their earlier destiny seemed to have found their own solution. Even that which I'd pretended didn't exist (the old septic tank) hadn't caused too much hassle or heartache.

I consulted my construction plan, an average, run of the mill notepad that had now accumulated all of the information pertaining to my build. In the back, to account for the people and how they would contribute, was a mini-rolodex for trades people, contractors and other general knowledge. A little further along was a crude calendar I'd scratched out onto the page, and still further along, the log of events leading up to the build, and the tasks and milestones that had been achieved.

From what I'd been accustomed to doing, this was the best way I knew to organize my thoughts. Occasionally I traversed the same thought patterns a few times, but at least the thoughts were recorded for posterity. Because getting the idea on paper was one thing, executing the plan smoothly was another matter entirely. Now, instead of planning the building process, I was in the thick of meeting out its execution. Maintaining composure and making decisions from afar was one thing, being mindful while in the midst of the pandemonium was quite another.

Seeing the springs on the back of the van breath a huge sigh of relief, I tacked the two by four back into position. If moving the shed was now of paramount importance, the best thing I could think of was to find a local farmer who was already equipped with a backhoe and loader. Surely, in this small place, if the guy up the street didn't have one, he'd know the whereabouts of someone who did. I crawled back into the van and sped off.

On the north side of the Richibucto River, a little farther downstream from its namesake town, there rests a gas station next to a local bridge crossing the river. An Irving gas station (in this place where the name reigns supreme) is the landmark for direction. From the Irving in town, one road leads west into the New Brunswick hinterland along the north shore of the Richibucto. On the outskirts of town are the Bonar Law historical grounds. The historical grounds are a farm museum in honour of the first (and only) British Prime Minister to have been born outside of the Isle's.

As the road continues west the farmland gives way quickly to forest. From there, right through the heart of the province, it is a challenge as to who and what commands the land. If left unattended for even a short spell of time, the quickly reproducing softwood forest immediately assumes occupation. The preeminence of clay makes farming and other cultivation difficult to rest from the thickets.

The favourable cost of the land makes it too tempting not to try.

Coming up from the river, I stopped at the corner before making a right at the stop sign. The farm I approached always seemed to house substantial activity, and a loading tractor seemed inevitable. I drove up the way before parking in the driveway. I got out of the car and walked to the door. I rapped at the entrance several times, waiting for the inevitable shuffling of feet to make a response. Nothing. I waited a few more minutes before trying again. Again, nothing. I walked back to the van, wrote some instructions on a sheet of paper and attached them to the main door.

I got back in the van, left and tried my luck across the street. On the north side of the highway, along with the farmhouse, a small mechanic shop was also in operation. Before even approaching the farmhouse, I sauntered into the shop to find out if anyone knew of the whereabouts of its occupant. I explained my situation, cutting through the French/English language barrier before being invited to sit down. Maurice was called in from the back shop.

"Yeah, I know de guy you wan' to talk to," he said. He sat on the opposite side of the desk, plunked a phone down in front of me and ordered me to dial.

" 'es a real character. Got a loader, can help you out. Bruce Hickey," Maurice informed me as I dialed the numbers

When I got through on the other end, Bruce Hickey was on his cell phone. In between being a farmer it seemed he was also in the employ of a gravel truck. As I explained the situation, he nodded and said "yes, we can help you out."

"For an agreeable sum.." I ventured to add at the end of the conversation.

"Good enough, I'm a bit busy, but when I'm finished I'll come out and see you," Bruce said before ending the conversation.

Thanking Maurice, I hung up the phone, elated. My first unforeseen obstacle was quick to find a solution. I hustled out of the garage, being profusely grateful along the way, and sped back to the property. I wasn't sure in what capacity Mr. Hickey would be returning, but all the more reason to be as prepared as possible for when he did arrive.

A mangled poplar clutched to life at the front of the shed. It would need to go first before I could crawl underneath and free the shed from the plumbing that held it underneath.

Swatting away at the labyrinth of six and eight legged creatures who weren't so pleased at my decision to do away with their home, I hacked, cut, bit, chewed kicked and cursed the twisted phylum. It wasn't long before it toppled over and I hauled it away to the burn pile.

Next, I lay down on the ground to get a good survey of the plumbing pipe into the ground. 'Hmm,' I thought to myself, 'this is pretty straightforward.' I pulled out my hacksaw and did away with the PVC. Halfway through, my concentration was broken by words that preceded the individual.

"Mr. Hamilton?" the voice called.

"Yup, that's me," I replied, drawing my hand back out from underneath the shed. As I rolled onto my back and moved to get up, Bruce Hickey was standing at the corner of the shed.

"Is this the shed you need moved?" Bruce got to the point.

"Yeah, it's kind'a in the way," I said making my way to my feet.

"That shouldn't be a problem," he said.

"Great, y'know for a nominal fee," I threw in the offer.

"Perfect, we can call it a campaign donation then," he said.

"Campaign donation?" I said quizzically. I wasn't exactly current with the local political scene. (My only previous political experience was with the local mayor of Rexton, David Hanson. He thanked me profusely about an article I wrote on the area for *Saltscapes* magazine.)

He stood over me with his webbed baseball cap, his patterned shirt and scruffy jeans, hardly the look of the politico. Not even as one dressing down to 'be one with the people'. He was the people. But for all I was aware he was throwing his hat into the ring for the Lions Club.

"Yup, I'm running in the next election."

And before I had the opportunity to naturally play to his query, he continued his diatribe as if I'd already requested the sermon.

"Did you know he tried to sell NB Power? Sell the provincial utility. You have absolutely no idea how pissed off he's made everybody here in this county. Sell it out to the Quebeckers. I mean, did he forget what Quebec Hydro did to Newfoundland? Turned around and sold power from Churchill Falls to the Americans. Just to save a few bucks on the debt when we all know it was going to cost us ten times down the road. No, it's got to come to an end. We've got to throw him out of office!"

I had to give him credit, much as he talked the game, as other political beasts are want to do, he was actually going to march into the political ring. He was also, as I continued to move about the property in preparation of getting the shed moved, very passionate about the upcoming clash. The one-sided conversation continued along as I nodded and tried to be polite, but really wasn't lending my ear to his platform.

Unfortunately, as everyone else treats the drive-through province, I too was completely ignorant of the provincial political climate. (My last understanding of any issue was from a former Toronto ex-patriot who was living in Saint John. His mother's property was directly in the path of a pipeline the mighty Irving machine was trying to get built.)

It reached a point I was struggling to find a reason or a distraction to reel in this runaway soapbox and get him back on topic.

"So what do you have to move it and how soon do you think you can do it?" I finally blurted.

"We've got a hundred horse tractor with a loader that should be able to take care of this no problem," Bruce declared.

"Wow, that's great. What a relief," I sighed heavily.

"I've got a short trip and I should be back by Wednesday. Will Wednesday be alright?" Bruce said.

"Shouldn't be a problem. I've got your number and if I don't hear from you by then I'll be giving you a call."

9

The Disappearing Yurt Fiasco

Despite his bravado, I was to discover Bruce Hickey was a decidedly cautious operator. I arrived at the property early Wednesday morning, all slop and drizzle, staring at the shed that would not move. All the meditation, all the visualization techniques were not going to make the simple 8' x 12' shed move by itself.

Remembering very well my uncle's fifty-odd year routine in farming, I made a point to wait until Bruce was finished his morning's chores before placing a call. Though it was the first, most important step, I held every confidence I could pry Bruce and his tractor away for a couple of hours when time allowed. I turned the page to the rest of the construction schedule.

The temporary power station just could not lose itself from my focus. A mast, supported by lumber, and then several protruding stakes and braces made it look like a giant upside down Tolkien-esque hieroglyph. Under the meter base was a short, weather protected plastic pipe to a switch and then a U-ground 20 amp outlet. Three cable ends hung down from the top of the mast waiting for attention.

"Uh, alright. That's that. It just needs to go from there to there," I nodded from grid to mast, "but we have a little air gap."

Surely it wouldn't hurt anyone's ego if I called the utility to find out when the temporary power was going to be hooked up?

"Did anyone explain to you how the process works?" came the voice deep in the bowels of the NB Power customer service building.

"Uh, well, I was in touch with a couple of people. I didn't have the best cell phone reception at the time so I thought I would wait until I was in the province to get the ball rolling. My electrician has the temporary in the ground and it just needs to be hooked up," I offered.

"Well, we have to send an estimator first to see how close you are to the grid…"

"Oh, it's not far at all. My neighbour has a post on his property and then it goes to his shed for power."

"Okay, that's promising. I'll find who the estimator is in your area and then he'll get in touch with you."

"You can't just send the truck to come hook it up?"

"Oh no. The estimator needs to do an assessment first…"

"An assessment. Right," I conceded before providing my phone number.

****

Away from our property for a couple of years, the sight was not without the necessity of maintenance. In this, the province thought to have witnessed the evolution of the tree and still absolutely dominated by them, any plot, any rock, any crag, any nook was fair game for a seedling to find purchase and take over. We were saved from an encroaching forest by our neighbour Harry who dutifully mowed our land a few times a year to keep it tidy.

The ditch was another matter. Perhaps nothing was happening on our property because the vegetation at the road had mutated so much finding the place was impossible. If there was little I could do to advance the build, then maybe by clearing the land and taking back our influence over it, it might welcome progress. New age hocus pocus aside, I had nothing better to do. It was either that or dig through all the lumber from *Stuck* and pull out thousands of nails, screws and whatever else was lodged into the used wood. That's all right; I'll take the bushwhacking.

I rooted amongst the mess of tools that littered the bottom of the shed.

"I know my Dad would laugh at this," I said as I pulled out a couple of modest tree shears and pruning cutters, "seeing as he was always more privy to a chain saw. Especially when it came to home renovations."

As I set about allowing my body to operate the tools on autopilot, my brain relaxed to allow the passage of time. For anyone whose ever asked a writer how he/she gets their ideas I'm sure most have a Zen task that brings them to the perfect mental space to conduct creativity. Washing dishes. Mowing the grass. Mopping the floor. The more mundane, the more repetitive the chore the easier it is for the conscious mind to somehow slip away and the unconscious to teeter into all sorts of tangents of exploration. And somehow, someway in that place where the conscious mind takes a vacation, the actions that have been cast in motion have a way of catching up with you. (The great Leonard Cohen is said to begin his morning by washing the floors. Simple. Repetitive. Zen.)

It wasn't long before the estimator from NB Power arrested my efforts.

"Hi Jason, you're in Upper Rexton?" the estimator, Mike LeBlanc said, "Perfect, I'm not too far away. I'll drop by in a few minutes."

****

"The way it works is we're responsible for the first pole onto your property, if you need one. After that, the cost is yours," Mike said.

"Ouch."

"Makes a lot of guys who want to camp out in the woods go solar or wind but don't worry, you won't have that problem."

"Cheaper I bet."

"Yup. Okay, so I'll send this in and administration will contact you about the hook-up."

"Any idea how long?"

"Hard to say. About a month."

I gulped. "A month? Yeah, I can't really wait that long. I'm supposed to start building this thing next week. I need power."

"Well, the best I can do is give you the file number and keep following up with administration as to when they can get out here. Hassle them, keep calling, it's the only way you'll speed things up."

"Okay," I said solemnly.

His truck sped off. Should I bother contacting Bruce about moving the shed?

"Oh hi Jason," he said without cause or thought to the verbal agreement we'd reached, "sorry, I've been meaning to call you. We've got a little check engine light on in the tractor. I'm sure it's just a minor thing you see. But well, the tractor is on a lease. Haven't had it for very long and I'm just afraid that if we go and use it while we know there's something amiss and it really fouls up, well I don't want to be making lease payments on a field ornament."

"That's okay," I said, "I understand. New tractor and everything."

"But, the guy told me he'll be down tomorrow to have a look at it. I'm sure it's nothing, but we want to make sure," Bruce continued.

I chuckled to myself. A hundred years ago this conversation might have made some kind of sense. A traveling doctor to tend to the four-legged engines of rural life. No, this traveling tractor doctor was somehow indisposed.

"Okay, well I'm going to be around so, when you get the tractor fixed you just let me know and we can get this shed moved," I said before hanging up the phone.

I ploughed around the property, devouring and sculpting every piece of shrub and vegetation I could find as though some form of physical exhaustion might ease the situation. As the small forest crashed down into the ditch the gleaming satisfaction of a job well executed was obvious. For the first time since we owned the property I was able to see the road. Wiping my brow, I allowed myself some positive reinforcement: The shed was going to get moved, I started to tell myself, then the Postech people would arrive, then the floor would be built. It was gonna be great!

At least that's what I was telling myself before Sylvie, Dustin and the rest of the Mazerolle family decided to drop in.

Face down in the mud, a low rumble emanated from my back pocket. Though I had been away from people for a few days, I didn't miss or cry out for human contact. I was rather enjoying the solitude of hacking away at my property on my terms, my schedule. I could pause whenever I felt, wander on down to the shore, plunk the kayak into the water and add to the serenity by paddling the river.

I stood up in the mosquito infested roughage and pulled the soon to be antique flip phone out of my back pocket. Sylvie was charging through her monologue before I could respond.

"We're coming out tomorrow," she declared.

"What!?" I responded incredulously.

"What do you mean what? I'm all by myself. I can't work because I've got Dustin to take care of. I've got no car and no transportation for my kit so I can't work," Sylvie continued.

"But that's not what we planned," I protested.

"I changed the flight. We'll be there for the long weekend. You don't want to be alone for the long week-end do you?"

I stayed silent. She powered along.

"Good, because it's Flo's birthday. They're joining us at the cottage for that weekend. Fern wants to drop off the bathtub we ordered from Costco," she went on.

"Er, uh," I stammered.

"What's up?"

"Well, I've hit a bit of a snag," I replied, "The shed is in the way and I'm having a hard time getting it moved," I finally blurted.

"I thought you got a local to move it?" she questioned.

I paused. How much did she need to know? It wasn't just the shed that was fouling up progress. After all, I didn't retreat to attacking vegetation after one silly setback did I?

****

"It was a month ago in the gravel pit when I called Postech. They didn't just want to know that it was a yurt and round and canvas and funky and cool, but how much did it weigh? What kind of beam and flooring would we be building on top of the posts in order to construct the yurt?

The auger piles weren't a completely one size fits all. They had different diametres that could accommodate different structures."

Sylvie nodded.

"What could I say, we didn't have a budget then because the house wasn't sold. I had to get a breakdown from Kent building supply first before I could get one from Postech. I gave Julien our plans and asked him for two quotes: One with the deck and one without.

The first quote was ten grand. Seeing as how the yurt was not going to be our permanent residence, it made sense to me that the wraparound deck could be added later."

She was still following my logic.

"I got the material list from Julien at Kent and forwarded it to Andrew at Postech. Postech had a few scenarios for me to consider: diameter of the posts and height out of the ground. The quote went from eight to six to four grand. And that was without the extra posts for the deck. All I could think of was Flo: Don't do it cheap."

Sylvie nodded, chuckled and allowed me to continue.

"Andrew said: You COULD take a chance and use a combination of the bigger posts and the smaller one's. You would get some of the height you were talking about but then you run the risk of movement. You could use the smaller posts and stay closer to the ground. But again, movement. We know the third option is the most expensive: 21 large posts, but some will be sticking out of the ground three feet," I continued, "So I called him, told him I wanted the larger posts and booked the appointment. Or so I thought. I distinctly recall the conversations ending thusly, "If you could come on such and such a date, that would be great.

"I called Chris Hudson to remind him I was going to be needing him and he said, 'I'm booked on a TV series and I won't be available for another two weeks."

Sylvie started to shake her head with the 'You should know better than to trust film people' look.

"I don't know anybody else hun, I thought I booked him! I called to confirm with Postech right after Chris and the guy told me I wasn't even in the system. At least HE made the mistake and he admitted it. Still, he can't get me in until next week. And even if he could, hey, we don't have any power. I assumed Bill would hook up the temporary because that's how we did it in Ontario. No, here, it's gotta be NB Power. I don't know what I got through to them from the gravel pit, but apparently they only came out to take a look, say, 'there it is' and that's that."

****

"You're coming out tomorrow? But I have so much work to do!" I defended, wondering, how, in fact, I was going to fill out my days with no posts, no carpenter, no materials, no plumber and no electricity.

"I don't want it to be a month before Dustin sees you again. He's going to forget who you are," she explained.

The Dustin logic. If any of her other arguments could be beaten down in a court of law the ace up her sleeve would be the Dustin logic. I couldn't argue. There was no point. Oh, but how I tried.

"I want you to be here too, but Cap Lumière is in the middle of nowhere. There's no park, no playground. No human being for many miles. If I need the car all day, what are you going to do?"

The defence was staggered.

"It's right by the ocean. We can go along the beach. We can take the car. You're going to be working, and I can go into Richibucto," she countered.

What she didn't notice wasn't that I didn't want her and Dustin to be a part of the building process. I'd been in New Brunswick two days and was already a week behind schedule.

Though she had all the best intentions in the world, "You build it and I'll decorate it" the woman knew no such restraint. She would not become personally responsible for the decisions and actions that would need to be taken, but would puppeteer me instead. Accentuated the more I flailed at my efforts. But what could I do?

"Doesn't matter, I've already booked the tickets," she continued.

"Okay," meekly, "I'll pick you up tomorrow."

"Great," she said nonchalantly, "and Mom and Dad are coming for the long week-end."

I gulped. She was pulling out all the stops. Four adults, one toddler, all crammed into a cottage no bigger than a shoe closet. Nothing good would come.

****

"You talk to de guy and after 'e said 'e would move de shed now 'e can't do it?" Fern insisted.

I squirmed, coughed, wheezed. Nothing could hide the facts.

"Yup, that's pretty much it," I concluded.

"Ah bin Jase," Fern left his words hang in the air.

I reclined on the picnic table, letting the aqua blue sky of late May wash over me like a comforter. I snuggled up to my beer, content to have it escort me into the next month.

Fern wasn't feeling my love of leisure.

"Let's go take a drive. Mebbe I can move it wi' de truck," Fern said, "it can't be dat heavy."

"No, probably not too heavy, but I don't know how soft the ground is. It's been quite wet," I said.

"Let's go see," Fern insisted.

Rolling the beer on the table, showing little enthusiasm, Fern could read my apprehension as if it'd been spoken.

"Jase, you can bring de beer," Fern reached for a couple of travelers.

I leaped to action, called our intentions to the women folk and dashed into the truck. I was in, strapped down and humming a tune before Fern could blink.

It had been a day since I'd pulled into the driveway and much to my chagrin, the scrub of vegetation that invaded the ditch at the road was showing signs of rejuvenation.

In the stubs of chopped stump, a few green sprouts were already feasting on the energy of the deceased mature shoot. It was painfully discouraging.

Fern took little notice of the progress that had been accomplished. He drove the truck right up to the shed, pulled into his customary abrupt stop and charged out the door. I scrambled to keep up. Fern flopped onto his stomach beside the shed.

"Frrrmm uunnnderrr," Fern addressed the underside of the structure, "Shit. Tabernac!" he exclaimed as he rolled over.

"What?" I queried.

"De stupid fucker who build de shed put de jois' de wrong way," he cursed.

"How's that now?" I asked, not hip to his conclusions.

"De shed is sitting on de railroad ties and de jois' are going dat way," Fern said and made a perpendicular motion with his hand, "if dey were goin' de odder way den would could just pull it wi' de truck."

Slowly, as thoughts passed through layers of fatigue and beer buzz, I understood his wisdom.

"Do you have any two by six?" Fern asked.

"Oh, probably," I said, acting cool. One of the little projects I'd managed to undertake in my spare time was to clean some of the vast amounts of screws, nails, staples and other hardware out of the timber. Brimming with enthusiasm, I hauled a couple of choice pieces over to the shed and dropped them on the ground. Looking around, confused, I'd somehow lost my father-in-law.

"Get in," Fern said, the truck running. I managed to strap myself to the seat just before warp speed.

Fern didn't hesitate, "we're still gonna need de tractor."

"Oh?"

"If 'es got a tree point hitch, we can lift de shed and put de two by six underneat," Fern concluded.

Coming out of hyperspace, the truck cruised to a comfortable stop in the driveway of my trusted farmer/politician. It was Victoria Day Monday, a holiday, and extremely unlikely that if anyone who was available to work was capable of performing.

As we sat staring at the house a figure appeared from the corner of our eye. He was younger, rounder, and noticeably fatigued.

"Hello," I called.

"Yeah," the young man ambled up to the side of the truck.

"Hi, Jason Hamilton, I talked to your Dad last week about moving a shed, is the tractor fixed?"

"Well, eez not feexed yet, but de guay from th'dealersh'p sez there's no problem ta jus' goahead'n'useit," the young man responded.

I paused to look at Fern, wondering if he noticed the thick accent. Seeing no reaction, I shelved the observation until after the dialogue.

"Oh, okay, that's great. Do you think you might have time to swing by and move it today?" I asked hopefully.

"Yeah, shoore, I'll checkwith theoldman," the young man said before walking away.

"Thanks, and by the way, what's your name?"

"Uh." I could see the cobwebs starting to clear, "gimmeaminute. It was the fireman's dance last noight and 'am a bit, uh, hung over. Right, name's Mike, lemme go chick with Dad. He knows where'syaslive?"

"Yup."

"Okay, we'll meet'chathere."

It wasn't long after we returned, emptied the shed of any unnecessary contents that the large tractor rounded the corner. I was expecting a modest tractor for a small farming operation. Instead a massive 125 horse beast rumbled the ground beneath our feet.

Mike drove the front of the tractor, with its wide front loader, to the back of the shed.

"Dis what'chawant moved?" Mike called down over the rattling spatula of the diesel. We shook our heads. Mike cranked the emergency brake and joined us on the ground.

"She doesn't sound like she's on death's door," I gestured toward the iron beast.

"No, joose makin'sure dere'sno problem," Mike said.

My head buzzed, going through accents real and imagined, trying to pinpoint his place of origin.

"So, if you can lif' it up, I don' tink it's attached to de railroad ties. We'll have to get dem out of dere anyway," Fern said, shifting our focus.

"I ken getin widdebucket and lift'her up," Mike said. We all looked at one another, perhaps tired of the accent game, shook in affirmation of the plan and set about the task.

With barely a shrug of effort, the shed lifted from the railroad ties. Fern and I scrambled and pulled the ties out from underneath. Mike held still a moment while Fern attached the two by sixes to the floor joists. Two ski's jutted into the air.

From safety, Fern nodded his head before the shed was humbled to the ground. Mike looped the tractor to the opposite side of the shed and hoisted it up. Fern pounded a nail, gripped the chain around it before the shed settled. The chain was lassoed to a hook on top of the loader. Mike lifted the rear of the shed as the two by six skis bent underneath. Ever so gently, the shed slid up the hill

Repeating the same steps in reverse, the shed was positioned and leveled by the time Bruce arrived to survey the situation (and collect the money). Relieved to see the terrain cleared, I seized the opportunity to use the tractor loader to my full advantage.

"Hey Mike, d'you see all that drainage gravel there?" I said.

"Yup."

"Think you could spread that out at the driveway?" I asked.

"Shoore theeng," Mike said before turning to scamper back into the cab.

"Hey Mike," I interjected, "where are you from? I've never heard that accent before?"

"I'm barn and raised roight haire," Mike said casually.

"My gawd," I said, trying to save some face (and keep from insulting the poor guy) "I thought you were going to say Newfoundland."

"Nope, Kent County NB," he said, bemused, before scurrying into the tractor. The stone was scooped and leveled while Bruce was left to finalize the contract.

"Thanks so much, Bruce," I said gratefully.

"Shoore, no problem," he said with a toothy smile. Stowing the money into his wallet, he cast a mischievous eye toward me, "So, are you going to be living in my riding when the election happens this fall?"

****

"You're problem is you're too wishy-washy!" Sylvie sounded off, her words gaining momentum, "could we, should we, how about this, what about that. What do you think if we did….Nu,nu,nu,nu,nu, nNO. Do this or don't do that." She exclaimed.

Sylvie could only bear to overhear a few conversations until her observations inspired her to action. And I naturally, had no means to mask or hide the mistakes. Without much prodding, I eventually caved. Actually, it was a phone call from Kent Building Supply that indicated more than a few things were amiss.

Much like the Auger Piles, I'd requested a couple of quotes for lumber supply. One quote was for the sub-floor. The second quote included the much more extensive 180 degree deck. Balking at the cost, I went with quote number 1: sub-floor only. Or so I thought.

When the time came to deliver the order, the driver called my cell and asked me details about location and what would be included in the delivery. As the list of materials was announced, I got stuck on decking materials.

"Decking materials?" I asked.

"Yup, sez here you're getting seventy-five pieces of decking materials…" the driver replied.

"Seventy-five?" I asked again. I didn't know the exact numbers, but I was fairly certain seventy-five pieces of decking would hardly skin the surface of the proposed deck.

"Yep, seventy-five. And we've got some two by fours…" he continued.

"Okay, hold on. Let me talk to Julien. There's a problem that needs sorting out," I concluded, my frustration rising.

"Hi Julien it's Jason, the yurt guy…we have a mix up. I got two quotes, decided on the first one and it looks like your driver has a mixture of the two."

"Well Jason, we apologize," he said coaxingly, "we can take it off de truck. It's no problem...."

"Yes, please take it off," I insisted.

"Okay, no problem. Y'know you can always send bac.." he continued before I cut him off

"Sure, but it's still on the account. I still have to pay for it until it's back in your shop," I continued, "let's just leave it there until I figure out whether or not I'm going to build it. Thanks."

And I abruptly hung up the phone.

"Jeesus Christ!" I finally blurted.

"Jase, Jase," Sylvie said, "the boy!"

"Aww I know, but the lumber guy screwed up the order."

"Hmm."

"What!?!"

"You don't get that upset over a lumber order."

I'd managed to hold out, Sylvie could see the look of bewilderment.

"Of course it's not just the lumber order. It's the posts that can't be installed until next week. It's the carpenter that I put on hold who isn't available. The electrical hook-up that's not going to happen until gawd knows when. We don't have a plumber. The guy's who were recommended don't want to do it. It's fucking everything!"

Sylvie could see the thread of commonality and focused her sights: No pussyfooting, no sugarcoating, and no sparing of feelings. She took aim and let fly.

"Did Chris know he was 'on hold'? Does he know what that means? Does the lumber guy know you weren't going to build the deck? Look, the only thing I'm getting from you is you can't be decisive. It's 'maybe we should do this. What do you think about that'. You're the one in charge. You make the decisions. This isn't hard. Just say it and mean it and move on," she concluded.

We let it hang in the air for a moment. I stewed in relative silence.

Dustin lurched about in the tiny space. If there was one saving grace, there was a television with modest reception and a high-speed wireless Internet hook-up.

I slipped onto the couch beside my boy, wondering how in the world a constant repeat of Mickey Mouse clips on YouTube could be amusing. But there he sat, his shock of blonde hair bouncing while listening to the same song over and over and over again. When you escape the feeling as though you are going completely insane, a numbed acceptance grips you. Zen or blatant denial.

I could sense Sylvie had more to say. Would she dare utter the words and bring attention to the matter or respect the unspoken silence?

I closed my eyes, hoping for some kind of dimensional hole to take me back in time to put right that which I'd managed to screw up. If only it were that simple. Gradually, some levity took over my consciousness. I was making peace with the mistakes and trying to find ways to cope with what was happening instead of bemoaning what wasn't.

When the early tugs of a relaxed grin started to spread, Sylvie knew it was her opportune time. She didn't pounce. She didn't force the thought out. Timing was critical. If I was too euphoric, the news might completely pop my exuberance. If I was too 'down' then the onslaught would be too much to bear.

She huffed out a deep breath to call my attention.

"Have you heard anything from the yurt people yet?" she asked.

I flinched as though I'd been punched. Sylvie knew it was going to hurt and there was no way to cushion the blow. She backed up and took a defensive stance.

"No," I said meekly. The words came slow, as though it was my introduction to a yurt support group.

"I haven't heard anything recently."

The delivery of the statement was somehow therapeutic.

"I got an email from them a month ago. Nothing seemed out of the ordinary. I figured no news was good news."

"After all that's happened, do you really think that that's a good policy?"

"We made the arrangements, we told them the delivery date. You were there with me when we did it. We gave them Flo's birthday so it would be easy to remember. I know it's coming from British Columbia, but, unless I get on a plane and fly to BC myself, there's nothing I can do about it."

We let it slide. As the date of delivery drew near, the carnage of missed quotes and other non-yurt related mishaps warned us that perhaps those issues should be the least of our worries. Ever fortuitous, perhaps there was a way to get things done that didn't require materials or shipping or hook-ups or anything else that had to come from away.

"Hi Roger," I said into my phone, "Do you think you can install the well a little sooner? My schedule is wide open!"

****

The Vautour Well Drilling Syndicate arrived en masse, drew up to a corner of the property and plunged their drill deep in the ground. I nervously clutched my phone; anxious it should be in my hands and no excuse not to get the call.

Like others we had heard about, water was first reached at a depth of only about twenty feet. The roar of the truck slowed and Roger motioned to me for consultation.

"You 'ave water 'ere now, but it no goo' for drinking," he said and returned to his machine and crew. The engine whipped up to speed and continued to spin the bore into the ground.

I continued to pace. Habitually, I checked my phone. Had I missed a call? Was there a text, a voice mail? I dialed and texted OUT to other people, just to make sure the lines of communication were working.

"Give me your phone!" I commanded to Sylvie, who without needing to delve deep into her pool of instinctive indicators, knew I was consumed with the whereabouts of the yurt.

"The guy in Memramcook said he would call when it showed up. Remember, you called yesterday to make sure he had your number," Sylvie defended.

"But maybe there's an email," I wondered.

"Jason, relax," she finally said, "after all, what are you going to do if it doesn't get here in time?"

****

At or about four hours later, Roger was welding the identification plate and attaching the cap to the top of the well casing. The slow cadence that I'd become accustomed to on the phone was a little quicker in person. Either that, or with my mind occupied elsewhere, he might have been speaking Chipmunk. There was something about shocking the well, offering to hook the water feed up to the pressure tank and other such information emanating, but it was like listening to the car dealer when you pick up your first brand new vehicle.

A lot of words may have been spoken, but few, if any, were retained. I quickly thanked Roger who left his billing information before heading out.

The silent cell phone could not stop ringing alarm bells in my ear. The end of the Friday, May 28th workday was clocking down and not even the hint of the imminent arrival of a yurt was in the air. Surely there must be an explanation.

First I called the delivery company, er guy, Paul.

"Have you seen my yurt?" I asked. It took him some time before it registered whom he was talking to, since it had been a month from our last conversation.

Paul would have been the first person to know if anything arrived. The yurt would be spilled from a truck onto his loading area in Memramcook, and then onto another truck and delivered to Rexton. He would know before I would if the yurt had arrived.

"Nope," I haven't heard anything. (That was as elaborate as he would get EVERY time I called him, which turned out to be at least a half a dozen times over the next two weeks.)

I had some investigating to do. The dealer was next in line

"Heard anything?" I asked Lorraine, "Has my yurt been delivered? Where is it?"

She sounded as though this query wasn't unusual. The stock answers and explanations were rehearsed, ready and regurgitated.

I became emphatic: "This is unacceptable! How can you run a business like this, are you serious, BE PATIENT! It might take as long as two weeks for it to arrive, that's insane! Should I have picked a moon to deliver it by instead of a day on a calendar! No tracking number. You won't have a number until it probably reaches Ontario! So what you're saying is you don't even know where it is!"

I was exasperated. Lorraine never flinched. In hindsight, I admired her for her ability to stick to the party line. I don't know if I heard anything that was being spoken to me or waiting for my opportunity to rage like a geyser. Even now, I'm not sure of the facts. What didn't get messaged into the dialogue was the situation of our lives had become slightly more complicated than the last time we passed through the dealer showroom.

10

Circle Power

While many (perhaps the reader included) had expected we were chucking the chains of civilization to live in a yurt it was never our full intention. With time, shelter, and no pressing urgency (except the onset of winter) it was the most opportune fashion to re-invent ourselves professionally in our new land. At least, that was the idealized version of how the venture was going to unfold.

The truth is sometimes we know EXACTLY how it's going to unfold. We know exactly that if we strap and lug over a thousand pounds on a Mazda 5 over 1800 kms the money we save on shipping will somehow be exacted elsewhere. Like a new set of tires and rear shocks that aren't initially a part of the budget. But mostly we know, if we take the time to listen, everything we set in motion will not happen as we expect but happen only when we expect it won't!

The incessant drizzle, the pain of inactivity and the boredom of being the only sentient being for many kilometres eventually drove us to Moncton to seek employment. While I held a more casual approach to employment, certain as I was I could always make a living with my hands, Sylvie was decidedly nervous about my prospects.

"You don't speak French Jase," she repeated.

"And, so what, you don't need to speak French to wire a plug!" I defended.

"No, but you need to be able to get along with your co-workers," she continued.

"I'll be fine."

"Remember, this isn't film. If you don't like someone you can't just call the union and say 'can I go to another crew'. You won't just get another job tomorrow after quitting one today. It doesn't work like that. Word gets around," she reiterated.

It was the first time I'd seen her worried and preoccupied. Either I'd been so immersed in yurt construction that I missed it, or she managed to wear her concerns with a little more dignity.

Though insisting I stay at the yurt to orchestrate some, as yet, undetermined action, she managed to convince me to make the pilgrimage to the commercial capital of Acadia. She had a meeting with an old acquaintance, she reassured me. Just a chance to catch up and see what prospects might exist in her field of work.

****

"I got a job," Sylvie declared.

"Uh, huh, what!?!" I exclaimed.

"Yes, I got a job. How rude of me to want to be an active and productive member of society. Isn't that something you'd say," Sylvie responded.

"No, that's not it. I'm just a little flabbergasted. A little caught off guard," I defended, "would you care to elaborate…"

"Well, way back, before your time."

I looked at her sideways, spare me the preamble.

"I contacted my old teacher. They're expanding and my timing to get in touch with her was perfect. She needs to add staff."

"Why don't you start by telling me what your job is."

"That's the thing. It's a little undefined yet."

Pause.

"I'd be teaching esthetics."

"Teaching make-up?"

"No, they don't teach make-up, they teach esthetics. It would be skin care. Nails. Waxing. The whole range of esthetic services."

"That's not make-up."

"No, it isn't. But it's close enough. It's teaching customer service. It's teaching colours. I think it will be great."

"Well, if you're happy then I'm happy."

"You don't sound happy."

"I am. I'm ecstatic. You just got a job a lot sooner than I'd planned."

"Oh no, it's not starting right now. It would be for the fall."

"Ohhhh, then that's perfect. That still falls within our construction schedule."

"Mostly."

Another pause. Sylvie licked her lips. A tell. She was most definitely NOT holding the Ace of Spades as her hole card. She'd bluffed me until this point, but now I was onto her.

"Would you care to elaborate?"

"I start training in July."

I gulped.

"That's cutting it awfully close."

"I know. Now we really have to get the yurt finished, because I AM NOT going to commute to Moncton from Cap Lumière!"

****

And so Lorraine couldn't know the timeline for the completion of the yurt had changed from leisurely to imperative. It being May 28th and no yurt, she wasn't aware we were to fly to Toronto on June 6th, close the sale of that home, sign all necessary paperwork, finish packing, say last good-byes, get everything onto a moving van, and ship it all out to New Brunswick.

Back in Acadia June 13th we would have to store all of our possessions in Moncton, travel back to Cap Lumière, build the yurt and have it livable by the first of July. Even repeating it now I was having a difficult time keeping track of the logistics. The calculation of hindsight told me we had fifteen working days to put everything together.

No pressure.

If we could only track down the whereabouts of the yurt, the prospects of meting out such an ambitious objective might begin to materialize.

There are, in many endeavours, the moment where the resistance to difficulties, hindrances, etc, is shelved and the need to acknowledge the changing situation creates a new euphoria: That time when the obstacle isn't the issue so much as the need to change expectations in order to accommodate said obstacle. The "Happy Accident" moment when a circumstance emerges that is out of your control that ends up being beneficial.

I didn't see it then, embroiled as I was in trying to both pinpoint the location of the yurt and then determine its arrival. Friday's tirade at Lorraine had produced no tangible results beyond satisfying my need to vent. Even though we would be homeless after we sold our house, it was still only June at Cap Lumière. Not yet peak rental season. We would still have accommodation.

The other tangible reality was even if the yurt had arrived when scheduled, the property was in no way ready for its arrival. We had a septic system and a well installed. The rest were a bunch of stake's in the ground where an as yet to be materialized yurt would eventually morph.

But in order to install the piping in the dirt that would feed the plumbed water to the septic system, those things would have just been in the way.

I just happened to be lucky enough that a plumber pulled up next door when I was muttering through the injustices of a build that wasn't going according to plan.

I didn't know what Bouctouche plumbing was doing at the near naked plot of our neighbour but I wasn't about to waste the opportunity.

"When are de post to be installed?" Euclide Cormier said cutting through the meat of my blather.

"On Monday." I said nonchalantly.

"Oooh," he awed, "today is Wednesday, dat's cutting it awfully close."

He must have seen the 'ah ha' moment take place in my head as though a thought bubble had formed.

"We need to get de unnergroun' install before de post arrive," he said in his raspy French accent (a forty year smoking career might be responsible.)

"I dig de pipe Saturday," he declared.

I consented, knowing full well I had little choice in the matter if I wanted to get the project back on some kind of schedule. Much to my surprise (but completely in sync with a nugget of insight my soon-to-be friend Chris Hudson was about to share with me) the people performing the work was not the problem.

The common dialogue, the "Brand' of Atlantic Canada if you will was one of a laid back approach to pretty much everything. ("How do you starve an East Coaster? Put his EI cheque under his work boots.") Pace of life, obsession with wealth acquisition and other such noble qualities were somehow not so dear to the hearts of East Coasters. Or so you would be made to believe. In fact even before taking office Prime Minister Harper took direct aim at this underperforming sector of the country by referencing it candidly as a 'culture of defeat'.

In the circumstance of building the yurt I was soon to realize the challenge wasn't getting the work performed in a climate stereotyped in such a fashion, it was getting the materials to arrive IN ORDER for the work to be performed.

Not to babble about the fine points of plumbing for the inner technician in every reader, but the trench was dug, the pipes laid, connected to the sewage collection tank and covered over again all in the space of four hours. In four hours the rough in of the underground plumbing was complete.

When the Postech boys arrived the subsequent Monday, they too landed with a purpose. The coordinator of the company shouldered his part of the scheduling blame and decided to send two men and two rigs to install the posts.

When two pick-up trucks arrived pulling ATV sized trailers I must admit I was a little taken aback. I was expecting a bigger operation.

Bigger equipment. Bigger package. So long as they were comfortable with the size of their gear then I would have to be satisfied as well.

Seeing the stakes sprouting out of the ground the two trucks pulled up on either side of the proposed building site in a V shape. (Y'know, attack plan Delta.) While one rig, the mini hi-ho, was a much-scaled down version of a large excavator, the other was a simple ATV. The mini hi-ho I could appreciate. It had all the same appearances of its larger cousin on a more modest scale.

The ATV was more than a surprise. Brian saddled onto the back, fired up the engine and practically leapt off of the trailer. More designed for fun and play, I wasn't sure the unit would be of much use in this application.

Brian wheeled the ATV to a jerky stop before idling its testosterone-fuelled small engine to a subdued burr. He got off, went to the front of the machine where a small engine stuck to the front of the four-wheeler like a canker sore. Somewhere, in the soul of the ATV was a gallant, vibrant racehorse whose best attributes had been harnessed to a manure spreader. Inside it was aching for freedom and wild terrain, on the outside I was seeing how extremely versatile the machine could be.

From the back, a mini mechanical arm extracted itself from its harness and reached down to the earth. The lad killed the engine once again and traipsed off to the back of one of the pick-up trucks.

His partner unshackled with a good deal more dignity and less fanfare. The mini hi-ho was resting comfortably while Dave wrestled the long thick tubes of galvanized steel from the back of the truck. From the look of the clenched teeth and arrested breath, the posts weren't on the light side. Snapping out of my gawking daze, I stepped to it and helped Dave hoist the post over the side and toward the building site.

"This where you want your posts to go?" I was asked as the outside row of posts was laid to the ground.

I took a nervous gulp. I'd been so accustomed to asking my superiors and leaders for direction that I'd no idea how to command said efforts myself. I was terrified of making a mistake and was half expecting them to take charge of the situation and determine the layout. It wasn't happening.

"Uh, where they are is where I want them," I finally replied before continuing, "Do you guys level them? I kind'a thought you would know where they're going to go?"

"No, we put 'em wherever you tell us to."

"Oh. Okay well then put them wherever you see a post."

Brian slapped two sharp, short pointed stakes on either side of the first wood stake. He made his gauge before walking back to the ATV. As I watched, the arm jerked to life. Brian attempted to lift the post where he could hang it from the short circular tube that was at the end of the arm. Again, snapping to attention, I marched over and held the weight while Brian pushed a cotter pin through both the short finger on the end of the arm and the post itself.

I stepped back as Brian uncoiled the remote control and braced his other arm against the post. The ATV bobbed and leaped as it countered the heft of the post draped from the arm. In a few more bleeps and bloops the end of the post, hollow and sliced to form a sharp point made a stab into the soil. The arm arched up as Brian hopped the post into position.

As the point punched into the surface the two large circular augers arrested its further descent. I walked over for further confirmation. Everything looked good. I remembered my tape measure, my command as the head of this endeavour and told Brian to halt for a moment.

When I returned, somehow with a renewed confidence (knowing no one was around to question my authority) a few nuggets of information managed to dislodge from the far recesses of my brain.

"The plan calls for the posts to be about seven feet apart," I said, holding not just the tape, but also a paper drawing of the layout of the posts.

"The beams will go on the posts and then the sub-floor will sit on top of that."

"Okay, whatever you want just tell me where they should go."

"It's good where it is," I declared, somewhat surprised at my newfound confidence.

Brian held a square level against the post as the finger of the arm slowly started to turn. In just a few short spins the auger slipped beneath the surface of the topsoil and disappeared into the earth. With each successive turn the auger burrowed deeper and deeper into the ground. Occasionally the post would stop turning and Brian would adjust the level. The surprises of the machine continued as, even though half the post was in the ground it was still able to manipulate its angle to the ground.

"Just like that," I thought to myself as the steel stopped spinning.

Brian looked at me and matched my nod, "yup, just like that."

"How do you know when to stop?"

"We have a torque pressure gauge. The ground will always tell us when it's too much."

"So you could have only a few feet in the ground or all of the post in the ground?"

"Yup, I'll sink 'em in and Dave will come around and do the torque-ing."

"Yessir!" I yelped before continuing, "so, you guys arrived here at noon, do I have to put youse up anywhere? Are you staying overnight? Is this a lot of work?"

"No. No. And No. This isn't really a lot of work. We'll be finished today." I gulped.

"Will I have to wait for them to settle or can I build on them right away?"

"Ha ha, you can build on them as soon as we're finished."

As he continued to speak, he drew the arm down to the ground and locked onto another of the posts. Drawing it up into the air, I helped him stabilize it once again as he smashed in the cotter pin.

"I can start installing the sub floor tomorrow?"

"Absolutely," Brian spiked the post into place.

I stood, transfixed as the metal slowly worked itself into the ground once again.

'Amazing,' I thought as I lost myself in the moment, continuing to let my brain wander off, 'I can start building the sub-floor tomorrow.'

"Holy shit!" I finally said aloud, "I can start to build the sub-floor tomorrow."

"Excuse me," I blurted to Brian before reaching for my phone, "I've got to call my carpenter."

I flipped through the screens and finally accessed Chris Hudson. I was about to start to dial his number when I looked over at the lonely temporary power station.

"Fuck," I said, "I haven't got any power. Maybe Mr. Hickey has a portable generator. Wait, I've only pestered NB Power every day this week. Is one more call going to hurt?"

Before I could negotiate the phone directory a white boom truck lumbered down the gravel road. I pocketed the phone and walked toward the commotion.

As the truck slowed, I walked out to greet them.

"This must be 99 Wilson Road," the truck driver declared.

"You bet'cha. Did you have trouble finding it on the GPS?" I joked.

"The supervisor told us where it was. I don't think you can find this place on Google Maps," he responded.

"No, I don't think so. It's probably an old logging road that's never been documented before," I responded.

He leaned back into the truck and lurched it ahead on the clutch. I hopped down from the step and pointed him toward the direction of the temporary station that was awaiting hook-up.

I marched back to the Postech installation team and resumed my duties as the unofficial apprentice. Keeping a watchful eye on the power technicians, they too had lassoed the grid, clipped it to the temporary and were down the road in short order.

****

By the middle of the afternoon we'd shown good progress. Over half of the 21 posts had been installed. As Brian took out a few of the stakes near the plumbing pipes sticking out of the ground, it occurred to me that the buried PVC could be compromised.

"When you're screwing those into the ground, is there any way for you to know when you've punched through piping you're not supposed to?" I asked.

"I wish! There's no way to tell until it gets destroyed," Brian declared.

I looked the situation up and down. The upturned earth from the underground plumbing was still fresh enough to indicate the activity contained underneath. But where, exactly, the six-inch pipe was in proportion to the three-foot width of disturbed earth I couldn't exactly say.

Brian looked at me with the post poised on the end of the arm and waited for further instructions.

"Hold on," I finally said and charged off toward the utility shed.

"There's only one way to know for sure," I said as I stomped the spade into the ground, "and this is a hell of a lot more forgiving than that."

The process slowed somewhat as I navigated my way through the layers of dirt, then Styrofoam before finally locating the piping. When I did, I surveyed the desired location of the post.

"Looks like there's about two posts that are going to be close," I announced before consulting my drawings. The blueprint for the posts had one supporting column every seven feet. How close did I need to stay to that curriculum?

"What difference is a couple of feet here or there going to make?" I said.

"Where's the weight going to be?" Brian answered back.

"The weight of the structure is going to be on the outside walls. Inside, well, a few retaining walls, but nothing that's going to be supporting any kind of a load," I answered.

"Well, I'm no structural engineer, but if that's the case then I don't think a foot here or there is going to kill it."

I nodded in agreement. "So long as the posts are in a straight line to accommodate the beams we should be alright."

We looked again before making our final decision.

"Hmm, but this one here, if we move it too far that way then we're only about two feet from the other post," I said.

"You don't mind if the post touches the plumbing do you?" Brian asked.

"How's that now?"

"Well, we can start the post off at an angle before we raise it up to the level you want it to be," Brian answered.

"You mean you can get the auger below the grade of the piping before you raise it straight?"

"Yup."

I considered it for a moment. Brian elaborated.

"Most of our work we replace old concrete columns under decks and granny flats when they've crumbled and failed. It's obviously cost prohibitive if we have to remove the old structure to install the posts. So what we do is get in underneath, on an angle, screw in the post before straightening it to where it needs to be."

My mouth fell agape. True to his word, he surveyed the pipe before angling the post toward the ground. The auger dove in a safe distance away from the pipe until it churned safely underneath. Ever so delicately, he hoisted the post until it went from a steep angle to a more obtuse distance from the ground.

"Well I'll be damned."

Brian paused for a moment and surveyed the results.

"This system is expensive, but the benefits sometimes outweigh the costs. Remember, you'd still have to auger the holes. You'd still be at risk for puncturing the pipes underneath. You'd still have to wait for the concrete to cure properly before you could put anything on top of it."

"Hey, thanks for reminding me, I've got to call my carpenter and get him over here tomorrow."

"Yeah, you'll be able to start as soon as we're finished."

That finish came a little after seven in the evening. The posts had all been installed, but the smaller unit broke down near the end of the day. Fortunately, the bulk of the work was complete. Dave and his mini hi-ho had a little more heft to his machine. He continued to torque the auger piles down to their necessary depth and grip. Much to all of our surprise, only one post snagged up on a small pocket of solid rock.

Dave was a little innovative with his approach to continue to torque the post deeper into the ground. His first idea was to clamp a plumber's wrench to the bottom of the post just above where it stuck into the earth. The teeth grip the object and pull it where you have the gumption (and intact hernia) to pull. He wrapped a chain around the handle of the wrench and around the front blade of the mini hi-ho.

"Now, I'm going to back the machine off, which should pull on the handle and screw the post further into the ground. I'll keep spinning the arm with the remote and between the two we should achieve the tension we require."

****

My concern was not immediate. Talk me through a problem, wave your hands with enough vigour and anything seems possible. I can easily get caught up in the enthusiasm of the talker and not question little things like whether an action may or may not result in fatality. "We've always done it this way," won't stand up in a court of law or the game of chance. A hockey player may engage in a bare-knuckle fight on the ice and only leave with a few welts or a busted nose. Chance it enough times and the possibility a heavy blow might knock you out and cause your bare head to whack off the ice (resulting in death or brain damage) will severely increase.

Just because you've survived it once doesn't always make it so.

It's not until you see the smoke rising off the pipe and the thick chain put under heavy strain does it seem obvious there's A LOT of energy coursing through that inanimate object: Something, something Newton's Third Law, equally and opposite reaction, something, something.

I only thought it was planets and cosmos and stuff, but apparently it does have a day-to-day application.

The Law doesn't change. It is and always will remain the same. It's whether or not those laws are being respected properly. My Father and Father in law have the shortened digits to prove their legitimacy. They've both been on the end of chains that had tension, and when something went wrong, they lost part of their fingers (and were lucky that was all!)

It is perhaps with that history that as the tension on the post mounted, I chose to keep more than a cautionary distance away from the action.

I recall one incident in my life that was far, far too close for comfort. I was working on a movie and a long-armed Zoom Boom got stuck in the mud. The best boy got in the bucket and extended the arm as much as he could before lowering himself to the ground. With enough leverage, he was hoping the arm would lift up the base and we could jam in a little flotsam and jetsam under the tires to propel it out of trouble.

But the arm trick wasn't working. It was sinking into the ground as well. We grabbed a few blocks of wood to put underneath the arm and give it, supposedly, more leverage. The best boy bobbed the arm down until the thick steel was touching the pile of wood.

He created a downward force on the wood. Only, because of the unusual form of both the earth and the wood, the arm was slipping from its perch. It did so with a sudden and forceful slip. Nothing major, but certainly noticeable.

One of my co-workers emerged to help load up the pile of wood again. Only this time, instead of trusting to fate, he gambled, hung in and held onto the stack to make sure it wouldn't move. The arm went back up and once again spotted down on top. We all concentrated on the base of the lift, hoping against hope that the leverage would lift it out of the ground. When I looked back at my co-worker, he was squatted beside the wood, holding on. Despite his efforts, the arm of the lift was slowly, inevitably starting to measure off the pivot.

"Pete," I yelled over the suffocating din of the motor, "get the HELL out of there."

Either by choice or by noise, my voice wasn't heard. Pete refused to look up. The arm inched farther off the wood, right in the direction of his head. I turned, hauled ass and pulled him back by the scruff of his shirt.

"It was going to slip. You'd have been toast," I said.

"I would have dove out of the way!" he retorted.

"You wouldn't stand a chance Pete! It would have flown off too quick for you to move!" I said, my nerves starting to settle. As the arm slipped off once again, further illustrating my point, the emotion died out quickly. Tom, after seeing me pull Pete away, saw the potential danger and called the operation to a halt.

****

The thought of Pete came back into my minds' eye the moment Dave lay down on the ground at the base of the post as he started to rev the engine.

When Dave saw me back away and take a rather concerned look to my body language, he shut the motor down for a moment to explain his thinking.

"I've done this before. Don't worry, the chain is rated for about 20,000 pounds of torque and there isn't but about 5 in the body of this thing," he said and motioned to the mini hi-ho.

Without hesitation, he backed up the machine. The chain tightened, pulling the wrench. The teeth gripped into the steel but the post still would not turn. He leapt off the machine and pulled out the chord to the remote. If he was confident, so was I.

"Y'know, it wouldn't be a problem to move it. We had to put a few others in different spots…"

Dave looked up at me, intense concentration on his face, his eyes not leaving the situation.

"I tried that already."

"Ah."

He worked the remote once again. The jib arm ratcheted to attention. Had I not known any better, I would have thought nothing was happening. I wanted to point that out to Dave who stayed transfixed on the ground. Maybe he was doing a Jedi mind trick on the thing and it was spinning itself into the ground with mental assistance.

"That's as much as she'll go," he said and put an end to his efforts.

He stood up and released the cotter pin before lifting the arm away from the end of the post. When he did, a steady plume of grey, smelting steel smoke echoed into the atmosphere.

Brian came over to survey the situation.

"Now that's some tension!" he exclaimed. He reached out to touch the post when his partner stopped him.

"I wouldn't touch that if I were you," Dave casually suggested.

"Oh no, I'm not that stupid," he said and brought his hands two inches to the edge of the pipe before he stopped.

"That's friggin' hot!" he exclaimed once again.

"Think I'll wait to take the wrench off the bottom," Dave said casually.

"Yeah, I'd recommend it. You could probably take the chain off, but anything that was touching that post is going to be pretty hot."

"It's probably absorbing a little heat from the sun too," I offered my insight.

"Oh for sure. Well, standing around staring at this thing isn't going to get this job done any quicker. We'd better get back at it," Dave said and released the chain.

"Oh shit, thanks for reminding me," I said and stole away.

"Hi Chris," I said a few seconds later into my end of the cell phone, "I had a lucky day. The posts are in and the temporary got hooked up. Are you available tomorrow?"

"Oh shoare," Chris let out in his customary over-the-top exuberance.

"Great, so what time do you want to start tomorrow?" I asked.

"Eight o'clock sounds alright," he said.

"Oh thank gawd, I was hoping you were going to say that and not some ungodly hour like seven!"

"Just because I work in film doesn't mean I think like film," he responded.

"Alrighty, I'll see you then,"

Of the 21 posts, only one proved to be stubborn and required more than normal attention. The only remaining question, as the ends stuck out at varying heights, was what should be the final level.

"I see your ground slopes a little to the south side," Brian said and demonstrated with his hands.

"Yeah, I'd like to have a little crawl space underneath. Y'know so we can get in and install the plumbing and the electrical," I asked.

"Well, if we go three feet on that side, then we're looking at about a foot and a half at the tall side," Brian said.

"Hmm, well, we probably don't need to go quite that high. Let's see, I've got the height of the beams and then the height of the subfloor. Maybe I only need to go about two and a half feet."

"Alrighty, then you'd be about a foot on the low side."

I considered it for a moment as my mind tried to discern the best course of action. After the pipes were cut, that would be it. Maybe an extension could be added after the fact.

"Hmm," I said surveying the low side. I walked over and knelt down to my knees. "I want to make sure I'm not sitting too high."

"I understand."

I looked down out toward the water. From the top of the hill where the yurt was going to sit, the ground sloped gradually toward the river. There was nothing to impede the view. We could see all the way into town where a canopy covered the bridge that crossed the Richibucto. It was the narrowest point before opening into the ocean. And the ocean could be dreadfully mean.

"The first time we stayed here we rented a camper trailer."

Brian looked at my quizzically, not quite sure what a vacation in a camper trailer had to do with anything.

"It was September about five years ago. Hurricane Katrina destroyed New Orleans and the tail end of that devastation came blitzing up the

Mississippi Valley. When it ripped through New Brunswick I think it was a tropical depression. Hundred kilometre an hour winds. Not hurricane force, but force enough. Staying in that camper trailer was like being in a plastic bag going through a car wash."

Brian laughed, now he was starting to get where I was going.

"Our yurt is essentially a giant tent. If it sits up too high then I risk the whole thing blowing away like a beach ball in a breeze. So, forgive me if I'm taking my time."

"Hey, no worries," Brian said.

I surveyed it once again.

"Two and a half feet is about as low as it can go and still have a crawl space at the other end," I finally said.

"That appears to be the case."

"Okay, go ahead."

Brian set the laser level, pulled out the grinder and set about cutting off the tops.

11

The Birth Of A Yurt

It would have been obscene to expect infinite sunshine on every day of our construction journey. Right after the last post was hacked to the appropriate height the bliss of warm weather, blue skies and comfort was enveloped in a thick shroud of Maritime liquid sunshine. The mercury plunged and the imminent summer that seemed so certain was packed away for an unknown unveiling.

The first day the clouds hung low, arresting the brilliant luminescence. Like the true film technicians that we were, we ignored the conditions as best we could, gussying up in our full suited rain gear to stay functional in the slow drizzle of precipitation. Knowing much more about local weather patterns than I could ever hope to appreciate, Chris' first order of business was a shroud for the chop saw. The low plumage was not about to dissipate anytime soon.

We struggled along in the mud and the mist. Crown up, the first twelve foot two by ten took up residence on the middle succession of posts. We stitched the other planks around it, along, beside to create a built-up beam, fully the length of the yurt, from one end to the other. The rain did not improve my mood, so too did the deliberate pace of my hired help. Accustomed as I was to the quick, dirty (and occasionally illegal and dangerous) world of film, the adjustments to the requirements of a permanent fixture were not easily appreciated.

"Hmm," Chris wondered aloud, seizing my attention. He crept beside one of the posts, examining the square topping.

THE BIRTH OF A YURT

"We'll have to make sure these rest perfectly on top. Can you show me the drawing of the beams again?" Chris asked.

He looked at them carefully, seeing the angles that they would abut. He took the pencil from behind his ear and made rough etchings on top of the steel.

"Can't we put a little piece of two by ten on top of each post to, you know, catch all the girth of the beams?" I asked and muttered under my breath (and speed this up a little bit).

"Well, as you can see, if we put the tops just right they will be wide enough to hold up all of the beams. We just have to make sure they're properly aligned and then we'll have to use some lag bolts to make sure they don't go anywhere," he said with his trademark nonchalance.

Doubtful I'm the only one who has the subtle gift of expression without words. Our body language sometimes deceives us the real thoughts that are forming in our minds. When I'm anxious and rattled, I probably resemble the little spinning top of youth. Flailing about wildly, all energy and action, somehow, someway thinking that if I expend enough of it, move fast enough, walk quickly enough, the problem will be quashed underneath its release. Rarely works. But I can't help myself.

It's really a physical manifestation of what's happening inside. As though I'm acting out my very own game of charades with the information fed to me providing the clues to an external audience.

"Yes, he's spinning around, picking up lumber. Carrying them, what, he's trying to pick up every piece of lumber in the pile. Uh, uh, I can't quite make it out. Is it a verb? He's allowed to nod his head right. Okay, not a verb. It's lumber, stacked. Y'now if it were all placed in the middle we could say it was a tee pee. Not a tee pee but he is nodding his head. Right, he's building a yurt, but he's stamping his feet, okay, I get it, he's not building the yurt fast enough! Wait, the lumber is all crashing down. He's knocked it all over. Oh, the yurt isn't getting here fast enough."

I would pause throughout the day, earnestly checking the phone, somehow thinking that my persistence in constantly monitoring my communication device would somehow make the yurt arrive faster. Chris could see me growing weary by the minute. Jovial and laughing, the façade was only going to work for so long.

"Hi Margaret yeah, I've been trying to get a hold of Lorraine at Blue Spruce and she isn't returning my calls. Listen, do you have any information on the whereabouts of the yurt. Anything at all" I asked desperately.

"It left the building. This is the first time I've dealt with these people. It's the dealer that makes the transportation arrangements. You'd think there would be a tracking number. We usually require there to be something the moment it leaves the dock..."

"That's what I was told as well. But, the last I spoke with her, she told me I would have a tracking number when it was put onto a train."

"Oh, okay, so they're going to ship it by train then?" she asked.

"I suppose. I don't even know who they've contracted to ship it. If I knew then I could get in touch with them and maybe find out something that way."

"Oh right, just because one company picked it up at the door doesn't mean it's the same company that's going to be shipping it across the country."

"Exactly."

"So really, it sounds like it's been subcontracted a few times."

"That's what I gather. But really, after the last few conversations I've had with Lorraine she isn't even answering my phone calls. She can really only repeat the same story and if the story hasn't changed I don't think she wants to continue repeating it. I'm as much to blame as anyone..."

"I'm really sorry to hear that. We just try to concentrate on the manufacturing and leave the other aspects of our business to the dealers. We don't do shipping, it's not our area of expertise."

"Don't worry, I'm not holding it against you. It's just that we're getting into a very serious time crunch. We fly back next week to close out the sale of our house and we've got nothing finished yet. My wife is losing her mind out in Cap Lumière. I knew there was going to be an adjustment moving from Toronto to New Brunswick, but aye yoye, I just want to know where the yurt is. Some concrete evidence of its existence so we can start to have an idea of putting everything together."

Margaret listened intently. I could read in her voice her level of sympathizing with our situation. Over the din of drizzle, Chris could see me pace back and forth. Occasionally I'd stop, pick up a block of cut material, maybe throw it or bang it against a part of my anatomy that still had feeling. He too was showing signs of concern.

I wanted to walk over to him after the conversation was finished and continue to pore out my frustrations, but Sylvie got to me instead. Hanging my head low, feeling around through the layers of rain gear that was beginning to hang on my body, I felt for the buzzing phone in my pocket.

"You've got to come home now," Sylvie announced.

"But Sylv, we're only part way through the day. Chris needs a helper or we'll be even slower than we already are," I pleaded, though my help wasn't entirely necessary.

"Dustin is driving me insane. There's no place to go. We're stuck in this fucking closet of a cottage, it's raining, I'm miserable…"

"Are you saying you want me to go home so we can both be miserable?"

"We need to find daycare. If I'm stuck here for the next four weeks by myself I'm going to go postal!"

And just like that the conversation ended as abruptly as it began.

I bit my lower lip, as I always do when anger and frustration has a solid hold on my state. Just as I was about to puncture skin, I released my jaw in search of another physical outlet for my frustrations.

I usually like to break things. Nothing feels quite so good as watching something tiny and nubile shatter into a gazillion pieces. I've always found a certain satisfaction in taking out all my pent up energy on an inanimate object. Punching things can feel devilishly good. Drywall is heavenly. It makes a whole lot of noise, there's ample evidence of your handiwork and it's easy to repair.

But my favourite material has always been a long wooden stick of some kind. Back in my days of youthful aggression, testosterone and angst, I'd take my worn out hockey sticks back into the woods and smash the hell out of them on trees and tree stumps.

Struggling mightily with a level of composure I'd surprised even myself in maintaining, I shuffled to the chop saw.

"How well do you think you can manage by yourself for, I dunno, maybe the next couple of days," I asked.

"It's no problem at all. The rain is a bit of a hindrance, but as long as it isn't too heavy I should be alright. And the wind," Chris said.

"Ah yes, there always seems to be a bit of wind here," I agreed.

"But this isn't too bad down here," Chris said.

"Oh?" I asked as his words begged for further clarification.

"I just got back from shooting *Belle Baie* up in Caraquet and man, you had to lean sideways into the wind on MOST days," he said.

"Wow!" I replied.

"Let's just say the Grips weren't flying anything much bigger than an eight by eight," Chris chortled.

"Thanks Chris, Sylvie is losing her mind out in Cap Lumière. She's in this tiny little cottage and there's nowhere to go," I confessed.

"Cap Lumière? Wow, that's far out there. Even for New Brunswick," Chris observed.

"Yeah, it's also a long way from downtown Toronto," I responded.

"Yeah, you won't exactly find a Starbucks around the corner," Chris chuckled again.

"Uh, no," I sighed heavily letting myself rumple to the sawhorse. Chris immediately took notice and paused in his work.

"The shitty thing is I don't know how much longer we're going to have to stay out there," I said before continuing, "We don't know where the yurt is. I was hoping to have it up and be working inside by now."

"You've had some delays on this end too. The posts just got installed yesterday. It's going to be a few days before the subfloor is finished," Chris reasoned.

"Yeah, we can plough ahead with that," I said, raising my hopes.

"If it makes you feel any better it's been my experience in props and sets that it takes about two weeks for anything to arrive in New Brunswick." Chris distracted me before continuing, "there isn't the infrastructure for film here like you have in Toronto. You call up the rental house and get them to send something else when it's broken. We'd often have decorators that wanted that one special item and we'd be sure to remind them, 'if you really want that you have to order it ahead of time'." I chuckled, the distraction worked. Chris smiled at the memory; shrugging his shoulders as he leaned back over the chop saw. The lingered thought, off in the ether of our conversation, floated back down to my consciousness.

"FUCK!" I bellowed. Chris turned toward me nonchalantly.

"Is there a problem?" he asked.

"We can't finish the subfloor," I squeaked.

"Oh?"

"The method behind the insulation is it reflects whatever heat you generate. Tin foil and bubble wrap, they use it in all the lunch bags now. The whole kit comes with a layer of this stuff on the outside. We also decided to order the r-foil insulation for the floor," I said.

We both let out an ooofff as though we'd been suckered in the gut.

"And we can't skin the subfloor until we have that layer of insulation to lay down underneath."

"And where's it coming from again? BC...." Chris said.

I sat down in a slump. Chris, (concerned but undaunted) continued. He moved to heft a joist into position on the post. Snapping out of self-pity, I moved to join him.

"Now, where were you when I was planning this? Had I known it was going to take so fucking long for everything to arrive I could have accounted for that in my building plans!" I barked.

Chris chuckled, "but I didn't know you then."

"Aww, excuses, excuses, excuses. You've got me thinking I'd better get my act together and get the hot water unit ordered," I said, filtering through the fog of frustration.

"Hmm, hot water on demand?" Chris asked.

"Ha ha, oh yeah, y'see part of our inspiration for this is to try and make it as environmentally friendly as possible. That and I don't want to pay for wasted energy when we're not using the yurt," I said.

"That's a good idea. You should go and see my friend Jerry," Chris said as we muscled the board onto the post, "I think he has two units."

"Really! I tried talking to a local plumber about this and they looked at me like I had two heads."

"I'm not surprised. We don't do too much like that around here."

"Trust me, I know. One day when you have time I'll tell you about the hoops I went through to try and get a composting toilet. So tell me about your friend Jerry," I asked.

"He's an interesting guy. He would also be interested in seeing the yurt. He's from Ontario, like you. He came out here in the seventies with a bunch of friends…part of the back to the land movement…." Chris said.

****

"It didn't last very long," Jerry said as Sylvie, Dustin and I paraded through his house.

An accommodating man, Chris had no doubt briefed him about our request and curiosity about the circumstances shepherding him to the province.

"There were six of us in university in Waterloo and word had gotten around that land was cheap and plentiful here. Lots of people were making the pilgrimage, to throw off the shackles of civilization and get back to nature," he confessed.

As he spoke he ferried us around his own unique structure. His original building was a simple frame house that he continued to add rooms and space. As he built, like others who've been concerned about the current energy philosophy, he created a home that was sensitive to the possibility of scarcity.

The seventies saw the initial energy shock in domestic oil production. Abundant and accessible oil had been extracted from domestic wells. That production reached its peak in the middle of that decade and the resulting spike in price greatly impacted North America. Some heeded the depletion of fossil fuels and shouldered that reality into how they lived their lives.

Jerry, in particular, allowed the event to shape his construction philosophy.

"I have piping in my floor that feeds into my wood furnace. The tile on top of the floor is a terra cotta."

"It's incredible," Sylvie interrupted, "I feel like I'm in California."

"It absorbs the sun energy and stores it during the day. It also transmits the heat in the pipes to keep the rest of the house warm in the winter."

"How did you manage to do that?" I asked.

"We use the water bladder on the back of the wood stove."

"And you're on a slab? There's no basement," I questioned.

"We didn't feel we needed a basement. Actually, at the time I was starting to build the house I just didn't have enough money for one. And then, y'see the whole thing has evolved over time. First there was our room and the main room."

"It really was a rustic wood cabin," I surmised.

"Oh yes, absolutely."

"Was this what you built when you moved out here?"

"Well, it wasn't quite like that. Yes, there were a bunch of us. About six core people that moved out here from Waterloo. We were all very much in the spirit of the movement of going back to the land. C'mon, I'll show you the hot water system," Jerry said as he opened the cabinet under his kitchen sink.

"I have two, that way neither system gets overwhelmed. This one just takes care of the kitchen," he said, continuing back to his earlier story. He left the cabinet open for a moment and let me investigate the contents.

"We got here, got settled. It was the spring of the year, right after school finished. We started our little garden and growing our own crops...."

"Homesteading!" I added with a muffled voice from underneath the kitchen counter.

"Exactly. The forest was wild in those days. As you can see not a lot has changed here..." Jerry let the effect of his words sink in.

"No kidding. If I wanted to go on the lam, New Brunswick is the place to do it. I'd just make sure I had a lifetime supply of mosquito repellant..."

"We got this piece of land for next to nothing and then, well, reality started to sink in..." Jerry let his words linger.

"I grew up on a farm. Was it the back-breaking labour they didn't like?" I asked, "the romance tends to wear off pretty quick when the sweat is pouring off your back and all you're doing is picking up rocks, or mowing hay. It's very physical and very taxing."

"I remember my Grandma Dodette's chicken coop. The smell!" Sylvie exclaimed.

"Yeah, that was part of it, but I think the work was kind of a relief. Most of us were a bunch of suburban kids that hadn't done a lot of fieldwork. You hate it or you love it. I used to do some farm work back in Waterloo so the work wasn't that big a deal for me. No, we just didn't know how to live together," he finally said.

"What, you hippies didn't like sharing lovers or what?" Sylvie laughed as Dustin squirmed.

"There was that of course, but it was the simple things of who was going to be responsible for what. We'd done all this research on how we were going to live on the land and spent no time at all as to how we were going to live with one another."

"And you were young. Cripes, I'm almost forty and I'm just now starting to figure out what I like," Sylvie confessed.

"What is it they say about youth, it's wasted on the young," I offered.

"Yeah, true enough. Anyway, after about six months I think I was the only one left," Jerry shrugged.

"But you stayed?"

"I went back for a bit, but something really stuck for me here."

"It was a girl wasn't it?" Sylvie said.

"I suppose. We met while I was out here. I went home to Waterloo for a short time, returned and then never left," Jerry said, "now, what have I done there?"

In front of him, the door of an upright freezer stuck out of the wall. Jerry stepped beside it, reached up and pulled a section of wall paneling down. Held on with Velcro, in behind was another small hot water on demand unit.

"On the other side of this wall is the bathroom. I have a teen-aged daughter now and so far this system hasn't had any defects. She gives it quite a go. I'm going to tell you the secret to giving yourself a fighting chance of making this work."

He left the panel on the floor as I gawked up to investigate the machine further. I grimaced a little. I had hoped he was going to show me a replica of what I wished to install and make my decision easy. Instead he had incorporated a variation of the hot water on demand to suit his own needs.

Beside the stand up freezer was a door that led to a 'cold' room.

"What's the secret to keeping the room a constant temperature?"

"I didn't know there was a quiz with the tour," Sylvie blurted.

"This part of the house sticks into the side of a hill, and earth in general, makes for the perfect insulator. It keeps everything at a constant temperature."

He opened another door to his left. A waft of cool air greeted us.

"That's where we keep our preserves. I keep that warm with a light bulb in the winter. Just make sure it's an incandescent and not a CFL. Out here in this little adjoining room I've made another minor alteration. Do you remember seeing the back of the freezer?"

"Jase, help me out, I can't keep up!" Sylvie confessed.

"Just turn around and look behind you."

Spinning around to stare at the space that should have been a wall, the bare contents of the rear of his stand up freezer greeted our presence.

"Ah ha!" I said understanding his thinking.

"Ah ha what?" Sylvie questioned.

"The way the hot water on demand works is to heat up only the water that you need. As you are no doubt aware, the temperature of that water as it enters the unit from the ground is about 10 degrees. To get the temperature we desire, we need to heat our water upwards of 45 degrees," the tour now having turned into a lecture, Jerry peered over his glasses at the struggling student.

"That's a thirty-five degree difference?" Sylvie said meekly.

"Precisely. Now, how does a freezer work?"

"It makes everything frozen," Sylvie guessed, wilting under the pressure of the pop quiz.

"It removes heat," I said.

"Precisely. Haven't you ever wondered why the floor is always warm under the front of your fridge?"

"Ah ha," Sylvie said, starting to piece the information together.

"In this utility room I had my plumber install an ambient tank. The heat from the freezer increases the temperature in this room another five degrees."

"And that's five less degrees you have to....I get it!" Sylvie said.

"Wow, very clever," I commented.

"Thank you, but it was my plumber that did all the work. If I can share one small part of information it's that the pre-heat tank is absolutely critical. It will help you get more life out of your on demand system."

"Good, I'll try and remember that. What about living as a communal hippie. Think you'll be able to help me with that?"

"No, I failed at it once, It's doubtful I'll be folly enough to try again!" Jerry laughed.

"And you're an accountant now!" Sylvie cried incredulously.

"Yup, go figure."

****

"Are you going to have anything for me to do once the subfloor is done? I got quite a bit of it finished when you were at Jerry's the other day." Chris asked.

We huddled under the shroud of the tarp. The occasional blast of wind, crashing the fabric into the air crackled our conversation. We scrambled for the edging, trying to prevent the blue sail from lifting off of its' makeshift attachment. I synched down the spring clip, doing my grip brother's proud as the flapping abated and the wind subsided.

"Oiy, and if I lose you to something else, I won't get you back will I?"

Chris shrugged. If I couldn't give him work and couldn't pay him not to go someplace else then it stood to reason he had to find a means to support himself.

"Well, I don't want to lose you. I've been sure to tell you we won't be here next week, right. I was pretty clear about that?"

"Yes, and I have something that will keep me busy for next week. Just a little project, and then we'll be back on when you return correct?"

"If the stupid yurt ever shows up!" I grunted before continuing, "Okay, I've been mulling over what to do and I think we might as well build two sections of the deck. What do you think about that?"

"That should get us through the rest of the week."

"That's what I was thinking. We're going to eventually do the rest of the deck anyway," I sighed, "we can't go any further on the subfloor unless I buy the insulation…"

"No, don't do that. The two sections of deck will keep us busy. Do you know what we're going to put the beams on?"

"Waaay back in my ideal world, I wanted to put them on the auger piles, but I KNOW we don't have that kind of money in the budget."

"Okay then. Have you heard anything more about the yurt?"

"Only the exact same story I've been getting from both ends of the spectrum. The manufacturer has only ever been able to tell me that it was picked up. It's not in B.C. anymore. The dealer, when I do manage to get through to her, just keeps telling me to be patient. It takes time. It's on its way."

"Wow, that's it?"

"Yup. A week after it was supposed to arrive and they don't even know where it is. It could be in the fucking Arctic for all I know. It's somewhere, but no one can tell me where. It's a Schrodinger's Cat riddle. Somewhere, in a crate in Canada a yurt exists. In that very same reality the yurt does NOT exist. It's funny when you're philosophical. My only hope, only, is that it will present itself before we head back to Toronto on Tuesday."

Chris, savvy film technician and all round perceptive individual, saw through my ruse, "and if it doesn't, who's going to be here to meet it?"

Staring straight at him, hoping against hope he had it in his heart to be accommodating to our desperation, "Will you be around next week? You won't have to do any lifting. Honest!"

"I could be available. So long as you aren't crushed when I tell you I have no further interest in working in this slop."

****

The slop that Chris was referring to was a week and a half in the making. From the moment the last post was installed on Tuesday, June 2 the cloud cover descended like an annoying mosquito. It hung low and wide. Whether it was a mist, a fog, a drizzle was in the details. The precipitation formed and expired simultaneously. The optimism of sunny climes was washed. The mercury plunged just north of freezing once again. The winds of the North East, low and merciless over the vast expanse the Gulf of St. Lawrence, sunk her dagger into all who braved her fortitude.

A day of hope, a day to cease the conditions was not imminently in the offing. Even in our shelter the musky, dank halo of humidity stuck to the walls of our small rented cottage and engulfed us. When all we needed was an afternoon, a few hours to open the windows and allow a little evaporation to make the experience somewhat more bearable, none was forthcoming.

THE BIRTH OF A YURT

On the East Coast they say there are only two seasons: Winter and everything else. Ask anyone who's lived in these parts for a significant amount of time and almost all will agree: Summer truly starts, and ends, in July. In other parts of Canada the summer kicks off at the end of May. Sure, some years when hurtling off the end of the deck in May might be met with ice shards and slush, but it is generally expected the heat will soon follow thereafter.

New Brunswick….. not so much. And what do you do? Plan accordingly. Hence the ease with which we were able to secure our lodging in mid-May. The owner of our cottage at Cap Lumière was ecstatic to have someone to occupy one of his cottages in the shoulder season. Alas, though the temperature indicated the place was livable and the heat made it so, physics was not in our favour.

The van pulled to a stop in the driveway. As I gathered my things and prepared to step onto the porch, I was greeted at the door. Sylvie charged out of the cottage. She took one glance at me, made a gesture as if she was going to speak and bolted past. The door to the van was open, the motor humming and she was peeling out of the driveway.

With no time to digest what had happened, let alone why, the wailing from inside the cottage brought illumination.

I opened the door slowly, listening intently. The wailing stopped for a moment. I eased my way into the cottage. I let out a breath I didn't know I was holding and was met with a thunderous crash on the other side of the door. My head rattled off the doorframe.

"Dustin!" I bellowed.

"No Papa," he called back, still pushing with all of his weight against the other side of the door.

"Dustin. Open!" I called, shaking my sore jaw back and forth. "Man, for a year and a half you are awfully soggy!" I declared before summoning the strength to overpower him and force my way in.

As I stepped in the rest of the clues as to Sylvie's rampage were evident. Toys were strewn about everywhere. The round kitchen table was awash with crayons, colouring pages and an attempt at a supper.

After a full day braving the wind, the rain and the cold all I hoped for was a warm meal, ready to eat. Instead: a few pots, a few pans, food in various states of preparation took residence on the kitchen table and beyond. It was as if, in the instant I returned home, she made a hasty decision to make bolt. But was it temporary or permanent?

"Dustin, where did Momma go?" I asked my young son.

He said nothing, instead hauling me by the hand to what was entertaining him. The laptop was open on top of the television. Was this another clue? As I looked at the screen the familiar Mac Beach ball was spinning. Behind it, stuck, was a screenshot of YouTube and the Mickey Mouse Playhouse.

How many times had the same clip repeated itself? Here, stuck out in nowhere, child and mother beyond civilization, the five-minute video clip could be repeated ad nauseum. Entertaining one, torturing the other. How long had she been subjected to those methods, and would army intelligence be calling to investigate the latest thing in interrogation procedure? Could it be more effective than the US Marine's blasting Noriega with high voltage AC/DC?

My son engulfed himself in some other program. I saw his shift in focus as an opportunity to salvage something out of supper. I shuffled over to the kitchen. It was hopeless. Like an inspector not wanting to disturb the crime scene, I abandoned those preparations to rely on a simpler solution for my hunger. I plunked the peanut butter down on the counter.

"Dustin, do you want some supper?" I called.

"Where's Mama?" he cried back and in that instant, his lip turned to a quiver, a snarl and then the long, loud note of a desperate howl.

"Great, isn't that just what I want when I step in through the door," I muttered to myself before trying to console him. When I stepped next to him he pushed me away and charged off into the bedroom, bellowing, sobbing and howling the entire way.

Wrestling with whether to interject or not to interject I thought aloud, "What should I do now?"

"Don't do anything!" came the voice from the door.

I turned and Sylvie, the crazed look of someone who'd been cooped up in a tiny cottage at the edge of nowhere for far too long, came stumbling back into the room.

"He's tired, he hasn't napped. He hasn't slept for a week. He's sick and so am I. I'm making Kraft Dinner for supper and after that I'm taking a nap and you're looking after our child!"

"Okay, I guess I won't bother to tell you what kind of day I had."

She glowered at me.

"And I don't need to bother telling you. I haven't heard anything more about the…"

"It's somewhere in Ontario."

"It is!" I said excitedly.

"Yeah, but that's not exactly here now is it!" she barked.

"Is it getting hot in here or is it just me," I tried my best to distract her.

"Don't! You'll only let in more humidity. It's probably why Dustin isn't sleeping."

Sylvie and I looked at one another for a moment, reaching the same conclusion. She left the pot on the stove and walked with me into the spare bedroom. Dustin had rolled himself onto the bed in a ball of linens.

"I think he might be passed out."

"Has he been that sick?"

"He's been feverish, frantic. He's been at my leg, playing Mickey Mouse songs a hundred fucking times. We can't go anywhere, it's windy, it's wet, and it's cold. We don't know anyone. This place is smaller than a Vietnamese prison. I wanna go back to Roden!"

I stiffened. At her best, Sylvie was not the stay at home type. Especially with a boy who would rather crash cars and slam on the bed then sit and make flower decorations. How much longer would they be able to wait out this weather before an unfortunate event occurred that wouldn't have been possible had mother been of sound mind?

My mind clawed at answers. Hope. Solutions. It was latching onto something. Something was amiss.

"I bet the floor isn't insulated."

"Ya think! How else do you explain the condensation on the floor…" she said and stopped. Her gaze reached mine, drawing the same conclusion.

She stood over his playpen: His playpen that was functioning as his bed. She pulled up his blankets, feeling them in her hands.

"Is it wet?"

"Hard to tell. I think it was less humid in the jungle's of Thailand."

She set it down and pulled up the small nylon layer of foam and folded cardboard that encompassed the underside of his bed. Underneath, forming noticeable collections of water lay the root of the problem.

"Oh good gawd," I thundered and hauled the folding bottom piece out of the playpen.

"It's soaked! No wonder he hasn't been sleeping well and he's been sick. Cripes! Look, over there," I said pointing, "there's a pool of water on the floor beside the bed. That explains it. We're probably too close to the ground, there's no insulation, and when the damp air meets the warm air inside the cottage, bam, instant condensation."

"Just fucking great!" Sylvie exclaimed, "how much longer before that yurt arrives?"

"Well, you said it was in Ontario somewhere, didn't you?"

"Yeah, somewhere, but they still don't know WHERE exactly."

"We've gone as far as we can building the subfloor. Chris and I are going to start building a couple sections of the deck…"

"And I'm going to put Dustin in daycare for a couple of days a week. We both can't stay here full-time. It's unhealthy. I checked the Internet and there's no end to this rain."

"What about the drop in centre in Richibucto?"

"It's open one day a week for half a day!"

"Right."

"We need to get out of here. The more heat we create the more condensation we're going to have."

"And what are you going to do hanging around Chris and I all day. Think you'll be able to help?"

"I'm sure I can find something to do."

12

Does It Have To Be Exactly 32 Feet?

Being a lawyer isn't all about the courtroom brawls and high stakes drama. Most practicing professionals make their living cleaning the slop of paperwork in their own unique language. Language, who's sole function, I'm fairly certain, as to be impenetrable by the general public.

And when you've been getting your hands dirty building and organizing sometimes the great antithesis of all that effort are the movers and shakers who are able to quash such energy merely by a pen stroke. It pains me such little labour can have such dire consequences. Doesn't what lawyers and bankers do seem such a load of fiction?

Or is it that they've bamboozled us with their mathematics, schematics and fine print that no one has thought, hey, what are they there for? What is money anyway? You can't eat it. It's a very elaborate piece of paper that says to the world: I promise! I promise to exchange that note; that funny, ink blotched little paper with an image of a dead important person for something of real value.

Ho Hum! And yet, to have the luxury of building a round canvas structure from the ashes of a sale of a Toronto home, i.e., exchange one for the other (with some extra working capital besides) would require the use of such services.

It hardly seems the stuff of romance. Packing boxes, seeing friends, celebrating the change: that we can all relate to. It's tangible.

Forwarding mail, finalizing mortgage payments, service title changes, mortgage title changes, sale documents, insurance stuff, credit balances:

hardly the stuff of legend. They're numbers on a page, that, when brought down to that level, look painfully insignificant. But the swath of havoc they wreak! Like a lumberjack felling a forest, only these are for documentation. Numbers.

But it was the pain of their necessity I was feeling. We'd been living in oblivion of the one and only number that mattered: The balance that remained on our home. The entire operation was like Robert Rodriguez' first film. We'd financed everything with credit. In so doing we'd joined the list of millions south of us who'd stretched themselves to the absolute limit only to have the elastic snap back in their faces.

We at least had a balance. But in purchasing materials, buying food, gas, and doing what we needed to do to complete the build all of the documentation of what and how we were doing was completely unknown. The line of credit was secured against the house and when the sale was finalized the account would be closed and the cash diverted into our pockets. We'd been spewing out cheques like a drunken sailor on shore leave. Only all too soon would we know the extent of the damage.

We'd know because we were back in Toronto, chasing paperwork to close out one chapter of our lives in order to kick-start the next.

We were running across the street to catch the bus when the real pain of the last scramble struck.

"Ooh, ouch," I said hobbling.

"What's wrong old man?" Sylvie said as we sat down on the bus.

"I heard a pop," I said, as the concern on Sylvie's face grew.

"The last time that happened my knee swelled so bad I was on crutches for a week," I said.

"That's not good," she said.

"Tell me about it. Not that it makes much difference, the yurt hasn't arrived yet anyway."

Sylvie shrugged.

"Don't worry, I'll be alright once we get all this running around done. Okay, so I won't be doing much running. Once we get all of this bullshit paperwork taken care of we can take our time, pack, catch up with a few friends and have a little serenity before we head back to N. B."

I stretched my leg out on the bus. A decent range of motion. Perhaps it was manageable. I attempted to pull the leg back into a bend. It stopped half way.

"Hmm, that's not so good," I declared, "I'll need to get ice on it as soon as I can. Some rest."

Sylvie looked down at her ticket.

"It's a day pass. We won't be home and rested until next year."

****

We were back in our nearly empty Toronto home, lives filled to the brim in boxes, bags and packages of all kinds, regaling our friends with our yurt misadventures.

"Well, I'd be ranting and raving at them," Larry Smith (who's always looking for a reason to perform such wanton acts of verbal assault) was the most blunt.

"I did that already," I said, "and still no yurt."

Sherry and Linda were equally as perturbed, "If they don't know where it is, tell them to send another one!"

There is comfort in knowing your friends are feeling, though it isn't happening to them, the pain of your discontent. "There you go Atlas," they allow in turn as they stoop under the world, "you just let me take this for a few minutes. Give you a rest. Take a smoke break."

And it somehow lessens the burden, brings a little humour and levity, wondering exactly how they might have handled the same situation. But, sucker as I am for the underdog (damn bleeding heart, Larry barked) I was starting to see the situation from the other side.

"It took them six months to be two weeks behind. Has it been two weeks? Anyways, if they're this late with the first one then a replacement isn't exactly around the corner. Y'know, now that I think about it they did say it might take awhile for it to arrive," I babbled.

"They should offer to refund some of your money, something, anything..."

"I know I should ask, but honestly, I'm not on good terms with the dealer…" I confessed.

"Oh," Sherry said, "Yeah, you won't get any of your money back."

"Jason," Linda pointed with a soft scolding, "well how are you going to know when the yurt has arrived?"

"I'll get a call."

Sylvie interjected, "Well, lemme get this right. The shipping company is going to take it to place with a dock. The dock is in Memramcook. Don't ask, but Jason has a funny story about Memramcook. They'll somehow get it onto a local delivery truck. The delivery truck will drive to Upper Rexton where our friend Chris will greet it and it'll slide onto our property."

"Yes, all that will happen after they find it."

"It was in Ontario sometime last week. It's gotta be gettin' close now."

****

It was impossible to get angry. I tried even, but Paul was just too damn nice and I was just too relieved to hear the yurt had a physical location in New Brunswick.

"Uh, okay, so it got there yesterday?" I questioned.

"Yeah," Paul said.

I was pulling for the confession. Instead I was met by a tight-lipped witness who needed me to walk him through the crime for concrete evidence the yurt had left the quantum world of possibility and arrived in the one of actuality.

"Was everything alright? You must not have been able to get it off the truck," I gathered.

"No."

From the kitchen window, Sylvie could see my reaction and immediately locked the doors in case the infection might spread.

"Was there a problem? It's not broken or anything?" I continued.

"No, just hard to get off. Had to go back to their dock. Don't worry, we'll take care of it," Paul finally elaborated.

'Could you tell me why? What was wrong,' were what I wanted say.

Instead the words came out as motions with my hands, thankfully it wasn't a video call:

"Good, I need to know to have somebody meet it in Richibucto."

"You're not there?"

I threw the phone up in the air.

"Sorry, a little reception problem. No, I've been waiting for two weeks. I'm back in Toronto closing our house. So if you could please tell me when you're leaving Memramcook I can get my friend to meet you at my property."

"Sure."

"Great. Thank you."

'Sure! Sure what?!' I thundered after I hung up the phone, 'why can't these stupid little fucking details ever be easy. You call me. I'll call Chris…'

And then the anger turned to elation: the yurt had finally landed!

For the first time in weeks, I felt relaxed and at ease. My knee, which had swelled earlier in the week, had subsided with rest and ice. Though I'd been champing at the bit, trying to get to site as soon as we left the plane, staying in Bathurst for a few days to recuperate brought the swelling to a manageable level. And for added bonus, Sylvie decided to remain up north with Dustin. I traded the two of them in for Fern. I now had a crew of three.

When I arrived on site, I could see why the crates were such a hassle. The framing looked acceptable, square, two by fours and plywood. It was the underneath that was the problem. The long crate sat on top of a succession of palettes that housed the log rafters. The palettes were attached to the frame, but not to one another. From loading docks to shipping means to whatever movement had occurred to get the product from the west coast to east each of the six palettes had determined themselves how best to arrive: Crooked, off kilter and hanging on by will power.

No wonder Paul couldn't get a forklift or a pump truck underneath the crates to move them where they needed to go! We all enjoyed a good laugh and wondered aloud what those good folks in Hope BC could possibly be smoking to have concocted such a shabby housing for such a fine product.

With great satisfaction, I grabbed my screw gun, a pry bar and started to open the crates. And started. And started. Screw after screw. And when I thought I'd gotten them all, tried to peel off the layer of plywood, another, hidden screw held fast.

"Ah," I finally observed, "so that's how it managed to stay together long enough to arrive."

When the first layer of ply managed to peel off I was somewhat afeard of what dangers might be lurking within. Considering the rough handling a bit of damage from the long transportation could be expected.

"You can look now Jase, dere's only two dat's broke!" Fern informed me.

Out of dozens of rafters and studs, only two were broken.

"All things considered," I thought, keeping my composure, "and hey, maybe they had enough foresight to send a couple extra just in case."

"Shoore," Chris said, "now where do we want to start?"

"The R-Foil. I see the roll here. We'll tack it down with staples and then we'll screw the sub-floor on top."

"Okay, then before we put down the insulation, we should make sure of our perimeter."

"How's that now?"

"Does it have to be exactly thirty-two feet?"

"I looked at the instructions on the plane, briefly, and that was the one thing with complete emphasis. It was in bold. The diameter has to be EXACTLY thirty-two feet."

"Okay," Chris said and set to work while Fern and I opened the rest of the crates to make sure all that was promised was delivered. As I dove into the last box of hardware I found a hard copy of installation instructions.

When I looked over my shoulder, Chris had fashioned a stick from some of the decking and asked for my assistance. I fumbled with the book to verify instructions. Was what Chris doing a match for the method outlined in the manual?

"Now, I've worked out the calculations so we can find the exact middle. We'll need to keep that through each layer we add onto the floor."

"Right," I said, trying to hold onto the tape measure with one hand and flip pages with the other, "because when we start to build the doors have to be in their exact perfect location. We ordered them for twelve and nine o'clock. And they're the first thing we put on."

"Okay, well, I've referenced our joists and we have the thirty-two foot perimeter. We should be good."

"Chris," I said, "I'm SO glad you're in charge of this and not me!"

****

It was a welcome relief, that second week of June, for the drizzle to part and allow maximum sunshine onto our build. That is, until the reflexive insulation was laid out, in pure unfiltered sunshine to burn the retina of anyone caught on the wrong angle.

"Aiye Yoye," Fern grimaced.

"Look, it's a massive reflector board!" Chris exclaimed, shielding his eyes.

"WOW," I said, "I wouldn't want to be a low-lying aircraft!"

"Hmm, and I've seen some around here too," Chris added.

"Oh?" I questioned as we wrestled the sheet.

"And they're not dusting for bugs like they used to," Chris said.

"But they're flying low?"

"Yeah," Fern added, "I seen dem too, when I was fishing. Going back and fort."

"Hmm, probably Google Maps," I said with confidence, "I know they were driving all around Toronto not too long ago. Every road, trying to get a street-level view of everywhere on the planet. I always thought New Brunswick was safe from big brother."

"You can still hide in the woods," Chris observed, "but you can never hide from big brother!"

Ka-Chunk! Went the stapler. It wasn't exactly the golden spike, but the first drive went through the insulation and into the floor beneath. Shielding our eyes from the intensity of the reflection, the layer of insulation was added without too much difficulty. Except.

Except when a regular floor is added to the joists there are a succession of lines on top to designate where to attach the screws. From the joists that stick out from underneath, it's easy to line up the ply, the lines, the screws and the joists. The added bonus of the exposed joists is they can be walked on to add the material on top.

We spent a few hours covering all those markers up with a material that was more hazardous to sight than a direct score from a laser pointer!

Fern was the first to misjudge his step and plunge through the reflective layer.

"Oh shit, sorry Jase!" he exclaimed, as much embarrassed as hurt.

"Don't worry about it, I hope you're alright, but don't fuckin' do it again!" I said with a laugh.

Fern chuckled as he neatly applied the tape to mask his error. As he finished I laid a line of excess two by eight across the joists.

"There, that should take care of that!"

"Just don't cover our centre," Chris cautioned.

"Wherever it ends up we'll be sure to mark the spot!" I explained.

"Here," Chris said and threw me his chalk line, "We'll have to mark the joists on the first row of ply."

Always the pragmatic one. Always a solution for something I'd have spent hours agonizing over an outcome. Instead, following Chris' lead, the only pain in tacking down the ply was my still tender knee that had yet to achieve a full range of motion. Fern allowed me the outside perimeter, with the chance to stand instead of crawl. Chris ripped the stripping that would encompass the outside rim and barrier of the diameter of the floor.

Sticking one inch above the floor, it would hold the lattice in place and prevent the bottoms from simply sliding out underneath (and collapsing the whole thing.)

Now that we had graduated from post to an actual subfloor, the curious eyes that cruised nonchalantly past the site were now starting to slow down to take a closer look at the project. And yes, the low flying aircraft Fern was talking about made an appearance. So too did boats along the river, drawn, no doubt, by the beacon of reflected sunlight that probably registered on the moon.

What they would find was two men crouched in the middle of the floor, measuring tapes extended, forming a triangle. And then, after pausing, scratching heads, those tapes would be picked up, moved and reformed in the exact same scenario.

Dipping into an ancient formula to find our true centre and our subsequent twelve o'clock and nine o'clock door positions (Pie and Pythagorean Theorem respectively) we paused for a moment before making our cuts out of the rim of the floor.

"We've double checked this, and these are our absolute door positions?" Chris asked me, "And we have to be as accurate as we possibly can be?" Chris questioned again.

"Yes, the manufacturer has it in bold. As a matter of fact, I think it's the only thing in here that they mention where they do ask for precision."

(Because naturally, when Sylvie and I were waiting to return to New Brunswick I picked up a magazine that featured an article on building a yurt. In his erection process (insert joke here) he got all the way to the roof cover only to find the door cut outs were in the wrong spot. He had to send the roof cover back to the manufacturer to have them repositioned!)

We both took a deep breath before allowing the decision to be final. Unlike a square home where a shim here and a cheat there can sometimes hide mistakes, what do you do with a round structure? If the doors, the anchor points, are out even a tiny bit, how does that affect everything else? In framing, mistakes in the project can be hidden with drywall, trim, caulking. Walls and floors can be crooked and still maintain structural integrity. What's the structural integrity of a circle?

We made the marks and cut the gap in the outer rim to accommodate the two doors. As the doors were leveled and screwed into position we took another pause to admire the extremely backwards process.

"Chris," I teased, "they're going to think you got into the screech again."

"What's that now?"

"Doors first. What are those Newfie contractor's up to anyway?"

With a chuckle, a shrug and the energy that bringing something to life can bring, we left the admiration alone and moved on to the next part.

Stretching out the first lattice piece I was relieved to find Yurtco got it right. We measured, stretched and then measured again to make sure we were following the prescribed instructions properly. That would be 10 ¼" to 10 ½" between lattice rivets and an even height all around.

We followed their guidance to the law. When the time came to attach the lattice to the doors, the connecting brackets weren't co-operating. Questioning, but not too much, the only solution we could find to make it work that wouldn't affect the integrity of the structure was to drill another hole into the metal bracket and attach the bolt and wing nut through the aberration.

Success!

Gritting with the second, larger, lattice section that spanned three quarters of the yurt wall, we heaved it onto the floor for unfurling.

We strung out the second lattice piece, stretching and manipulating the beast to the outer perimeter and into a fashion that was roughly of equal height. Except there was one catch: The overall height of the second lattice wall was noticeably shorter than the first. We were dumbfounded. Confused. We consulted the installation manual for clues and inspiration as to what was the guiding principle behind the yurt installation. After all, they were quite adamant about the door location, but how exact did the walls need to be?

We stood, looked, scratched. Perhaps the doors weren't quite in the proper positions as we measured. Again, I referred back to the installation manual.

The instructions in the installation manual called for us to 'take a measurement of the perimeter of the yurt, divide it into four sections, mark each quarter and then install doors on centre lines'. Chris and I both went, uh, huh?

When we had gone through the trouble of using ancient, but proven mathematical equations in finding our 12 and 9 o'clock door positions, the manual was using another mathematical equation entirely. After all, measuring the circumference would be the easiest thing to do. However, if the yurt wasn't exactly a 32' diameter, that would throw off the circumference, n'est pas?

Fern and Chris stared at our just completed doors and lattice walls.

"What if we moved the doors?" Chris said.

"I don't see why we can't," I replied and flipped the pages feverishly, trying to find a solution.

"If Fern can give you a hand I'll try and call the manufacturer, see if they have any more insight," I wavered a little nervously.

Down went the doors. We cut out our new position, stood and leveled the doors and continued to stretch out and reinstall the lattice walls. Voila! It worked.

Somewhat relieved, our day reaching its conclusion, we headed home. Except there was a nagging feeling in the back of my mind. Throughout the conundrum, I'd tried to get in touch with the manufacturer and get some input as to what our problem might be: but Yurtco was four time zones away.

I was racing through the aisles of the Richibouctou Village Co-op/Liquor store/gas bar/dollar store/whatever to scrounge up some beer and burgers to close out the day by the time a consultant could be reached in BC.

"You'll have to move the doors back," Darin said.

"I had a funny feeling about that," I agreed.

"The vinyl roof is cut out to match the door positions exactly. If they're off…"

I was unnerved. To get it right the first time, only to get it wrong the next, only to have to go back to where you had it right to begin with…I was a little annoyed. But in only confirming my suspicions I forgot to ask him why the difference in height of the lattice?

Before I arrived the next day, Chris had a grin from ear to ear, which told me he knew exactly the conversation I had with the manufacturer the night before.

"So we have to move the doors back?" he said.

Defeated, but ready to continue the fight, I nodded the affirmative. But, to confirm the distance, I went to the various bags of Yurtco shipped material, grabbed the top cover and started to undo the bag.

"What are you doing boy?" Fern asked me.

"Just trying to eliminate any possibilities, I responded, thinking back to the article.

I pulled the very heavy top cover out of its bag and spread it out on the grass. Stretching out the tape I was relieved at two things; the roof cut outs were in the right place and their distance matched the original placement of our doors. Relief, but that change meant the height question was back on the table.

I looked like a jones-ing cokehead as I clenched my jaws back and forth. What was the answer?

"I think we should cut the lattice," Chris opined.

"Yup," Fern agreed. "I tink it's de only way. If we cut it den we'll get de height we need."

My dependable crew had now banded together in this most improbable, and mutinous, fashion. We hit a complete standstill. It didn't seem like the best answer, but I couldn't prove my hunch. Knowing the walls would be up one way or another, we optimistically erected the scaffolding for the next stage of assembly (to try and make some productive use of time.)

It was still only ten o'clock.

The pressure to give in to the easy answer was becoming more difficult with each passing minute. Fern liked to remind me, 'if you're not working me den I might as well go fishing'. Chris, my carpenter, was on an hourly rate and keeping his skills idle was costly as well. I tried biding my time and getting us working on something, anything, that might make all of us stop looking at our watches. It was pointless.

I clenched my teeth; feverishly hoping Darin would pick up the phone at any hour as promised.

Not responding to his personal phone I waited until just after the company opened its doors to place a query.

"Hmm, really, that's the first that's ever happened." Darin said cheerfully. I was secretly praying he'd choke on his phone cord.

"Okay, we've got different heights and my crew wants to cut the lattice," I said dramatically.

"Oh no, don't do that, whatever you do," he blurted.

"One wall is noticeably taller than the other one…"

"How many vee's do you have?" he asked.

"Errr?"

"Where the lattice comes together at the top."

Chris counted, "24."

"Twenty-four," I repeated.

"Ahh, that's why." Darin said, not letting me in on his Ah-Ha Moment.

"It should only be twenty- three, but there's an extra one to match the other side," Darin explained in his flawless yurt-speak.

"Go ahead, make the walls as even as you can, and if one section of wall is slightly taller than the other, don't worry, the weight on the compression ring will balance it out," Darin said.

I turned to Chris and Fern and in my best annoying kid voice said, "Nyah, nyah, I was right!!" before summarizing the explanation.

Stretching, heaving, scratching and clawing, we settled the lattice walls into its perfect unevenness. The height difference was disturbingly noticeable. Before adding the compression ring, the inner engineer in all of us had to wrap our heads around how it all worked.

"No madder what your weight is still transferring down. As long as de bottom doesn't kick out," Fern added.

Our mental meandering was only tackling some of the skepticism that remained unsaid. It looked flimsy. The kind of engineering gaffe even IKEA would be embarrassed to sell.

And that was before I scampered to the top of our scaffolding. The scaffolding we had to scrounge from a guy who knew a guy. All of the quality material was being monopolized on the bridge renovation in downtown Rexton that I could now see from my view fifteen feet in the air. As Chris joined me I cowered for balance like a nervous spider spinning its first web.

"Wow, you could probably get a good few feet with that bounce," Chris said as his feet found purchase on the platform. With Fern attaching the rafters on the cable at the bottom, it would be up to Chris and I to hold the centre ring steady while also fitting the metal pin at the end of the rafter into the hole. But the two sections of staging weren't quite enough height.

Two sawhorses were hauled to the top of two stages of scaffolding. The centre ring was to rest on top until a few rafters could be secured to take the weight. And then, we had to get the angle of the pin at the end of the rafters just so in order to slide it into it's corresponding slot on the centre ring. All while leaning here, pulling and lifting the rafter into the slot, and leaning there.

And just for fun, Chris informed me very early on that his son was having a graduation ceremony that day and the latest he could stay was 5 pm. We pressed ahead. Fern worked vigorously below, while Chris and I tilted the bulky six-foot centre ring to accommodate the first four rafters. We set them in with great determination. It was almost lunch. I held tight to the centre ring even after the fourth rafter was in place. Chris stepped back, informing me he was no longer taking any of the weight. I was singlehandedly holding the goddamn thing together.

"Go ahead, you can take lunch. I've got this," I said hunkered over the ring.

"I don't know Jase, de rafters look pretty solid," Fern observed.

I slowly took my hands away. Mouths agape, we stared, the centre ring was self-supporting! Famished, I too scampered down the elevation.

Though it was only four rafters and the lattice bowed mightily with the weight, the results spoke for themselves. The concept of a place was now materializing! And by fuck, the shit was holding up!

The more geometrical the shape, the more difficult the construction: the previously unbalanced weight allowed us the leverage to muscle the top of the wall out to get the rafter slotted into place on the compression ring. More weight equaled less flex! And the day and the sun exacted their toll.

With haste and fatigue, one rafter that wasn't secured as another was being manhandled dropped out of place! Fern's arm, outstretched for balance, found the log fall directly into his hands: which wouldn't have been a bad thing except he was holding one already. I hopped and yelled as Fern grimaced to take the weight.

Chris, never in a panic, worked efficiently to attach the first rafter before helping Fern with the second. We breathed a little deeper, mindful the mistakes that can (and do) happen so quickly.

"I forgot to tell you," I called down, "it says in the manual you're supposed to wear a hard hat when you're installing the rafters. Guess now we know why."

****

I was nervous for mostly one reason: getting the layers of fabric on the roof in one piece. With the house sold, we were officially without a permanent residence. I had always envisioned being mortgage free before the age of forty, but being homeless wasn't in the equation. We had two weeks to turn a shell into a functional home. And unlike the other qualities of the home and their human scale, the roof was big, unwieldy and would require disparate persons and personalities to work together to complete. On Saturday morning, a day that promised to be sunny and most importantly, calm, I managed to wrangle two more hands from a roster of over half a dozen to help put the heavy vinyl layer onto the rafters.

The first layer was easy. Like putting a blanket on a bed. The cloth liner rested on the rafters before a small wisp of wind reminded us how thin that layer. Sensing our work could be quickly undone; Fern and I attached the fabric onto the wood with staples. The second layer, the R-Foil reflexive insulation, drew more attention from the elements. It too was grappled down.

Just as Fern and I were attaching the layer to the roof, Richard LeBlanc was the first pair of hands to arrive. Seeing us struggle, he bounded onto our temporary platform outside the walls to hold down the outside before staples could be driven through the material. Sylvie, Flo and Dustin arrived just as we were about to tackle the last, heavy vinyl layer of the roof of the yurt. Great, I thought, perfect timing. Much as I love my son, his infectious enthusiasm and lack of experience wouldn't aide the construction process. But then again, what 22 month old does?

We stopped for a moment before deciding how to best to get the large package up and in position. Fern and JC (Sylvie's uncle, Fern's younger brother) had different ideas, both perfectly valid. JC suggested we use a rope to pull the vinyl up from the side. Fern said we should fold it up in half, the way a trucker would use vinyl to cover a load: pull it up through the centre ring and unfurl it first one side and then the other. The way the manufacturer suggested. However, the manufacturer probably never put up a yurt with our stellar scaffolding. Scaffolding that so far hadn't maimed us, despite its best intentions. Between the scaffold, its deck and the rusted parts, the roof could catch and tear at an ample number of places.

I agreed to JC's plan. We lugged the roof to a side, tied it all up in bunches and prepared to haul it up the outside. The plan was not without detractors, but since I was the de facto crew chief, my decision was final. Men being men, I could hear Fern and Richard think out loud: "if it were me, I'd do it this way…" and if the situation were reversed, I know I'd have had my thoughts about the situation as well. But they said nothing and embraced the concept with zeal.

As Fern stood on the scaffolding looking down, I could hear faint, but stern words of caution: "Be careful Poppa!"

More nervous than I, Dustin stood and pointed at Fern as he and JC heaved on the rope. Richard and I lifted and helped from below until it was all in the hands of the men up top.

I couldn't stand to idly watch, but as one of the ground people, once the vinyl passed a certain height on the rafters, it was out of my control. I stood on the ground, looking up, running here and there to see if there was any place I could be of some kind of help.

I must've looked funny, like a career convict who'd just been released from prison, standing outside the penitentiary, terrified of the big wide world, looking for any way to get himself back in! In the process of running and seeing where I could be of assistance I was at least relieved the roof climbed without becoming snagged.

But judging by the amount of flailing and chattering I heard from above, it was far from smooth. The roof was in a big heap of a mess, like a puppy trying to hump a beach ball. It wasn't pretty. As in other moments of helplessness, my mental anguish manifested into physical energy: Up and down the scaffolding I climbed.

Fern looked to me nonchalantly while JC grinned his happy devil may care grin. I scampered back down. There was no more I could do or be doing. I muttered to myself about the wisdom in JC's idea when the roof gradually unfurled and found its way. It stretched out into place. I could finally find a place to grab onto an edge and exact some influence on the process.

"Is it in the right spot yet?" JC called to me.

"Uh, I don't know, where's the cut out for the doors?"

"Can you see dem from where you are?" the roof guys asked again.

Then the conclusion to the confusion. The shock and awe moment.

The big "AWWW FUCK!"

Flo ambled up to me slowly, no hint she was in possession of such widespread yurt knowledge and delivered a zinger, "Jase, are you sure it isn't upside down?"

With perfect timing, JC's cell phone rang and he was forced to address his caller. I got tagged into the ring to continue to wrestle with the unruly vinyl roof. I climbed beside Fern on the top of the scaffolding.

"Be careful Poppa!" Dustin exclaimed again.

I fumbled and flailed about with my father-in-law who could only delay my assault. I was hopeless and near hyperventilation. The whole mess we'd tried so painfully to avoid had sucked us into its vortex. I scrambled down to the ground and cursed.

It wasn't my concern for what MIGHT happen as opposed to what was ACTUALLY happening. And naturally, by being focused on what could go wrong, I neglected everything that was going right. Fortunately, the meddlesome wind, which gained some velocity, and hampered the boys on the roof, was preventing them from hearing me curse under my breath.

With perfect calm (or so it seemed, whether in anger or joy, the French always sound animated) the roof was steered around, flipped over, and eventually slid into its proper space.

"How does it stay on?" Richard asked as he brandished the staple gun.

When I saw the gun my heart skipped a beat, "You didn't staple anything on the last layer did you?"

A little taken aback, Richard responded, "No."

I felt my heart start to beat again.

"Sorry man, you just scared me half to death," I clarified before continuing, "When we get the walls up, the roof attaches to the walls, which then gets screwed to the floor."

"Ah, okay," Richard said in the exact same cadence as the other Kent county crowd.

In the shadow of the scaffolding, we sat and enjoyed our bounty of Subway sandwiches and a few beers. Satisfied. Now, more than the subfloor, more than the walls, I could SEE the space and how it was going to work. It was a beautiful sight. Dustin thought so too. Before any of us could see what he was up to, he started racing around the scaffolding.

Finally the black cloud around Cap Lumière that seemed to engulf us had broken up and lifted. At least for the moment.

13

Move In Condition

For two blissful days Chris and I mucked along the floor of the yurt. The roof was intact, the walls were open and inviting a breeze. The conditions were perfect for rolling out and laying down the vinyl flooring.

"I know you usually put up the interior walls first," I said to Chris as we crawled about on the floor.

"This makes more sense," Chris agreed, "there's nothing in the way. The floor will cure in the weather and we can just roll the vinyl floor where we need it."

"Okay, good, it's nice that something is starting to work out for a change," I said and enjoyed a loud, long exhale.

"Oh yeah," Chris continued chuckling, "it really takes a lot for a build to go completely wrong."

The pace of the van as it slowly rolled into the driveway should have been all the indication I needed. The rubber tires echoed the gravel back and forth in its unforgettable sound. I heard the click of the latch, the door jarred and then closed again. On my knees, applying glue to the floor, I grimaced as I got to my feet. I straightened my legs for a moment, encouraging motion. My knee was stiff, but holding up.

I saw the look on Chris' face first. It was a face that just saw something it wished it hadn't. It was then I knew everything was not alright. I looked over to the van. My wife was slumped over the steering wheel.

"Oh shit," I said.

The bellows and sobs greeted me before I opened the door.

"I…(sob) can't…(hyperventilate)..find…anyone…to…take..Dustin," Sylvie whimpered along.

"Oh crap!" I muttered.

Dustin continued his thing completely unperturbed. Sitting in the car seat, his long, wavy blond hair bounced with each crash of his dinky cars. The brows over his deep, chestnut brown eyes furrowed as some explosive story came alive in his face. He grunted and growled at each zoom or bob of his dinky cars.

"I..don't," Sylvie tried to speak again, the sobs slowing but more dramatic.

"Wait hun, hang in there," I said as I pulled her out of the seat, reached in and turned off the car.

"Know….what….to….do?"

As the sobs and howls became louder, the noise broke through the bubble of Dustin's story. He became very concerned very quickly.

"Maman!?!" he said and tried to crawl out of his seat.

Sylvie got out of the car, hung her head and started to pace in the driveway. I reached in, unbuckled our boy, and pulled him out.

I bounced with Dustin in my arms. He enjoyed the force and asked for more. His enthusiasm was contagious, Sylvie's wailing halted somewhat. It was time to test the waters for a lasting resolve.

"Did you try and show them how cute our son is?" I asked. Oops. Too soon.

Sylvie wailed, stumbled and tripped as she flopped down on the steps. Dustin crawled out of my arms to console, returning an evil look my way on her behalf.

It was far more serious than I thought. Concerned, Chris gave us a passing glance before continuing his work. I eased in beside and wrapped her into my arms. She curled in and tucked her head to my chest. The erratic wails abated quickly. She sniffled into my shirt.

"Mama okay?" Dustin said to me. Sylvie shook her head back and forth, sniffling simultaneously.

"I guess that..." and my words were interrupted as Sylvie sat back and snorted deeply. I looked down at my shirt, damp with tears, grief and mucous.

"Ewww, gross!" I yelled.

"BWAH, Ha hahhahahaha," Dustin howled in delight and pointed at my shirt.

Sylvie found a chuckle.

"It's gonna be all right hun," I said with half-hearted certainty.

Her body shook with another sniffle, a longer chuckle and then giggles as she pawed at the misery on my shirt.

"I'm just tired hun. I'm not made to be a full-time Mom. I'm a good part-time Mom..."

"I know. I wish I could help but I'm tied here..." I offered.

"And I'm tied elsewhere and I don't know anyone..."

"So what did you do before? Remember when you first came to Toronto and I tried to get you to go to places for work..."

"Yeah, and I wasn't ready yet and I was in over my head," she barked at me sharply, "I almost moved back remember!?!"

"Right, maybe that's a bad example. But you never let it stop you. It was what I always loved about you, that feistiness...."

Her eyes drooped in painful desperation. "What, do you think I've lost it?" she said with thick irony.

We both chuckled.

"Y'know what, screw it. I don't care if I have to beg or bawl we absolutely NEED someone to take Dustin for a couple days a week. You're working here full-time, I start in Moncton in two weeks, we need to find a house."

I nodded along with her. Her sadness was turning to resolve.

"Somebody has GOT to understand. I mean, half the people in the daycares are mothers..."

"You mean you've only been calling on the phone so far?"

Her eyes caught mine. Neither of us was particularly good at taking 'No' for an answer. Nor were we afraid of barging in where initially we were uninvited.

"I'll bring Dustin with me and if I've got to bawl my eyes out in front of them then that's what I'll do!"

****

"You're asking me to build this thing with one hand tied behind my back!" I grumbled.

"Well how can I get my career going and pay for this friggin' yurt if every time I have to do something work related you freak out about it!" Sylvie fired back. It was a standstill.

"I just can't afford to lose a day like this!" I said, trying to hold serve in the argument, "I mean, why didn't you get daycare for early in the week so I can get some work done?"

"How the fuck are you going to take Dustin to and from day care? You're bike! It's twenty kilometres each way!"

I said nothing. She had me. The offence continued, relentless.

"Be happy we have any daycare at all! I tried everywhere and not everyone wants to take on a kid part time who isn't two and isn't potty trained."

"I know but....it's just frustrating. Finally we have the yurt and all the material and I can't get to it."

"Do you have any idea what I had to go through to get a spot for him? I called every place in town, and nothing was available. I start training next week."

"I know. We don't have a home remember. We move out this weekend, and the cottage is booked until the end of summer."

She glared me down. Back on the attack.

"I broke down. I was balling on the steps of the daycare. Balling. I was having a fucking breakdown..." her eyes welled up during the recall.

I cowered, waving the white flag. She paused and gathered her composure.

"We're going to Moncton, I'm meeting my boss, and you're looking after Dustin. Daycare starts Thursday. If you don't come you might as well move into the yurt by yourself!"

****

"What do you want!?!" the voice responded abruptly. I was hardly surprised. I was at a McDonald's in Dieppe, trying to make the most of my day off. I contented myself trying to organize the other aspects of the build (plumbers, electricians and such). Sylvie was across town, socializing with her soon to be new boss having already made the next step in our transition.

Dustin screamed and scrambled in the play set while I forged on, cell phone stuck to my ear. I'd finally learned, from earlier fiascos, that being proactive was a way to abate panic BEFORE it set in rather than beating it off AFTER it'd taken residence.

"I'm looking for someone to dig a trench," I said nonchalantly. Why? Why was I not chewing this brain-dead hic a new arsehole for being so rude on the phone?

Because it was a response I anticipated.

When Bob picked up the phone, it was the third time I rang. The response leading up to the greeting was an all too familiar déjà vu.

I called once with no response. The second try it rang once before the machine: someone was attending but screening calls. A third ring indicated I was someone with legitimate business. I was right on all accounts. Bob begrudgingly picked up the phone on my third try.

Some might take offence at being treated so rudely. I found it comical, the disdain of instant communication revealed much about the people in this new land. These rural dwellers, with one foot in the hunting stand, were ferociously defending their choice to remain of a 19th century mindset. How would I navigate that in the workforce and on a social level?

Construction season was in full swing, and naturally, for the trouble of dealing with one so inconsiderate, it wasn't a surprise they didn't have the time for my small job anyway. Bob could afford to be both rude and busy. I had to laugh it off.

How could I be mired in Dieppe while my story-telling device of a deadline dictated I should be barking orders at contractors in Richibucto? And why was a trench so suddenly important? The deadline was very real. From the moment the roof was finished we had a two-week window to complete the rest of the yurt: electrical, plumbing, walls. Complete it at least to a point of function.

For that function we only needed to construct and erect one two by six wall between the bathroom and kitchen that would house the majority of the plumbing.

This we did in order to facilitate the other trades who could begin without my direct input. And then someone jumped the queue.

I've said it about Larry that I've never had to work so hard for his money. Larry, you might remember was my transient friend from Saint John who, despite his disposition, factors favourably here and in my life. Without Larry (and to a lesser extent Daniel Baldwin) I wouldn't have met Sylvie, fell in love with her and spawned a child. But my affection for my short, bald, pudgy friend continued beyond his initial influence on my fate.

Larry was also the primary tenant of our old apartment.

It was a mutually beneficial arrangement: for a reduced rate Larry would sometimes get me work on the shows he was working on (and sometimes not) and we would let him have the apartment for a reduced rate. He would have an audience for his rants, and we would let Dustin run around above his bedroom at very early hours as an impromptu front desk courtesy wake up call.

And of course, Larry would be kind enough to keep an ear out for Dustin and allow Sylvie and I to go to a movie on occasion, and Larry (who has some intestinal issues) would destroy our plumbing. Larry would eat bad food and work long hours, and then blame Dustin whenever he was inflicted with 'The Plague'.

It was a mutually beneficial arrangement.

Back when we sold our house for a substantial amount over asking, we cut Larry a break and allowed him to stay in the apartment rent free for the remainder of our ownership. Larry was ecstatic….and ingratiated.

Since he drove back and forth from New Brunswick to Toronto for work, he offered his empty truck to ship materials as a means of gratitude for the free rental of our apartment.

For his troubles I made sure to load his truck full of building material (my barn board collection) that I intended to use in the yurt.

"What in the fuck are you going to do with this junk?" Larry quizzed me. He wished to satisfy his gratitude for the favour but didn't want to be TOO put out in the process.

"That stuff is gold Larry, pure gold," I said, completely aware how much he didn't want to be responsible for anything but himself.

"Well, whatever you're going to do with it, be forewarned, this truck is on its last legs. I don't know if I'm going to make it home in one piece. If it falls apart in a heap, I'm gonna leave it there and make other arrangements. Don't send anything valuable," he declared.

Value was in the eye of the beholder. Most of the materials were worthless to anyone but me. No matter. Larry must have felt some genuine penance (perhaps one destroyed toilet bowl too many) for when I spoke to him after he returned to Saint John he made me an offer I couldn't refuse.

"Who's installing your water pump?" he asked.

"So far no one..." my old Hamilton Spidey-Sense could detect a deal was in the offing. And if there's one thing we Hamilton's (okay, me) cannot seem to avoid, is once the scent is in the air, it's almost impossible to ignore it's effects.

"I still feel like I owe you for the apartment. You didn't have to do that," Larry confessed. Bless his heart, despite the gruff exterior and repeated assertions he boldly proclaimed he 'didn't play well with other's' he really was an old softy.

"Uh, well, if you want to install the water pump you come right up here and fill your boots," I invited.

"Well dear boy, I want to come up and see for myself what a giant hundred thousand dollar ten looks like," Larry said. I laughed.

"That and I've got to get rid of your shit in the back of my truck. Some of the wood doesn't look too bad. Y'know if I don't get rid of it, it might actually end up in my garage."

"I told you it was gold."

"I wouldn't fuckin' go that far dear boy," Larry asserted and continued, "You'll need to get the trench dug out. If you think I'm digging it out by hand you've got another thing coming!"

"Sure, sounds reasonable."

"And you'll have to buy the pump kit. I'm only gonna install it for you. The kits aren't expensive. I put one in a while ago that might have cost me a thousand bucks. If you get the plumber to do it, I guarantee it'll cost you a couple grand. Just go to the Hardware store and ask for one of those well kits, and they'll give you everything you need." Larry said.

Now Larry had me on the hook with the smell of saving a dollar. Or, in this case, close to a thousand. But, as is often the case, the hidden cost of saving a few bucks was going to be the running around looking for the kit and finding the materials. Both of those commodities were in rather short supply.

And Larry was also being slightly demanding with the time frame. The back of Larry's truck was still full of my 'building material' and he was loath to unload it before he came to drop it off. Larry was rather particular about handling things twice, even on those occasions when he was being paid handsomely to do just that.

I was and I wasn't quite ready for him to do the work. My attempts to find a trencher had proved difficult. The rude guy was too busy and the other contact I'd found was way up river with no cell phone access.

Not to mention the other contractors would soon be swarming the site to meet out my instructions to get the yurt to a point of functional habitation.

I followed Larry's instructions and started with the local plumbing specialists, GL Caissie in downtown Richibucto. Severin Cormier and I paraded around the store, picking up pitless adapters, O-Rings, valves, stems, and some personal lubrication for sexual gratification for all I knew.

"I have a friend who's going to install my pump. He said you guys would know what to get me," was all I could utter. By this point, the pressure was starting to get to me.

The pressure was, of course, time. With a naked interior, we had to make the yurt a functioning cottage in less than two weeks. Sylvie would start her training and I would be the sole provider, entertainer, parent of Dustin, all alone in Upper Rexton. It was a daunting prospect. I'd always said I wanted to camp and rough it with my son. The opportunity would soon be at hand and the anticipation had turned to dread.

And money had suddenly become a factor. The house had closed, we'd handed over the keys, but nothing in our account had changed. The line of credit and its limitless consequences had vanished. Everything was coming out of one simple chequing account and no money had been transferred into it. We thought we'd done well, but every time I made a purchase of a few dollars, my account told me I was up shit creek, deep into overdraft. A week had passed, how long did it take for bankers and lawyers to shuffle paperwork? Where the hell was the money and how much was left?

With the collection of rings, valves, hoses and clamps, the final tally was rung in.

"Eighteen hundred." Severin said with a tone of remorse in his voice and hope in his eyes.

I said, "thank you" spun on my heel and left everything at the counter.

****

"How do I get there dear boy?" Larry asked me.

"Uh, go to Moncton and turn left," I responded with a touch of humour. I was at a loss to go into specifics. The sight was abuzz with contractors, trades people and a never-ending stream of questions. Wasn't this Larry's home province? Surely he must have been around here once or twice in his life?

"Uh, take the Trans-Canada toward Moncton and when you see the sign for Miramichi take it!" I said casually. "How fuckin' hard can it be" I said aloud, "figure it out."

From another of Chris' contacts I'd managed to get the trench dug out to the yurt. Larry was swiftly shuffled back to his place in the queue. But it wouldn't matter if the pump was installed if there was no electricity to run it.

****

My initial phone consultation (from deep in the gravel pit north of Toronto) gave slight evidence Bill was a different breed: As an electrician? Yes. As a resident of rural New Brunswick? Yes. As a middle-aged white guy? Yes. All of those factors seemed to put him in direct conflict with the evolving, information obsessed reality that was non-existent in his part of the world.

I explained to Bill the yurt wasn't a conventional build. He understood.

"I can email you the plan," I offered.

"Naaa, don't have email. You'll have ta maaill it to me," he drawled then.

No email. Right.

"Oh, and you called my cell phone beforrre. I'd preefer it if ya called me on maiy hoome phone," he continued, "only use the cell for emergencies."

Except for the missing twang, I thought I was calling south of the Mason/Dixon line. But the real pain was when I mentioned the crown jewel of my green living/money saving concept.

"Aiill haave ta check, buut aii doon't think a Hot Water on demand is allllowwed unnnderrr code," he countered my enthusiasm.

But he was licensed and he was recommended. He just needed to get it stamped and I could make it how I wanted long after everyone else had left.

Bill and I walked through the yurt, newly complete with interior stud walls, making marks and deciding what was going to go where.

"So, as soon as you get that utility room built I can get to work," Bill announced.

"Huh," I said, "You mean you can't start before then?"

"Well, I won't know what material to order until I know how far I'm going with it," he said, oh so annoyingly calm.

'Uh, have you ever heard of an expense account' I thought to myself.

Instead, I pulled him outside, showed him the trench, waved my hands and said, "THIS is where it's going to go!"

I allowed him to consider the revelation while Larry buzzed in my pocket.

"Uh, where is Harcourt? Am I anywhere close?"

"Chris" I called. Chris scrambled down the ladder. I tossed him the phone before taking a much-needed breather from the activity.

I sat down in the grass, trying to find some tranquility, trying to find some peace.

"Larry's close. Y'know when I spoke with him I forgot how many ways 'fuck' could be used in the English language. Are you alright?" Chris said as he handed me back the phone.

"Yeah, I guess I just never thought of myself as a contractor. Now that I see what they have to deal with…." I said.

"It's like being a director. You always have to have AN answer. It might not always be the best one or the right one, but you always have to give them something," Chris said and understood.

"Well, I thought I did. Is Bill doing anything now?"

"I think he just left."

"I hope to hell he's going to order some materials!"

****

"Jason, I take it all back. It's actually pretty neat," Larry confessed as he gazed up at the vaulted ceiling of the inside of the yurt.

"Well thank you Larry."

"I still think you're right out of your fucking mind," he continued.

"You and me both dear boy," I agreed.

"Now, where do I put this shit that's in the back of my truck?"

"Right this way," I said and led him out of the yurt.

I stole a glance over my shoulder for a moment where the plumbers were gathered deep in a huddle. It wasn't lunch. It wasn't late and suddenly the buzz that gripped the sight for most of the morning had ground to a halt. Bill disappeared into the mist. Chris was outside, continuing to hang the exterior walls and close in the yurt. The only sound of activity was Otis, (Larry's dog) as he scrambled around the truck waiting for his master.

"He needs to take a dump," Larry said matter-of-factly.

"Do what you need to do, just try and keep it out of the way or pick it up. I don't want Dustin to think it's something he should play with."

"Sure thing dear boy," Larry said as he hauled Otis out of the cab. I opened the garden shed doors and started stuffing the materials in with the rest of the mess.

The plumbers spilled outside and gabbed away in French. They appeared to be a fun bunch, with the occasional hijinx, which needed no translation, to help keep things light and fun. I saw Nick, a stout fellow with thick, curly brown hair and glasses, sneak around the back of the plumbers' cube van. He said nothing, but in a few moments, as I silently observed, he jumped out from around the van to scare the shit out of one of his co-workers. I laughed while trying to keep my composure.

I was toiling silently, waiting for Larry to reappear when all three plumbers descended on me. Maybe they were looking for a Quarterback to translate the plumbing scheme.

"Do you know how we're going to vent this?" they asked.

It was a moment I'd been dreading. It asks a very simple fundamental question about plumbing. Plumbing needs access to air to be sucked in to allow the flow of water that isn't under pressure. Basic stuff. Every building has a one-inch plastic pipe sticking out of its roof to appease that function. I've only seen that function satisfied one way: Straight up.

And that means a hole in the roof. Which wouldn't seem so bad, except how do you patch a vinyl roof? When the wind whips up a fury, what prevents the flapping fabric from creating a larger gape? Unfortunately I couldn't think of a better way.

Perhaps it was the heat, or maybe it was the look on my face, but they saw me sweating and decided to enlighten me as to their intentions.

"De vent doesn't 'ave to go straight up," they said. I was more befuddled than usual.

"So long as de vent pipe EVENTUALLY goes up, we can twist it around corners, y'know, whatever."

I still wasn't getting it. I'd prepared myself for the reality they would have to cut a hole in the roof for the stink pipe.

"So I tink we'll run it up, connect all de feeder lines, go down, out trew de floor, to de utility shed and back up trew dat roof. No hole in de yurt. I jus' don' know if Euclide is going to like it."

"Lemme get this straight, you knew what you were going to do but you were just too afraid Euclide wasn't going to like it?"

"Yeah, 'e's kind'a old school."

"Who gives a shit about Euclide. If it's going to work and it's to code and it doesn't put a hole in my roof."

"I's jus' going to look funny, de pipe going up and over and down den back up,"

"So what, it's going to be hidden in the wall isn't it?"

"Well yeah."

"Fine, you have my blessing. I'll duke it out with Euclide if I have to."

The boys laughed as I scampered over to the trench.

"You got everything Larr....oh, hold that thought," I said and reached into my pocket. Sylvie was calling.

"Mind if I swing by Bernie's and pick up a few things for the yurt," she offered.

"It's two o'clock hun," I said, "where are you now?"

"The wedding started a little late then it went a little late. But the bride loved what I did for her make-up and she gave me a good tip. I'm just leaving Shediac now. I'm going right past the store. You always tell me I shouldn't waste a trip," she argued, "and wasn't Bill asking what we were going to be using for a stove anyway."

I considered it for a moment. From the back of the yurt I turned to look at the river. I walked toward the front of the yurt, checking underneath. My bike was there, as was the chariot. I hadn't used either since we'd arrived. It was like carrying a backpack full of clothes for two months and you had that one special outfit you desperately wanted to justify bringing.

"You always said you wanted to pick him up with the chariot," she reasoned.

"This wasn't exactly what I had in mind...dear," I patronized and paused "....fine, go ahead and get it."

****

"Grr, she's doing it to me again! Friggin' trying to build this yurt with one hand tied behind my back. I should let her build the damn thing! Oh, that's it, I think I'm gonna have to kill her! SYLVIE! SYLVIE!"

I was screaming into the wind. No one could hear me. It was delicious therapy. I was on my mountain bike, child chariot in tow, struggling home from the pick up. The distance didn't seem too far but I forgot to factor in the wind. Barely fifteen miles direct to the ocean, on a wide tidal river, the Acadian Midlands were always breezy. Not little ten or fifteen kilometer puffs, but usually anywhere from 20 to 40 km/h winds. I happened to pick a day that was consistently 60. I wouldn't have cursed her so much if I'd been in some kind of shape.

I begrudgingly said yes with a gross misunderstanding of my physical conditioning that my ego failed to recognize. Sure, I COULD pick up Dustin, but that would assume I had enough spare time in my life to get into some kind of shape for the idea to not almost kill me.

At my back, I made record time covering the 20 km distance getting to Dustin's day care. I made it in less than half an hour. The wind did not abate for the return voyage with the extra fifty pounds of baggage. Dustin got a comfortable hour and a half nap as I gritted my teeth through the constant head wind.

As I struggled back to the yurt, I was barely able to get off my bike safely. It careened slowly into the deck where I used the structure to take my balance. The place was deserted: Larry, the plumbers, the electrician, only Chris remained. He was horrified to see me, laughing and sympathizing with my misfortune.

"Y'know, it's probably too late offer it now, but you could've borrowed my truck," Chris offered.

I struggled to find breath. I reached for the water bottle on the bike. I opened the spout to rejoice in its bounty. It was bone dry.

"We….forgot…the car seat…"

And I couldn't finish the sentence. Sharing that extra pain, Chris scrunched up his face like he'd been kicked in the groin. The phone rang.

"I got a fridge, the counter top stove. I just spent all of the money I made on the wedding," she bubbled, "did you get Dustin?"

"Sure," I huffed between breaths, "No problem!"

****

"You always said you wanted to rough it with Dustin," Sylvie observed. The vitriol, somehow, had subsided. A little levity had returned. Perhaps it was from the necessity of the situation. There was no room for anger.

It was Friday. We would move out of the cottage and officially into the yurt on Sunday, July 4. The yurt would be livable, but far from finished. Sylvie would start work on Monday while I parented in the backwoods of Upper Rexton.

The plumbing was roughed in. It would need to be inspected before Chris and I could install the wall paneling and close in the rooms. The Hot Water on Demand unit had been ordered, and would hopefully arrive in time for both the electrician and plumbers to install it: The electrical was roughed in. The utility room was built. Bill could start building the mast and meter base.

The movers could be contacted to dig part of our possessions out of storage and lug it to the yurt. That would be the project Saturday.

Boxes and boxes of an IKEA kitchen needed to be opened, assembled and blessed that everything was necessary to complete their function.

It looked good on paper. It being Rexton and Bill, instead of making the drive (one hour) to Moncton to get exactly what he needed, he chose to order his materials locally instead. And his local source didn't have everything he needed to build the mast. When those materials would arrive was anyone's guess.

I also assumed that despite the yurt not being completely finished, Bill could still call NB Power to declare a date for hook-up.

"Nooo," Bill droned, "I caan't do that. Case I get inspected before I'm finished I could lose my license."

I hung my head and inquired at NB Power how long it would be after the request was submitted until hook up.

"It takes 10-12 business days after we get the request before we can send out a truck to hook you up," they replied.

None of these issues was critical to our survival. We would live. Long ago our neighbour Harry had allowed us use of his water and there was always a barbecue for cooking. Sylvie was not so content. In the process of building the yurt we'd discovered a little flaw that wasn't quite present in the literature.

When we were asking our questions, trying to find out as much as we could about yurts, our focus always seemed to be on how we were going to heat it.

"Look," I said at the time, "there's a couple with two kids living in one in Alaska!"

We found yurts all over northern, frigid climates. Somehow, some way, they were able to survive those harsh conditions. The reflective insulation, so long as there was a heat source, did what it was intended and that was return generated heat.

But there was one, teeny, tiny little catch we didn't think to ask about. How did that process work in the summer? With no tall trees and a suddenly uncooperative wind that until July was howling and blustering everyday, the slow, hot air settled on us just as we were about to move in.

Our only source of ventilation was two back windows that were now sectioned off into the bedrooms, two doors that had no screens and the rooftop dome that could be opened slightly in favourable conditions. The heat was oppressive. Dustin still needed his naps, but, more importantly, to bathe. Sylvie was relentless where I'd given up hope.

"Uh, no, no, no, no, no, no, surely Bill can do something to give you running water and maybe an outlet for the fan."

Bill could not so easily be dismissive of my wife as he could of me. I was the United States government when it came to interrogation methods. So long as it occurred on foreign soil I never questioned her tactics. I was elated that Sylvie managed to convince Bill to have running cold water and one electrical outlet for the floor fan. Hardly a champagne bottle busted on the hull for the maiden voyage, but an inauguration nonetheless.

****

It's always those little things, things you thought you'd dealt with long ago, that somehow find their way to make themselves known at the most inopportune time, that really make you scratch your head. I was rolling with the issues now. The plumbing inspector wasn't available until next week. Good-bye functioning washroom. But there was that one phone call.

"Hello, is dis Jason?" came the inquiry.

"Yes, yes it is, who's this?" I asked.

"It's Roger, your driller," he responded, "I 'ad a problem with you cheque."

I stopped dead in my tracks. My mind quickly racing through dates, times, places, and I wondered: "How long ago was that?"

"Dey said de account was closed. I was surprise since you were such a nice guy," he went on, "I didn' expec' no problem."

"I'm so sorry Roger. I'll get you a certified cheque right away," I said, still in shock.

"Dat's okay, we'll get it from you in a couple days. Jus' call me when you have it."

My mind raced, how long ago had I sent that cheque? It was before Toronto. Roger drilled the well May 28th and left an invoice the same day. I wrote and mailed the cheque the very next day. He only made the attempt to cash it the last week of June. How long after it wouldn't cash did he decide to contact me? A month, I said to myself, I wish I could forget about four grand for that long.

All things considered, I thought, it wasn't too bad only one cheque got lost in the shuffle.

****

It was the noise the yurt made that surprised us the most.

"It's just like a tent!" Sylvie said. Indeed, every wisp of air, every droplet of rain, and in the morning, every hoot and screech of every bird was there for us to hear and feel. The highway, many kilometres behind many trees, at times felt louder and closer to us than downtown Toronto.

And then there was the river of fire.

Even without the benefit of windows, the harsh, blinding hit of the red sky jolted us all awake before the sun crested the horizon. The deep red hues tickled off the river. The sun pounced on us at 5:30 to remind us the day had started.

"Just keep him alive for three days until I get home," Sylvie said. Those were the departing directives. Don't bother trying to be father of the year. Just keep our son alive.

"It's ten degrees warmer inside the yurt than outside!" I told Sylvie over the phone.

No matter what I did, nothing could alleviate the heat.

"R-Foil insulation," I said to myself, "barbecue material."

There was barely enough opportunity to create a cross breeze. The two French doors at the front of the yurt had a six-foot drop underneath. Opening them (and inviting all sorts of insects) would be an attraction to a one year old to explore the possibilities. All I could do was open two back windows and one in the side door.

The heat was stifling. We had no television, no Internet, no transportation and no other children for miles. Even the river, warm and inviting, was off-limits: how could I adequately clean him with no running water?

I was stymied. I wanted to 'rough it' with him, but….

It was Dustin and Poppa for three days with no connection to the outside world.

"Just keep him alive. Just keep him alive!!!!"

14

The Ghosts Of Toronto

Typical. I could kick myself. I fell for it, hook, line and sinker! The city of Charlottetown had been romancing the *Regis and Kelly* show for about two years trying to lure them down for a week to film. When they finally succeeded in securing the show July 12-15 the rest of the Maritimes took notice and it was a hot subject on the radio while we were building the yurt. It was as Chris and I were building the floor that the scale of such an approach hit me. The only local film crews were in Halifax. I had this stupid crazy hunch I would get a call to work on the show. It never came.

But Sylvie did. Two weeks before the show was to touch down she got a call from her agent and was booked with a hotel, per diem, travel, the whole nine yards. After all the hoopla from moving and building, we took it as the perfect opportunity to ship Dustin away for a day or two and go on a 'gypsy' vacation. Three days before the show was to hit town my phone rang with a Nova Scotia area code.

"We're short manpower. I don't know how much gear they've ordered. I've got Larry Smith who told me to call you. Can I put you on 'hold' until I find out more?" the Rigging Gaffer Steve said.

"Particulars. If I do say yes."

"$300 a day, based on ten hours, hotel, per diem, travel."

"I'm in."

After two days of hearing nothing and our own departure date approaching, I gave Steve, who promised he'd let me know either way, a call.

Nonchalantly he said, "Sorry, I had you on hold in case we needed extra guys and it looks like we won't."

Larry didn't take it nearly as well as I did.

"I'd like to know who the PM is who hires these idiots. What, we're not good enough? I can only go to Toronto and be a best boy on some of the biggest features and TV shows that have ever been made in this country, but I can't get a job in my own backyard," Larry continued on in his own indignant manner.

I could appreciate his frustration, whereas I wasn't quite so disappointed. In the fit of excitement of being wanted I'd already allocated the money I was going to make. Forgetting the golden film rule: the money isn't yours until it's cleared at the bank. The sudden rejection was the final evidence that getting out of film was the right path to take.

But fifteen years in show business is fifteen years. And there is an excitement that can't be replaced. All of Charlottetown was buzzing as we pulled in and took our own guided tour of set. Security here. Security there.

"Sorry, you can't go in. Not without ID badges," they declared as we walked up to an entrance

I chuckled at the pimple-faced representative. The sudden authority draped him like a bad fitting suit. My experience has told me that if you show enough bluster and bravado you can practically march through the front doors of the White House.

"I'm looking for the lighting crew," I said casually.

They were dumbfounded. I spoke a secret code they knew nothing about. They shrugged and let me pass.

"Never mind. I'll find them myself."

"Admit it Hamilton, you miss it," Sylvie needled me.

I hated it when she was right.

We spotted the trailers and as it turned out, half of the lighting crew was from Toronto.

"Don't tell Larry I'm here," Johnny 'Stets' Stezjnmiller said, fearing verbal retribution.

"Okay Sylv," I said as we drove away, "maybe I do miss it a little bit. I remember that high you'd get, the adrenaline. And not just from meeting the stars or hanging around famous people. I loved being involved and seeing something come to life. I miss that. Always will. But for the past five or six years I've been living on the periphery of that. It's painful to see others get a chance to do their thing when you think you have an idea that just needs a chance," I confessed.

"I miss it too. But I don't miss the drama. I really liked being in fashion. I'll take a strung out, anorexic model over an actor or actress any day," Sylvie said and we both laughed.

Something more serious struck her attention. In the light moment she summoned her nerves: "I always resented you for going back to work so soon."

"What do you mean by that?"

"I mean before we had Dustin I was just starting to navigate my way with my agency. I was just starting to get my career to where I really wanted it to be. And then we had Dustin…and poof. It was gone. You went back to work, all of the Mommy friends went back to work and I didn't have anything."

"Uh, uh," I stammered, "I didn't WANT to take your career away from you…."

"But you did."

"I made what I thought was the right decision. I was busy. I had Gaffers and all sorts of people calling me while I was still on parental leave. I didn't know what to expect from the business when my benefits ran out. I didn't want to take a chance at neither of us getting work."

Sylvie sighed.

"It was steady, it was guaranteed. There wasn't a lot of work in the city at the time," I continued.

"I know. And we didn't have family and even in fashion there's always that chance a photo shoot could go late. So if you were at work and I was at work, who could pick up Dustin."

"Yeah. So, unfortunately, only one of us could work at a time. That's just how it went. I never meant to take your career away from you…"

Another pause.

"Is that why you've been so adamant about getting something right away, so you wouldn't have to get sloppy seconds?"

She laughed. It broke the mild tension.

"I want to have my chance."

"Fair enough. We've just put so much into the yurt. Heart. Soul. Money. It seems like we're abandoning it before it's even finished."

"I'm not taking any chances about my career."

****

Regis & Kelly wasn't quite the Gypsy vacation we had hoped for. Sylvie's call time was VERY early Monday morning. 6AM. We made sure to retire at a reasonable hour, but it didn't matter. Film people, thinking everyone operates in the same bubble, tend to forget the sanity that frames the rest of the world.

The production manager, in his wisdom, thought he was doing us a favour by calling to inform the call time was pushed by a measly half an hour. That he did so at 1230 am, waking us from a deep sleep, because HE was still awake and we weren't, seemed absolutely lost on him. However, say what we will, it was nice to get away from all things yurt, even if it was only for a few hours.

Because as soon as we landed back in Moncton that afternoon, a communication I wasn't expecting jogged me from my mental break.

"Jason, it's Bill. Do you have the number for your building permit?"

I was so used to lugging around my office bag I'd actually brought it with me out of habit. I opened the bag, tore through a mound of paperwork before finding the right piece of information. I gave Bill the number.

"That doesn't sound right. It should have more numbers," Bill retorted.

"Well, that's what they gave me."

Something wasn't adding up. I often wondered about that building permit. But another thought was taking hold.

"Why do you need the building permit Bill?" I asked.

"So I can put in your application for electrical hook-up."

It was the second week of July, it could take a month for the permanent electrical hook-up and he was only just submitting the application. First it would have to go through the bowels of NB Power, analyzed, queued, sorted, fluffed before a decision rendered an action. It could be four more weeks of living like a pilgrim. I about choked on my own tongue.

****

Back in exile, Dustin and I discovered berries.

Sylvie had mentioned it, but it wasn't until Dustin and I went on an adventure walk by the road did I realize how abundant wild berries were in New Brunswick. Raspberry bushes choked the ditches beside the road, and for the first weeks in July the crop was thick and inviting.

I didn't know whether Dustin would like it or not, or how long it would take before he got bored. I took a bowl, thinking perhaps I could pick some berries to have later.

The bowl wasn't necessary. They were no sooner in my hands before Dustin was shoving them into his mouth. We spent every day from ten until noon prowling the ditches for berries. It was part of our extended mission to walk to pick up our mail.

The intention was to keep him away long enough so that Chris and Fern could work on the deck. The deck had become necessary when at first I'd axed its construction. Every time we opened the French doors to invite a cross-breeze, Dustin looked at the six foot distance to the ground with curiosity.

By the time the week was through, Chris and Fern had all the joists up and part of the deck skinned. Dustin, with the daily evidence in his diaper, cleared the ditch of raspberries singlehandedly.

All things considered, as the heat blazed and the boredom burned, the solo time with my son cemented our relationship. It pained me, absolutely pained me, to be living in a space that still needed so much attention before completion. But what could I do? My son was and is a people person. I was his only people.

I could look toward the door and imagine the three windows on either side with the panoramic view of the river all I wanted but willpower alone would not complete the task. I had to learn I could only do so much. Getting to that realization wasn't easy.

Every parent harbours their fair share of guilt; Guilt that they're not doing enough for their children; Guilt that they're trying to compensate for some lack. We microscope them to death with our mistakes to always see where we can do better. Be better. Ensure they live a better circumstance than what we've achieved.

We're always preoccupied with the next thing, stage, event in their lives ("it's gonna be so great when he's older and we can do this...") that the current one, the one we know we'll never get back, always gets overlooked. The repetition, the mindless games our children can do for HOURS become one more thing we have to endure until they get a bit older and it becomes a little more fun for us.

And then that thought hits like a stone. The thought of all the times as a kid when you said you'd never do what your parents did and there you are behaving just like them. And what is that? What is that one thing a child wants from their mom and dad that seems next to impossible for them to give: Their presence. Their undivided attention.

And damn, but didn't the gravity of that thought pull me out of bed, shake me awake and not let go until I was blubbering like a baby.

"What's wrong?" Sylvie muttered half asleep.

I couldn't find the words. It was as though the whole time it was he and I was interference to more important things: getting the yurt finished, getting a job. I was inconsolable. My body jerked and the tears flooded.

"I'm a bad father!" was all I could think to say. I repeated it over and over again, crying harder with each utterance.

Sylvie soothed the pain. There had been no prompt. No event. No trigger. Was it fatigue? Or was it the slow realization that happens to every parent when they know they could be doing a better job?

Yurt or not, he was only ever going to be this age once.

****

Language and culture have a way of misappropriating original meanings and bastardizing it into a form that's simpler to digest. Take karma for instance. Webster's Dictionary defines karma thusly: the power, resulting from an individual's volitional acts, which determines his cycle of reincarnations before he attains release from this world. The sum total of the acts done in one stage of a person's existence which determine his destiny in the next stage.

Broken down, bastardized to a more Western/Christian concept we interpret karma as a sort of check and balance of our good/altruistic behaviour versus our bad/selfish one's. Then we throw in a little Newton for fun. We tell ourselves that as we act we create a sphere of influence on future events that is directly attributable to the actions we take in our present situation.

For the purposes of story, most of what we consume follows that line of logic. Very little of our fictional popular culture strays far from the good versus evil melodrama. Hollywood serves as the interpreter for how we view our characters without letting too much crowd the senses.

And why wouldn't they?

Leave too much to interpretation, to ambiguous an ending and will the audience leave satisfied? We're very much groomed viewership in that regard. We invest little of ourselves into thinking or allowing that our stories should remain anything less than pure entertainment. And not grounded into anything approaching a remote likelihood of possibility. "Better not," the executives say, "because life doesn't wrap up that easily."

Life most definitely does not follow the plot line quite so neatly.

Or does it? Is there a running fault line under our lives that really does dictate how it unfolds?

Is there a place for that messy interpretation of karma? One that doesn't simply play off those conscious choices to be good/altruistic vs. bad/selfish. And what the hell does that have to do with a yurt?

A yurt, like a story, has an intention. A life, like a stream, has a flow. A reader, through the summation on the back jacket, is tempted by the promise of what interesting read might lie inside the pages. But it is not done blindly. A reader then approaches a story with a certain belief of how it will unfold.

(Part of the reason our popular culture is enraptured with a predictable ending in our tales is to have certain expectations confirmed. Psychologists have now proven that our stress levels decrease significantly when we watch a re-run of our favourite show. We allow ourselves these enjoyments for the comfort of knowing the outcome.)

We wrap up and lose ourselves with the full knowledge an order of things exists in the fictional world that doesn't in the real world.

As much and as hard as we conveyed the message our yurt would serve as our cottage it was as if our efforts fell on deaf ears. Once you read the history of the yurt and understand that its' purpose was to house nomadic people's and a certain belief is met. Reinforced by the flight from the big city to the rural coast.

That, in itself, might not be such a hurdle: simplifying our lives.

But because we so quickly built, and then abandoned, our yurt, perhaps we were challenging the fates. Not just with the yurt, but with our friends and family as well. Life has its flow. Rhythm. Our efforts, beliefs, confidences, fears, loves and hates all conspire to shape the barriers and boundaries to its flow.

Along for the ride for short or for long, our family and friends shake the quality and speed of that flow. Circumstance makes those relationships happen. Circumstances from birth and life that bring us together. The more aware we become of those things that make us, us the increased likelihood of inviting people with similar circumstances.

When you wish to dramatically alter those circumstances….well, it's been my experience it takes much time until the tributary finds its path again. We encounter it in our various life stages: leaving home for the first time, starting a career. Marriage. Kids. Our friendships change accordingly. Some people stay in our lives. Others go. Each alteration. Each desire to reach out for something new results in the small loss of who you once were to try to become something different. Maybe better, maybe not. But in order to attain something sometimes you have to give up that which you were.

As the summer ambled along and our various life luminaries arrived to visit and share in our life changing experience, I found a strange parallel to a very popular work of fiction. It somehow unfolded I was in a bizarro remake of *A Christmas Carol*.

Preceded by our parent's, our visitors would follow in succession as representing our lives in past, present and future.

****

Under normal circumstances, I would be overjoyed at having company, but the first guests to arrive at the yurt weren't the easiest to entertain. Since the blow up I'd forged a truce with my parents, but given the unfinished state of things (and the yurt), it wasn't a surprise I was nervous about their arrival at the end of July.

I tried to abate that anticipation with a prediction as to what words, exactly, they would use when they first stepped in the door to take in the experience.

Delivery people, service people, inspectors and just plain curious folk came through our doors at various times during the construction process. And without a word of a lie, (with perhaps the exception of Larry) almost everyone who stepped in to look around said, ad infinitum, "That's different." I kid you not.

So, naturally, when my Mom and Dad walked in and said exactly what everyone else had been saying, I couldn't help but laugh. (Sylvie and I had put odds on the first words, and damn, but didn't they deliver.)

With no hint of our last visit they took in the yurt experience as I prattled on about the state of things, including the most recent setback with NB Power.

"They were supposed to hook us up on Thursday, the 22nd last week," I said, "then there was rain, so, crazy me, I thought they'd come the next day. Nope. So I called Friday afternoon, they said maybe Monday. Today's Monday, they said maybe Tuesday, but not later than Wednesday. So, unfortunately, I kind'a have to stick close to the yurt in case they show up. I have to call the electrician so he can disconnect the temporary power that's back feeding into the panel so the boys don't fry a transformer when they're hooking us up."

"That's alright Jake," my Dad said, "'cause y'know we're a bit tired after that drive, it's a bit longer than fourteen hours."

"Oh right."

"No, we came here to see you and see just what shenanigans you've gotten yourself into."

"Well here it is."

Preferring to let things lie, I didn't press them for their opinions on our project, allowing instead an insight to manifest itself later that would just about melt my heart.

Sometimes it isn't easy belonging to a family that's not the most adept at acknowledging their emotions and letting those close to them know what it is they're really thinking or feeling. By no means is my family unusual in that regard. What's difficult is what's said and what's done don't always match. On the one hand, one of their best qualities is showing, by their direct action, that which they can't express with words.

Dustin was the star of supper. In a quiet restaurant overlooking the Richibucto River and only a few other patrons as his audience, my son, probably just as happy as I was to be in civilization, was flirting and giggling up a storm. Normally my Dad was only more than happy to chat up whoever comes within earshot, but with the boy commanding all the attention, he was upstaged a little.

It wasn't until we got to the cash register to pay the bill, did I really know what agenda he had on his mind.

"Don't be surprised if you start to have some guests at your front door," Dad said before turning his attention the waitress, "So, have you been up to see the yurt?" he blurted at her.

"The what?" the waitress replied.

"My son here built a yurt on what is it," he asked me.

"The Richibucto. Just up river," I said.

"It's this big round, TENT. Like a cottage. You've got this nice view of the river. It's quite something," he went on.

"He's been telling everyone he sees," my Mom whispered.

I could see the sparkle in his eyes, the gumption in his words. Not in my direction, but at least in my vicinity, and worth more than they could ever know. They were proud.

****

"We just bought a house," Sylvie's voice came over the phone, "I got the appliances, the window treatments, the air conditioner, and the washer and dryer. It closes the 1st of September."

"Perfect, right for when Pierre and Baxter arrive."

"You're kidding. Four visitors this summer and the yurt isn't even finished."

"It's kind'a like the ghosts of Toronto past…" I tried to wax philosophic.

"And then no one will see us next year."

"Meh. It's too bad the yurt won't be finished, but I'm not going to say no to anyone."

"So long as they don't mind helping us move."

"You're gonna miss the move again aren't you?"

"I'll be prepping for the first week of school."

"Great," I muttered.

"Hey, if you want to go to work instead…." She continued.

"Just because I'm unemployed, doesn't mean I haven't been working!"

I hung up the phone and turned to face my Mom and Dad. It was burning in me to illustrate a point and maybe dig up a little misconception and false information.

"So there you go Dad, we're not going to be living in a yurt. We just bought a house," I turned to Dad and said.

"Well, I didn't know, that's just what you told us," my Dad defended himself.

"Or a silo for that matter," I let the words linger.

"I didn't know what yuz were building, y'see," he feigned ignorance.

"Uh huh," I mumbled, "Yeah, Beth blurted out something about us living in a silo. We got the whole confession on tape."

Dad was nervous and unsure where I was going with the interrogation. I admit it. It was fun to hold the upper hand for a change. I let him squirm before I delivered the punch line.

"What, d'ya think we're crazy! I've only been here by myself with Dustin for three weeks and I'm already starting to lose my mind," I said. Dad looked relieved.

"I mean, don't get me wrong, it's beautiful, the river is spectacular, but coming from a big city like Toronto, we need some city life," I said, "we're not ready to rough it. This is our cottage."

"That makes a little more sense. We didn't see you going right from Toronto to here," Mom says.

"Uh…NO," I grinned.

Unfortunately, for much of their visit I'd hoped to take them to 'Le Pays de la Sagouine' but the NB Power delay tied us to the yurt a lot longer than anticipated. I was anxious to have, see and feel my very own hot water on demand system and if it was going to work. Imagine being a kid at Christmas who got a beautiful new toy but had to wait a month in order to use it. It pained me to wait so long.

But sure enough, just as soon as power got hooked up we had to blast off to Moncton so I could sign paperwork regarding the house. When we returned to the yurt the first thing I did was turn on the dishwasher (which I'd loaded up and emptied several times waiting for NB Power to install our power) and took a bath. Voila! The hot water on demand worked like a charm.

The next morning as I waited to show Sylvie our wonderful new system the power went out. We went into town to meet my parent's for breakfast before seeing them off and there was no power anywhere! As it turns out, the delay in our hook-up had nothing to do with whether or not NB Power liked me. A major transformer was being replaced and there were only so many crews to go around.

****

"Before we begin, putting everything aside, in your ideal life, where you didn't have to worry about money, what would you do?" Manon asked.

Unprepared for the question, without even thinking, I belched the first answer that came into my mind: "Novelist"

In Richibucto, in the Acadian midlands where the major industries were fishing, forestry and some farming, I'm fairly certain I was the first and only person to declare such an occupation.

"Uh, well, Mr. Hamilton…" she stammered, mentally rolodexing for the tab in the instruction book that deals with such anomalies.

"Hey, you said ideal. I was being idealistic. But don't worry. I'm sure we can figure out how to get from 'unemployed yurt dweller' to novelist. I am realistic about my situation."

"I was gonna say," she responded.

"But, as you can see by my resume, I have been in a rather unique profession that I don't know how to translate into the real world. I have some published freelance writing and other management experience…."

"There is a lot to work with, please understand, most of what I do is trying to find work for fishermen…"

"Right, should I just wait and start this process somewhere in Moncton then?"

"No, this is a good challenge for me. If you're looking to transition into a new profession altogether believe it or not but I've been very instrumental in helping those fishermen start new occupations."

"Not here of course."

"Some. The younger one's have had to go down to the city."

I snickered a little, "you mean Moncton?"

"Yes. Or Halifax. Montreal."

Coming from a large place, where large population centres have a certain reputation for being difficult and cold, I felt a certain swagger for having survived in its heart in such a challenging profession. The experience I had in life, outside of work, creating and executing my own projects and doing different things at times to make a living, gave me a certain appeal as a potential new hire.

That and the knowledge that qualifications were only a percentage of the ability to do a certain job. I certainly worked with greater talents (just ask them) in lesser roles who couldn't grasp the concept of co-operation needed to get the job done. I knew, without being cocky or overconfident, that my talents lay in being able to get along well with others. I had a vast network of relationships from producers to P.A's that could attest to that ability. But, pushing forty, forgetting it took me fifteen years to build and maintain those relationships, you tend to gloss over how long it took to open certain doors.

As a unilingual former film bum who was great at socializing the extras at the craft table, how much substance was there to perform a specific role in a specific industry? Worse yet, I couldn't even define what industry I wished to be a part of. Manon had her work cut out for her. But how does one go from being a yurt builder to a novelist and not go broke in between?

"I think we should start with some testing...."

****

I was aware enough to know I was skewing the answers toward the profession I hoped to achieve. It wasn't standardized math testing after all. But I wasn't lying either. Not surprisingly, the results confirmed for me what I wished to achieve. A career in advertising or radio or broadcasting or reporting or something of the like. The question then became, what opportunities exist and how do I access them?

By building relationships: In a strange land with a strange tongue. Challenging, but not impossible. Not for a big city presence like myself. I puffed up my own courage. It would be necessary for when the time came to hit the pavement and carve out a new career niche. And then, even before the investment in a new wardrobe and an updated resume a cousin of Sylvie tipped me off to an opening for a Creative Writer position at a Moncton radio station. A client of hers worked there and just happened to mention the position in passing. It was forwarded along to me and I could email him my resume directly.

'Huh', I thought to myself, 'piece of cake. I'll be just like Sylvie and land the first job before we even move.'

I polished up my resume as best I could, included some writing samples and felt confident it would cross those desks before being lumped into the pile of the general populace. I had a contact that could make sure I skipped the slush pile. We exchanged pleasantries and he informed me he would put in a good word.

"No need to worry about any more career counseling," I felt myself rehearse a little before my next consultation with Manon, "got this career thing all taken care of. I only had to sell my house, move to another province and build a yurt to do it, but hey, mission accomplished."

The silence was crippling. A week passed. Mom and Dad were long gone. I occupied my time skinning the deck of the yurt when Dustin napped.

Sure, it could take some time before all resume's were gathered and worthy candidates asked to interview, but two weeks? It was getting unnerving, particularly since I was without Internet access for three days a week. An email could be sent and answered in casual time when people were in the right frame of mind to answer them. A telephone call was abrupt. At work it's an interruption. The recipient is generally annoyed at having to take the call on principle and it immediately clouds the exchange.

I needed to know what was going on but only in the most subtle and delicate of fashions.

When Sylvie did return home for the week I booked my time in town and sequestered myself to try and find an answer. There had been no more messages from my contact. He'd gone silent. In the meantime, the job was posted on CareerBeacon for public consumption. I wasn't even in the slush pile.

It looked like I would be in the same circumstance as everyone else. What happened to my contact? He'd read my blog, knew my work and could vouch for my wit. He couldn't hire me, but he could damn sure get me to the front of the line.

I housed my disappointment for later and soldiered on with the application.

Two days later I was asked to compose and pitch a few short spots, which I immediately complied. And then I waited again. I was frustrated to learn I didn't make the cut for a formal interview. Bollocks! Since I didn't make the grade, what would it hurt to field a call to answer the riddle.

"Yeah, hi, Jason Hamilton here, I'm following up about the Creative Writer position."

"Oh, you mean the TWO positions? They were both filled."

GRRRR!

"Okay, I'd also sent my resume to Brad and he hasn't replied back. Is he dead or does he just have poor email etiquette?"

"Oh him, he no longer works here."

****

Starting a new career in a new province was not going to be without its difficulties. But before that next transition was to take place there was the matter of a few visitors that held strange continuity with the previous incarnations of our lives.

Sherry and Linda were our very good friends that in some ways were 'Sylvie and Jason Past', er, before children. Ever since we'd been talking up the yurt they'd made certain their time to visit us was booked well in advance. Such is life when you're childless.

Fortunately, in the way they carried themselves, the discrepancy in family situations was not an obstacle. Why? Because they also brought their own joie de vivre that included good food, good drink and an invitation to include all (no matter the age) who shared that vivacity. And not in an excessive, falling down, immature manner, but more in the full 'sucking the marrow out of life' fashion. Sylvie and I were both looking forward to their arrival.

Sherry lived in the top apartment of 105 Indian Road when Sylvie first moved in with me to the basement of the same address. Civil and cordial before Sylvie arrived, our friendship with Sherry cemented on the rooftop patio over drinks and cigars. A kinship in the building evolved over time….and circumstance.

There was The Great North American Blackout of 2003 that turned the rooftop patio into a haven. There were our Christmas dinners for the entire building. Our mutual shock and awe over a tenant who lived in the basement and whose partner was a knight in Medieval Times. But the most notable: a transaction between a john and a prostitute that did not fulfill all contractual obligations.

Linda met Sherry a few years later and in getting to know her discovered a small detail we found captivating: She once owned and operated a restaurant in Richibucto Village when she was in her late twenties. We thought we were a little different: How about a six-foot two-inch lesbian in rural New Brunswick? The very same village we passed through every day on our commute from Cap Lumière to Upper Rexton. Of all the random places she herself had decided to chart a new course.

At first blush, it didn't seem so unusual that a wayward soul might check in somewhere in rural New Brunswick, set up shop and get away from the break neck pace of the big city. It was/is the Canadian Dream: Get rich and build a home in the woods where no one can bother us. (And despite having a reputation for friendliness, most East Coasters seem to be living just such a contradictory existence. Go figure.)

Under a cloudless sky, the stars started to claim the night from the long summer day, we set our chairs around the fire, glasses full and armed with a convoy of refills. Sylvie and I, intent on knowing the full story, immediately got to the task.

"I was looking to start a business. Get out of the corporate world, get out of Toronto and start a B n' B. My friend's mother had this restaurant in Risheebucktoo Veellage with a place to stay. I jumped at it," Linda said.

"So we took over this restaurant in Risheebucktoo Veellage and surprise, surprise, I ended up working about 90 hours a week," Linda said and shrugged her shoulders.

"Uh-huh," we nodded in agreement.

"I satisfied my inner entrepreneur, but I was working just as hard as I was before, so I asked myself, 'what did I leave behind in the first place'. I guess, depending on how you look at it, I got what I was looking for. Clean air, no traffic. A beautiful beach on the ocean. Sand dunes. Water. Trails and roads where you're the only person around for miles!" Linda said.

"Yeah, tell me about it," Sylvie said, "we're about to do our shift change. I get to stay home with Dustin while Dad goes to the city to look for work."

"Oh, you'll be fine," Sherry said, "you can always do like my mom did and tie Dustin to the clothes line."

We all looked over at Sherry, she was nonplussed.

"Well I was a wanderer," Sherry continued, "I was always going off, getting lost. My mom says I would just get intrigued by any little thing and then I'd be gone."

"C'mon Sher, it wasn't any little thing," Linda teased.

"I know, I know," Sherry said, "It wasn't any little thing, it was Shiny things."

We all laughed. Not so much at the thought of seeing Sherry as a child wander off without prompt, but that it could still happen as an adult.

Glasses were refilled. We took a moment to recline back, gaze out on the river or just look up at the black pincushion roaming above. There were a couple of other fires along the water, but shortly we were the only ones left to hear our voices carry in the night.

"I guess I still had that need for culture and cuisine that you just can't get here," Linda continued.

"Yeah, I know what you mean. Not a lot of variety," Sylvie said.

"At first I did put some funky dishes on the menu to try and spice things up a bit, but they just didn't want it. Just take something, anything, deep fry it and serve it. That's what the customer wants. Nothing fancy. Nothing too out of the ordinary," Linda said and shuddered.

"People around here must LOVE the yurt," Sherry implied.

"If I could ever get out of here more than a few days a week I'd be able to know," I said candidly.

"Oooh, ouch," Sherry said.

"Hey, don't look at me. I had a contact, I got the job first," Sylvie replied.

"And so I've been trying to finish things up around here in between cooking and being a parent," I continued.

"Would that explain why the bathroom doesn't have a door?" Linda asked.

"It's in the works. Be happy the wall is covered," I muttered.

"Cut yourself some slack. It's functional," Linda replied.

"I was just hoping for it to be further along than it is now," I said with a sigh.

"What did your parent's think of it?" Sherry asked.

"That's different!" Sylvie and I said in unison.

We all chuckled.

"My Dad didn't like it too much because he thought it was waay too hot," I said.

"It is pretty warm, but we don't have any front windows yet either," Sylvie agreed.

"But, all in all, I'd say they're pretty proud of me. Us. That doesn't mean they don't also think we're crazy."

We all laughed.

"It's just hard to know what they think sometimes," I said.

"They're your parents. You've gone and done something completely unexpected and it looks like you managed to pull it off. Don't you think there might be a bit of envy?"

I considered her thoughts for a moment.

"I suppose."

"Jase, your mom has told me she wishes she'd had the chance to do even a tenth of what we've done in our life. She'd like to travel a little bit. She wants to go to Hawaii," Sylvie said.

"But they don't want to leave their comfort zone," I said.

"That's not so strange, North America is one great big bastion of a comfort zone," Sherry said.

"Yup, wherever we go we want to bring our culture with us, not appreciate or experience what exists in another part of the world. I'll travel anywhere, so long as I can get my McDonald's and my Tim Horton's," Linda said, "after I figured that out I was getting ready to pack my bags to head back to Toronto."

"Hoo boy, do I know what I've gotten myself into?" I asked.

"I just hope you have a back-up plan," Linda said.

"I tried so many different things to get out of film, get into something a little more stable, and the lure of the money always kept pulling me right on back. The yurt is my halfway house. I'm in film rehab."

"Drink up then," Sherry said.

"I only hope I didn't bite off more than I can chew," I confessed.

"You'd think our film experience would give us some sort of advantage," Sylvie mused.

"It might be the opposite. Someone looking to hire you might think 'will they get bored' and quit in six months?" Linda offered.

I hung my head.

"But you know how to network. You're both social. You'll be fine…"

"Yikes, I'm not so sure. I've got a job, it's him I'm worried about…" Sylvie pointed at me.

"Worry pas. I can always work in the trade. There's always a turnover of people. I'll be fine. We'll cross that bridge when we get to it. For now, we've got a little bit of freedom left, let's enjoy it," I said and raised my glass.

"Ooh, ooh, wait. We brought a pie," Sherry said and scrambled out of the chair.

"How come I didn't see it?" Sylvie said.

"It's in the freezer, we hid it from you," Linda said.

"Aaah, it's frozen."

"We'll reheat it in the fire," Sherry said and headed toward the yurt.

A few rocks were rearranged around the edge of the pit. Bold with the drink, the pie was placed safely near the fire. As we sat, waiting for eternity for the pie to heat up warm enough to eat, the conversation drifted off into all manner of whimsy: using gin to keep away mosquitoes. Cape Breton. Martha Stewart. Friends. It was easy to lose ourselves in the moment. The big picture and the big uncertainties of our near future wafting like smoke in the night.

But though the clock was ticking slowly on the time when we would have to make strides in the next part of our transformation, it neglected to include the pie.

"Oh shit, is anyone keeping an eye on the pie?"

It was mercifully retrieved. The din of the fire prevented us from knowing if it was burnt, torched or still frozen. We could only be sure it embraced the fire in some way. Ash flavoured blueberry pie.

"Fuck it, I'll eat it," I said quickly.

15

Along Came Earl

Without the need for a press conference, a press release or any other of the traditional means of communicating their plans, the rest can only stand and gaze at those dynamic individuals among us who arbitrarily decide they're going to do something and it magically happens. The beginning of my career change was to begin with just such an individual: Wendy Papadopoulos.

We first met on the set of *Stuck* in Saint John. She was moonlighting as a locations PA. (I say moonlighting because she negotiated a temporary leave from her full time position at Enterprise Saint John to work on the movie.)

A year later (2007), *Stuck* was premiering at the Toronto Film Festival. As part of the promotion of the movie, she got to travel to Toronto and we were able to get together for coffee. She was working with a mutual friend pitching a TV series and in the course of that process, she'd recently traveled to Dubai and Spain. Unfortunately, the series never came to pass, but I could only tip my hat in admiration at someone who passed through such corridors with ease.

We stayed in touch as Sylvie and I mused aloud about a potential move to the East Coast. Wendy eventually left Enterprise Saint John and started a Brew Pub business and a non-profit initiative called 'Elementary Literacy Friends'. (Some of us build yurts others conquer civilizations.)

The literacy initiative was in its infancy. The organization had some funding, but it was not made clear to me who or what was behind it. As I considered how well she traveled various social corridors, I had no doubt she felt comfortable approaching whoever was necessary to create the vision.

I'd already spent several days in Moncton, portfolio and resume in hand, getting my name into the rotation; so far no leads and no encouragement. I'd always fared much better when networking through channels I'd already established. I booked the time with her and traveled

We were seated in the brewpub: Big Tide Brewery. Feeling comfortable and relaxed after being landlocked in Rexton all summer, I almost forgot the trip was more than a social call.

I was two beers in and a little unprepared for the immediate needs of my services.

"We're going ahead with the project although we don't have any government backing at this time. No major funding decisions will be made until after the election," Wendy explained. Then came the paperwork, background information, and a host of other references to other literacy initiatives that ELF had been modeled after.

"But we can't wait."

"No."

The puzzled look on my face was begging for further explanation.

"I convinced Jamie we need to move forward. We've built some momentum, the returns have been excellent and we have to keep progressing. We're adding five more schools. We need volunteers," Wendy said.

"Er, uh," I was flabbergasted. I grabbed at a pen to try and stall the sudden avalanche of information. But the election idea lodged its way into my brain.

"What would the election have to do with teaching kids how to read?"

"That was precisely my point with Jamie. He's convinced that if the Liberals lose then we won't even get an audience with the Conservative government. I know, it's absurd but when you're an Irving…"

"Jamie Irving. He's behind this?"

"Yeah, I'm the Executive Director and the face of everything but Jamie is heavily involved."

"Oh."

I'd long heard about the tangled reach of the vaunted Irving family. Depending on who was compiling the stats it was estimated twenty percent of the entire eligible workforce in the province of New Brunswick fell under their umbrella: Everything from paper products, oil refineries, gas, building material, communications and transportation. As a family-run business they were not obligated to share the breadth of their reach with the public. They were known to run a very tight ship with their hands steadily on the pulse of their organizations.

"And the election is in September. If we can forge ahead with some strong results then it won't matter WHAT government is in charge. I need content for the web site. A stakeholder report and if all goes well a monthly newsletter to send to the volunteers."

My friend had become my client. I discreetly finished the last of the taster beer samples on the plate.

"Deadline?"

"How about the end of August? Think you can get it done in two weeks?"

****

From our group of Mommy friends at the Roden drop-in centre, Amie and her husband Mike were on the last leg of their summer vacation with family in Nova Scotia. We had been expecting their arrival for some time, and perhaps the hype, like an American pro football championship, made the reunion of their daughter Audrey and Dustin too much pressure for two two-year olds to have to live up to. We had been telling Dustin all summer that he would be getting a visit from Audrey. He'd been mostly alone with only us as his sole/soul entertainment for several months, could that really affect his behaviour?

As the car pulled up Dustin wasn't sure who had arrived until the doors opened and our guests stepped out.

"AUDREY!" he shouted.

Greetings, salutations, hugs, kisses and soon Dustin was charging around his play area, showing off for his first love.

As we started to unpack the car with all of their things, it soon became obvious our Ghosts of Toronto present were suffering from exhaustion, fatigue and too much family drama.

Perhaps at the yurt we could find them the sanctuary they needed. And for a time, that was the case. The weather was favourable, the kids played outside as the menu of food and drink was quickly tackled.

Mike and Amie had only a few days before returning to work. Sylvie had a week before she would be starting her job and I, through my meeting with Wendy, had an end of August deadline for my first writing gig. There was a lot of anticipation for what was approaching in our lives with a hope that the time before the bedlam would be peaceful and tranquil.

It was not a lasting love. As the fixers of this perfect match, apparently we skipped the most crucial element of a successful relationship. Sharing. Dustin had grown a little possessive about his toys. As Audrey would uncover something he hadn't cared about in weeks, Dustin would charge over and rip it out of her hands. A little surprised at first, Audrey thought perhaps Dustin just needed to get to know her again.

As she fixed her attention on something else, Dustin dropped the toy he'd just stolen to hoard anything Audrey was remotely interested in. It was hopeless. Soon Audrey was wailing at the injustice, Dustin was scolded and bellowing and there were no time outs to be had in a round house.

Mike and I turned to the drink and ducked outside to escape the racket and hope, somehow, our absence might quiet the fracas. To no avail. We couldn't run far enough. But at least the drink dulled our senses.

Eventually, with a great deal of effort and patience, the cranky children were wrestled down for the night. A fire was struck. We eased back, beverages in hand, and took in our remaining sabbatical at the yurt.

"Jason, that's an interesting bathroom you have there," Amie said.

"Yeah, it's great isn't it. A nice soaker tub, lots of room," I responded.

"No, it doesn't have a lot of privacy just yet," Amie laughed.

"Oh that, I'll get the trim around the doors sooner or later," I said.

"Even with the trim I could still have a pee and carry on a conversation with you guys in the other room. I think I'm going to take the roofs off of all my bathrooms," we all laughed.

Amie was trying, but fatigue was evident in her voice. Our poor children couldn't quite rekindle their spark. The love was gone.

"Guys, I'm so sorry the kids aren't getting along."

"Don't worry about it. Dustin's been cooped up here all summer by himself…"

"Well don't take this the wrong way but…"

"You're heading back a day early," Sylvie said for her.

Mike was a little surprised at not being consulted about the arrangement.

"I just wanna sleep in my own bed y'know," Amie pleaded.

"We completely understand. It's hard going from house to house," I nodded.

"Which isn't so bad when you're twenty. House to house, bed to bed, man to man," Sylvie said.

"What's in that wine and why is your glass empty?" I offered.

"Thanks guys, I'm exhausted. Next time I promise, we'll come to the yurt at the start of our vacation and not at the end," Amie promised.

It was sad to see them go, but it was a relief too. As you get older you mourn less over the parting of ways and the drifting of friendships. Sometimes the great swirl of the universe brings people together because of chance, circumstance and geography. A friendship might continue despite those obstacles. And sometimes those obstacles makes you rejoice in the circumstances that brought you together in the first place.

As newborn parent's we'd delighted in the magic and the manic that a child can bring. Where Toronto was going to continue along without us, Mike and Amie would return, less with the memories of our final rendezvous and more with the collision of events that brought us and kept us together. But the part of moving on is realizing that kind of circumstance can't be replicated.

Those thoughts were furthest from our minds.

Where Amie and Mike were looking forward to being back in their own home, we were looking forward to starting our new lives. It was the last week of August and we had a very busy week ahead of us. Sylvie officially started her first full week as an aesthetics instructor. The house we purchased in Dieppe would close Wednesday. My first writing assignment was due at the end of the week.

And company was coming. Our last visitors: Pierre and his eleven-year-old son Baxter, aka, the Ghosts of Toronto Future. They were somewhere in New England, buzzing corners on a motorcycle while a little disturbance in the Caribbean was hinting at an arrival.

****

Anyone with a modicum of customer service experience has probably experienced the gamut of human emotions: Degrees of screaming. Pleading. Crying. Threatening even. Unfortunately the news the secretary presented to me set me into gales of laugher. She wasn't amused.

"Mister Hamilton, we tried to process your cheque and the account was closed," the woman said

"Another cheque that didn't pass, you're friggin' kidding me."

I was driving in downtown Moncton, trying to find a place to park when this VERY unexpected call threw a monkey wrench into my thoughts. I was about to walk into the lawyer's office to sign the paperwork for our house. Having just arrived from Upper Rexton where I was taking some precautions over the imminent arrival of Earl.

I was hoping the keys would be made available to me so I could get in touch with the movers and get the move done that day.

"Wait, wait, who is this?"

"It's the Kent District Planning Commission."

I was dumbfounded. Surely there must be a mistake. Aside from ordering the yurt the first thing I did was apply for a building permit.

"Hold on," I asked, trying to be reasonable. I thought long and hard before I remembered a phone conversation that seemed somehow to relate. When was that? Where was I? What was I doing? It came back to me like a deep zoom with a dolly move. It was a parking lot. Moncton. Really hot. Stupid hot. I was careening around somewhere without my child. When was that? Why was I there?

We were at the mall. Getting back from Charlottetown. It was a month ago. It was Bill.

Bill said the number on my construction permit "didn't make sense".

"What does the date say on that cheque?" I finally asked.

"March 3rd," she responded.

I couldn't help but laugh. But the laughter wouldn't stop. Miss Kent County wasn't amused in the slightest.

"But you know what's really funny," I said, trying to compose myself, "I just drove from Richibucto to Moncton. I was at the yurt making preparations for Hurricane Earl. Tying down the dome. Had you called me even two hours earlier, I could have swung by and given you everything right then and there."

"Well sir, if you could clear this matter up…"

I was still laughing. "You know it's for a building permit don't you? And the building was finished a month ago. But what I really want to know is what happened to the cheque? I mean, obviously you guys had it the whole time. I didn't write one for March 3rd and send it at the end of August. This is too funny. Don't you find this funny? Where was it all this time, under a desk?"

She didn't share my amusement, "It is your responsibility to send us the amount owing."

I finished parallel parking the car.

"Look, I've got paperwork to sign for my house, a hurricane bearing down on my yurt…that isn't even insured yet. The only guy in the country who agreed to cover it is laid up in the hospital with chest pains. I need to move, find a job, finish a writing assignment and entertain guests all before the end of the week. You're asking me to deal with something that, frankly, isn't my fault. The date on the cheque says so. You'll get your money when I find the time…and maybe the inclination," I thundered before hanging up the phone.

I took a moment to compose myself. "Of all the idiotic," I started to say before I stopped, "just when you think you've tied up all the loose ends…"

****

"Hey guys, perfect timing," I said, the irony lost in translation over the phone.

"I'm just sitting in your town, enjoying a Timmie's," Pierre said, "and young Baxter is having himself a milk."

"You're still not letting him drink anything leaded yet?"

"Oh no, when he's older, he'll be sipping cappuccino's, wearing a beret, smoking cigarette's."

"OUR Baxter. Doesn't sound like it."

"No, that's me."

Some laughter, some excitement, but I couldn't shake that my mind was on other things.

"Where are you?"

"I think we're in Dieppe."

I almost dropped the furniture. "Dieppe. Really!"

"Yeah, I'm pretty sure. We were driving up from Hopewell Rocks. Did you know only a few hours ago we were walking on the bottom of the ocean? You're talking to some drowned people right now. And we just started following the road to Moncton. We went around the traffic circle, didn't we Baxter….And then oh look, perfect, we took Main Street, can't go wrong there. Cruised through downtown. It's cute. Nice, small. We thought we could find a place to park but you can't park on Main Street, so we just kept going and then hey, there's a sign for Dieppe. We went past the mall. Then something that looked kind of 'downtown' Dieppe."

"That's Dieppe city hall."

"And Baxter knew we were close."

"Yeah, no shit, you're very close."

"Instinct man. A GOOD driver doesn't need the fancy GPS navigational nonsense. With it I might have drove into the Bay of Fundy."

"Alright, I'm pretty sure I know where you are, I'll come meet you in about five minutes."

"Wow, that is close. Good thing too, we need to take refuge from this Hurricane that's coming. It's no place for two people on a motorcycle."

"Ha, I know. I don't know how the yurt is gonna stand up to it."

"The first hurricane for the yurt!?!"

"Yeah, I'm a little nervous, but guess what, I've got a house to move into. You're timing is perfect."

"I know, I've taken those set decoration calls. I've moved my fair share of furniture."

"Perfect, we're moving tomorrow morning. I've gotta make you earn your keep."

I tried to make light of it, but as we parked and made our way inside, the vast empty house arrested my attempts to be a good host.

Pierre seemed to pick up on my frustration, "Don't worry about it. Come on, an air mattress on the floor, it'll be just like we're at the yurt. Right Baxter, this is like camping."

"But on the floor. And you were the one's who bought the mattress."

"Ha ha. It's not like we can take it on the motorcycle anyway. Consider it a house warming gift."

He had me. Pierre knew what the situation was going to be like before they arrived. Boxes, boxes, everywhere boxes. It was just that as a host, you'd always like to be able to have the opportunity to show at least SOME kind of hospitality.

And what did they get in exchange for their long voyage? On Thursday morning I asked them to stay behind and receive a bed we'd ordered. I was helping the movers shift all of our things out of storage and onto a truck. Then when I arrived with the truck, Pierre and Baxter got to help me unload the truck, with all of our worldly possessions.

But they seemed to take it all in stride. Which is more than I could say for yours truly. As much as I was fixated on unpacking and getting our lives in order, what was really occupying my mind was the turbulent weather that was expected to touch down in the Maritimes anywhere from the Bay of Fundy to the coast of Newfoundland.

****

As we drove up highway 11 it was evident that Earl was more than just your average windstorm. There had been some conjecture as to where, when and how strong the hurricane would be when it touched down. As it turned out, it crossed right over the toe of Nova Scotia as a tropical storm with 85-100 km/h winds. No slouch.

The van rocked and rolled as the rain pelted into the side of the vehicle.

While the commentators, meteorologists and everyone else was talking of its path, it never occurred to me to consider WHERE that swirling mass might be drawing its energy. I was expected the winds to slam us from the direction of the hurricane's origin. The southwest. But the ripples in the rivers, and the heavy pelt of rain were all coming from the northeast.

Significance?

A few days before Earl's arrival, I decided to undertake whatever hurricane prevention matters I could. On the outside of the roof cover, the manufacturer's had two sets of eyelets: one circled the underside of the cover and held the whole outside vinyl shell together. The other eyelets hung over the wall to create an overlap and prevent any weather from getting into the yurt. When Chris and I were putting the whole thing together we kept asking ourselves what was the purpose of the other eyelets. As Earl picked up steam, I knew.

From the direction of the path of the hurricane (south-west), I weaved rope through those outside eyelets and attached the cord to the posts supporting the entire structure. Unfortunately, the wind would batter us from the other direction.

Splashing along the road, I was getting nervous as we approached the yurt. After a summer of extensive heat (and no windows to aid circulation) the dome on the roof was constantly being opened and closed. So much so a gust of wind lifted the dome and shifted its trajectory. I had to go to the trouble of borrowing a twelve-foot ladder (from Kent Building Supply) to re-adjust its alignment.

As we rounded the corner and the yurt came into view, I could almost feel my heart in my throat. I wanted to stop the car, get out, run, and yell. Instead, my head ducked deep under the front windshield and I peered long at the damage on the top of the yurt.

"Oh FUCK!!" I couldn't hold back.

Pierre and Baxter weren't sure what had me spooked. Like others who've come before, taking in the structure for the first time, they didn't see what I did.

It was only as we pulled into the driveway and I could barely park the van before bolting out of it, did they sense something was awry.

I was like a rookie cop that just happened upon his first murder scene. The forensic evidence lay in the grass at my feet.

A broken piece of clear plastic dome had blown off of the top of the yurt. Flapping in the heavy wind, a remaining shard was clinging to life and sticking up into the air in defiance.

"I bet that's not supposed to be like that," Pierre offered.

"FFFUUCCKKK!" I didn't care about young Baxter's tender ears.

"Do you have a tarp?"

Thankfully, Pierre was present and his mind sharp. Seeing the hardship, the challenge, and the great personal and financial risk all swaying in the breeze galvanized my humiliation and had me drooling like a fool. I couldn't string two thoughts together. All I could see was disaster. Another hair-brained scheme had been exposed for the colossal blunder it was. I set to my phone, sending calls of desperation all over the country: to Chris, Yurtco, Kent Building Supply, anyone who I thought might be able to help. It became clear this was no one else's problem but mine.

"Do you have any rope?"

I slowly came back into focus. The rest of the structure was still standing and could be salvaged. I fumbled for keys. I needed to get inside to see the significance of the damage.

"Yeah, there's some rope in the shed."

As I stepped into the yurt through the French doors, Earl's effects were all over the floor, but not as bad as I feared. Though the winds were harsh, the pelting rain wouldn't have any long-term impact…if we could close the gaping hole in the middle of the roof.

Pierre opened up the shed and a material inventory was assessed to determine a course of action. For all the cursing of the Grip department I did over the years, I damn sure wish I had a homeless one squatting in the yurt at that moment. Drunk or sober, at the very least a pair of shaky, yet experienced hands would be welcome.

"Do you have a small piece of wood we can throw over the roof?" Pierre asked.

Roof. Heavy object. Vinyl. Not good. I didn't like it. But I didn't have a choice. I paused for a moment. All I could recall were the sharp, jagged edges of two by fours that, in the course of saving the hole in the yurt, would undoubtedly create other, lesser ones. Then I remembered the short round cut-off stud pieces that I was saving for another application.

"Okay," I said, and scrambled to retrieve one.

"We'll tie it to the rope, throw it over the roof, attach the tarp and haul it up," Pierre declared.

"I'll throw it. That way if I put a hole in the roof, I've got no one to blame but myself."

I visualized the wood safely arching high over the roof of the yurt before falling to the grass on the other side. About to throw, my mind switched to disaster mode, and all I could see was the wood skipping off the fabric and puncturing a fresh opening with each bounce.

"Fuck it," I closed my eyes, and heaved for all I was worth.

The rope caught in my foot and the wood shanked close to the electrical service. Oops. I gingerly pulled it back.

"He's beginning to believe! Free your mind Neo."

I let loose again, this time I kept the trailing rope away from my landing position. It didn't quite make it, but it was far enough we could wiggle it to the ground.

"Any holes in the roof?" I asked. Even without the howling wind, from the other side of the yurt, Pierre couldn't hear me anyway. No matter.

"Some coils I found from the cable round, and we tied it to the tarp;
Some hope we gulped and the wind it whupped as the plastic punctured sharp;
The wind it screamed, and to me it seemed
Our luck would never hold;
But fought we did, and the tarp it slid,
Until perchance the blue gripped over the hole."

(With apologies to Robert Service.)

Before hauling the tarp over the opening we tied several other lines to give it a chance to stay rooted in place. Pierre and Baxter each held tight to theirs while I secured one of my lines. I gripped mine once again as Pierre secured the other side of the tarp.

Unfortunately, a jagged piece of the dome still clung to life. The tarp snared on top of it. We paused, like wet dogs, in shorts and rain jackets, to go inside, survey our progress, and take refuge. Each whip of wind sent fresh sprinkles of water cascading down onto the floor. I looked up and grimaced.

"We should get up there and put another tarp underneath to catch all the water," Pierre offered.

Hmm, catch it, I thought, but then what? I let Pierre hang there, gazing up at the roof, standing in his underwear while his pants swirled in the dryer, and went outside.

"Look, I know we're in our underwear, but is this really the time for a wading pool?"

Baxter laughed, giggled and bellied over. And why not? All I needed was a rubber ducky and some water wings, and the six-foot inflatable kiddy pool ensemble would be complete. Standing under the dome, I sized up the aim, and dropped the pool under the falling water.

"Ah ha, clever, now all we need is some beer and a few lawn chairs and we can have a hurricane party."

I took the hint and scrounged around the yurt for a few spirits to help pick me up. Luckily I managed to locate a few light beers and a cooler. Hardly our drinks of choice, but given the circumstances....

Sitting in our underwear, occasionally glancing up at the tarp as it and the yurt whipped and flopped in the rain, we were startled by a knock at the door.

The door opened and wading in with his rain jacket came Jack from Kent Building Supplies.

"You said you needed a ladder," he said.

Jumping to my feet, I couldn't even remember if I'd confirmed or cancelled the request. Not pausing to think about it, I put on my clothes and helped Jack muscle the 12-foot ladder into the yurt.

Staple gun in hand, green tarp in the other, I climbed the steps to the top.

As I looked up, I could see the blue tarp, still caught and snagged on the jagged piece of remaining plastic dome. The equally large bug screen, screwed to the underside of the opening, prevented me from being able to reach up clean and free the plastic.

I called for a knife and made a modest incision; just enough to reach up and free the offending piece from worry. I stretched and struggled, trying hard not to think about the wobble of the ladder and the twelve-foot plunge to the floor.

I reached my arm up, through the incision, careful not to tear it farther. Given the height, I used my free hand to cling desperately to the edge of the ladder. I gripped and tugged at the tarp, flailing madly in the heave of rain and wind. I pulled my hand down, the audience at my feet wincing with every move.

I shuffled my feet together, closed my eyes and took another deep breath. Again, my arm went up through the opening with precision. I bent to let my arm stretch as far into the damage as possible. Still the tarp wouldn't come free.

"This isn't working. Hmm, hold on, I've got an idea. Pierre, in my tool bag I've got a pair of pliers. I'm going to have to free up the plastic and everything," I called down.

I moved back down the ladder, hugging it as close as I could before stretching an arm down to receive the pliers.

"Do you need some help up there?" Jack asked.

I ignored his words, eager to finish the task. A little farther from the danger, I slowly unscrewed the jagged piece from the hardware that secured it to the roof. The closer I got to the end of the screw, the harder it was to loosen. The wind, the tension on the plastic pulled it as I reached the finish. I took one last look at the jagged plastic. It was almost released, but should it decide to cause havoc, it could easily puncture the vinyl on the way out of harm. But if I left it in place, the chance of it doing worse damage was inevitable.

I spun the screw one last twist and the plastic released from the yurt. It was out of my hands before I could recover it and hopefully pull it back inside. I looked down horrified.

"I'll go see if the yurt survived," Pierre offered and scurried outside.

I dipped my head down to see if there was any damage on the inside. My suspicions were confirmed when Pierre returned and announced, "All good."

I breathed easier. The potential for further disaster (the plastic flying off and puncturing the vinyl) had been alleviated.

K-chunk. K-chunk. Another tarp was quickly secured underneath.

In short order, the ladder was folded up, loaded back onto the truck and Jack whisked away.

****

"Why isn't their any more beer!?!" I asked, looking at the too empty fridge.

Considering the still howling hurricane and the drive back to Moncton, it was better that our supply of alcoholic beverages was limited. As I stared at the green tarp, now starting to bulge with water, no amount of booze could assuage my disappointment.

"Here," I said, and handed a Bud Light to Pierre, "you can have this, unless you want a blueberry cooler."

"Naw, I'll stick with this water here," Pierre said and snapped the cap off the pint, "Who drinks this swill anyway?"

"Fern. Look at it this way, you could be a girl drink drunk like me."

We laughed, happy the worst would soon be over.

"Hey, this place isn't bad, 'cept there's a little hole in the roof," Baxter said.

It was just water and water eventually evaporates. There would be no permanent damage. My psyche, on the other hand, wasn't willing to bounce back quite so quick. Everything we'd poured into the place: gone in a puff of wind!

I didn't want to start a solitary philosophical debate with company and thought the best way out of such an emotional spiral would be the Acadian delicacies I'd promised Pierre and Baxter since their arrival.

"Let's get some poutine and lobster!" I declared, "Acadian style."

We collected ourselves, assessing if anymore could or should be done to help save the yurt. The bulge in the second tarp was noticeable.

"Maybe you should put a hole in the tarp," Pierre suggested.

I climbed the bunk bed, held the rafters and walked on the top of the walls to the middle of the yurt. Wielding a kitchen knife, I leaned out into the yurt and punctured a few holes in the tarp as close to the middle as possible. The water gushed into the wading pool on the floor.

Pierre shrugged his shoulders at me, "I guess it'll have to do for now."

It pained me to see all of the trouble, effort and risk get battered around by Mother Nature so casually and not be able to do anything further. What we did would have to do. As the winds ceased and the hurricane continued its path up the East Coast, Earl's effect, minimal at the yurt, was a great deal more painful in other parts of Atlantic Canada.

As news broke of the destruction Earl created elsewhere, we sat in La Poutine a Lea, drowning in a heavy dose of Acadian Poutine Rapee: Cooked meat, wrapped in a ball of mashed and pureed potatoes and then all boiled in water.

"Okay then, the yurt is, uh, somewhat secure, you've had your Acadian culture experience. I guess the only thing left is for you guys to make it home for Baxter to go to school."

"Ha ha. It's Saturday, he won't make it home in time for school Tuesday."

"That's alright, the first day of school after summer vacation isn't all that spectacular anyway."

"Do you know how cool this kid is gonna be?" Pierre asked.

For two movie people who've made their own films and walked and hobnobbed with stars of various caliber and ego, neither of us could have envisioned the scenario about to unfold. Hurricane Earl kept Pierre and Baxter grounded in New Brunswick until Sunday morning. Monday was Labour Day and Tuesday was supposed to be the first day of Grade 6 for young Baxter.

Arriving Marlon Brando-esque, without a care for the education system or its rules, Baxter strode into class straight from the motorcycle half way through the second day of school. Still wearing his leather jacket, his helmet tucked under his arm, a yurt adventure closing out his summer holidays, I could only imagine the look on the faces of the other students. Before he even sat down I could picture twenty kids crumpling up their first essay of the year: "How I spent my summer holiday."

****

"What do you mean it's designed to blow off?"

I was apoplectic. Margaret, having dealt with me as we tracked the whereabouts of the yurt only a few months ago, had grown accustomed to my wild reaction to news and information.

"That way it won't break apart, like yours did, and puncture the fabric of the yurt," she explained.

Yurt logic. Like crumple zones in cars.

"Well I need another one because it didn't blow off but it sure as hell broke apart."

"Okay, I'll send one right away."

"Good, great, that will be a relief. I've got two tarps covering it in the meantime and I don't know how long they're going to last."

"Oh, didn't Darin get a hold of you. He said to just cover the opening with plywood until the new dome arrives."

Plywood, why didn't I think of that? Not quite as severe as the rivalry amongst East Coast and West Coast rappers, Atlantic and Pacific Canadians are not without their differences. Veterans of the Canadian Navy who've endured the swells and storms of the North Atlantic affectionately called their brothers stationed in British Columbia "Sandy Bottom Sailors". The term was hardly complimentary. Fighting hundred kilometre an hour winds, it wasn't WHAT I got the hole covered with, it was THAT I managed to get it covered at all. Imagine being at the top of a twelve-foot ladder, in the middle of a hurricane and gluing a solid chunk of lumber to a sail. Plywood indeed.

"Would you like me to send the dome to the same delivery place?"

"Memramcook?"

"Yeah, I think that's what we have on file."

"I don't need a loading dock do I?"

"Oh no, you shouldn't, though I've never shipped just a dome before…." Margaret confessed.

"Send it to Kent Building Supply in Bouctouche."

I made Kent Building Supply aware of my predicament and asked them to alert me when the dome arrived. And waited. Waited while hunting for work, going back over familiar tracks to follow up on previous leads. In addition to ELF I landed another gig. Perhaps I wouldn't have to join the ranks of the average working stiff after all.

I reveled in the continuance of my independence. It seemed too good to be true. Sylvie was not faring particularly well. Brash and impatient with others, she was having a hard time dealing with the mentality of the modern student. And administration. A rebel in her own mind, the new constraints of having to fit within something determined by someone else was a lot more challenging than we expected.

****

A week went by before I thought, once again, the lines of communication had somehow broken between Dieppe and British Columbia.

"Hi Margaret," I inquired, "I haven't heard anything from Kent yet, has the dome been sent?"

"Uh, no Jason, sorry. We're having a hard time getting it shipped. Please bare with us, I thought we could put it on the underside of a bus but it's too big for that."

"Okay," I sighed, "whenever you can get it up here."

Though it was a nice architectural feature to be able to reach up with a long handle and crank open a six-foot dome when necessary, I made my mind up right then and there to bolt the thing down when it arrived.

Epilogue

Bruce Hickey lost his riding in the election. In political terms I'd say he was a sacrificial lamb. His chief opponent was the premier of the province, Shawn Graham of the Liberal Party, who was up for re-election. His party went down to defeat, but Mr. Graham still won a comfortable victory over Mr. Hickey.

The low-flying aircraft, a feature of our construction progress, was not, in fact Big Google Earth Brother, but rather a means of gathering seismic intelligence: Turns out New Brunswick just happens to have massive untapped reserves of natural gas. Whether the people will allow it to be harvested, via 'fracking' is still a matter of considerable debate and fierce opposition.

The change from Liberal to Progressive Conservative had a reverberating effect throughout the land: not the least of which were contracts and the ideas they supported. ELF did not get further provincial funding. The uncertainty until that decision meant my one dependable client could not shuffle work in my direction.

The dome to the yurt arrived after a spell. I called on Chris to help me haul it back up to the top. I borrowed the 12' ladder from Kent Building Supply (again) and made sure to wire the plexi-glass piece shut so as to assure I wouldn't need to call on them again.

Feeling some confidence in my freelance writing career it was suggested to me I could (and should) attend a small business seminar and apply for a special program to help small enterprise.

EPILOGUE

The seminars were an awakening to my inner entrepreneur, but my focus was on the long-stated dream of full-time employment. I'd had enough of constantly being on the lookout for work. It was taxing, stressful and time consuming. And for a highly socialized being, painfully solitary.

I submitted my application and business plan and was rejected. My heart really wasn't in it anyway. But the window to my employment insurance was quickly closing.

Then there was the sting after sting of several interviews and opportunities that never came to pass. I was becoming demoralized. EI ran its course. I was truly a full-time freelancer.

Another follow-up yielded a little more freelance writing work, but eeegads, the solitude was starting to impact my personality….and not in a good way.

Earl turned out to be just one of three heavy wind days that fall of 2010. Sometime in October a plain ol' Nor'Easter whipped up 100 km/h winds.

Not to be outdone, a confluence of wind, full moon and high tide season produced a dramatic and traumatic storm surge just two days before Christmas. The tide, driven by the strong wind, heavy rainfall, full moon and gawd knows what else left the Acadian Riviera from Shediac to Miramichi deep in water damage.

Barely a week after the clean up started the first winter storm ploughed through the region. Two and sometimes three winter snow falls a week continued right until the end of March. 25-50 centimetres of snow at a time.

My Dad would call me often, cackling away, wondering how we were surviving our first winter. Had I worn out my shovel handle yet, he delighted in saying. In my words I feigned spirit, I laughed along with him but our situation was slowly becoming dire.

A deep need, the need of every male breadwinner, to provide for his family was whittling away. My carefully crafted plan, to target the places and businesses where I thought I could land employment, evaporated in a rush of frustration. I'd become the homeless man of job hunters, standing at the street corner passing out my resume. Nothing was working. Even as I sloughed away with my one client, I struggled to find my worth. (The Toronto film industry meanwhile, was having the best year on record.)

Sylvie was feeling it too. She'd stopped bringing her desperation home. Neither of us was listening much to the other. I was still wishing we'd cozy'd up in the yurt and resented her greatly at jumping the gun on our plan. Her misery begat mine, or so I convinced myself. If I had found decent paying full-time employment I doubt our partnership would have survived. Stuck in misery, breaking up would have made everything worse, not better; It was only that thought and not a deep, impenetrable love, that kept us together.

"When this happens, when that happens.." we kept telling ourselves. We needed Fern and Flo to move to have some more family support. We needed the conditions to be just 'so' in order for the peace, tranquility and stability we'd sought could be achieved. We forgot, nay, kyboshed any notion we could only be responsible for ourselves, for our reactions. "The Secret" be damned! I was so furious at the folly of "The Law of Attraction" that if I'd found one copy of the damn book I'd have roasted it in the fire. We did everything for the right reasons, we told ourselves, why, oh why, wasn't it working out like we'd hoped?

****

I wish I could say it was a moment. I wish I could say it was some sort of epiphany that brought me back from the abyss. I know what it was that scared the be-jesus out of me because it reflected back where I was and how close I'd come. And it was through that event, I could really see, for the first time, that I too had stared down that long, dark tunnel to oblivion.

It's an extremely difficult place to describe. It is not a physical element that has grass and trees and atmosphere. It is a mental construct of thoughts and representations that can and does have a fuel. A life. The thoughts of desperation are like a devouring monster. It feeds upon itself with a dizzying intensity. And worse yet, for me in particular, in a new land, with new values, new social structures, language barriers, those thoughts were like a barrier. A prison. It was as if I'd become captive to my own swirling funnel of, of…what, I don't know.

I tell myself NOW that it wasn't clinical, that it was an extreme of congruent circumstances that wasn't likely to repeat itself. A perfect storm of emotion I hope to never see again.

Those thoughts engulf you, overpower you, consume you in exponential ways that only now, with the currency of safety, can I fully appreciate their power. I felt I'd nowhere to turn. No one to call upon. I'd insulted my family, turned my back on my film community, by trying in a brash new sense, to reinvent myself, and in so doing, I'd completely, and utterly failed: Unemployed and unable to get an interview at the Second Cup kiosk in the mall.

I'd come to believe in that one ace up my sleeve, my ability to land work in the electrical trade come hell or high water, would always be there when necessary. Nothing doing. The massive precipitation of winter had given way to a spring where the rain simply would not end. I called around. I called every electrical contractor in the Greater Moncton area: we've got temporaries up, waiting for foundations to get poured…but the rain. And on came the responses. One after another: The rain.

The ace was a complete dud.

Sylvie was mired in her own misery. She wished to finish out the semester, get through the school season before turning her attention elsewhere.

That's when I started to get back in touch with my film friends. A man had to do what a man had to do, pride or not. It was just an inquisition, I told myself. How busy was Toronto? I called Larry.

"Jesus Christ Jason. How fuckin' soon can you get up here? You could take over for me and be a Rigging Gaffer on this show. I could keep you busy until Christmas!"

I'd found my spirit. It was crushed mind you, annihilated, with barely a sliver of life, but it was enough of a spark that I was aware of a definition between myself and the abyss.

"I can't come up yet, Sylvie is finishing her term. She starts a new job where she'll be on the road…."

But, supposing there wasn't just that one gig, surely there must be other work?

"Sylv," I finally declared, "I'm heading to Toronto for a few weeks."

"Okay."

"I have a flight booked. I'm leaving on Sunday and I'm staying with Trevor."

"Oh great. Yeah. Awesome idea. Do you have a job when you get there?"

"No, I hear it's really busy and I shouldn't have any trouble getting work."

"How about you get the work first and then book the flight, have you thought about that!?!"

"I know it's a little backwards, but if I book the flight now, I'll make some calls in the meantime and I guarantee I'll be working on Monday."

"Uh, phew, fine. Whatever."

And that's when all hell broke loose.

One of the first calls I made was to an old friend and boss who were working on the only feature in town. If I was going to stick my tail between my legs and go back to Toronto to work, you can be damn sure I'd try to get on a feature and make as much money as I could.

"You didn't hear?"

"No."

"We lost one of our brothers."

"Oh my god. Are you serious?"

"Yeah, Pierre Berube showed up today and told us Steve passed away on the week-end. No details."

But somehow I knew. Even without being told I knew he'd taken his own life.

****

EPILOGUE

I'm not afraid to admit how vulnerable I'd become. It's easy now. It's human to admit mistakes and accept results. I went to Toronto for three weeks. In three weeks I managed to get my feet underneath me. While I was there I landed several job interviews back in New Brunswick from one of the hundreds of résumé's I'd cast into the world. One of which resulted in an offer of employment. Too bad it was in Fredericton. Having just moved out to the East Coast I wasn't about to pull up stakes again. I turned it down, called every electrical contractor in the book and simply wouldn't quit until I got employment. It took a week, but it worked.

While I was in Toronto I got to salute my friend and raise a pint in his honour. None of us can ever know his state, but I'm sure he helped shove me back from mine. Whether you believe in such things is a matter of personal preference. Considering the world was flat until just over five hundred years ago and some Tea Party members still believe in the divinity of creation, I'd say we have some ground to cover until we have it all figured out.

The yurt has survived a couple of seasons. Wind one year blew the side door open and invited the elements inside. Adding a storm door to prevent a reoccurrence, the next year it too was blown asunder. I've finally learned to board the door shut for the winter.

In the course of all the tragedy and happenstance that transpired with the yurt it did open some very unexpected doors. During my small business seminar I met a young real estate agent who, somehow, was contacted from France to secure a piece of property in the Moncton area. The man had an unusual project, a little different structure that was well-suited to a smaller community. "What is it?" Sylvie Cormier insisted.

"You've probably never heard of it."

Since I was the 'Yurt Guy' at the seminar she already had.

But perhaps most dumbfounding of all the yurt conflagrations was discovering a manufacturer was open for business in Belleisle Creek, New Brunswick. On the same coast. In the same time zone. To purchase a yurt from him, it most likely would not have gotten lost en route somewhere in Ontario. Ho Hum.

The deep peaks and valleys of our earlier existence have finally smoothed out. It's a bit of a trough as we slowly adjust to both the financial constraints of starting over and the reality we're just like everyone else. More than a sanctuary, the yurt has taken on a life of its own. As one of the very few in this part of the world, we've let it out for rental and without the extra income we'd have barely survived financially. It's absurd sometimes to have to put in extra effort after hours for someone to enjoy your space, but such is the price of home ownership. It might also be the beginning seeds of some new enterprise.

But the joy of this new existence rests in the fact I've been home every Friday of every week to tuck my child in to bed and tell him I love him.

While I dedicate this effort to Steve Spurrell, I derive the inspiration for it from my son Dustin and my common-law heterosexual life partner Sylvie.

The Prince of Acadia & the River of Fire

Eco-Terrorists. Sabotage. Tanner's sixth-grade summer vacation just got interesting!

Warren LeBlanc wants to challenge his son Tanner and his friends with a 'rite of passage' along the legendary River of Fire. But what Warren didn't bank on was sharing his cause with an illegal mining operation. When the boys conquer the first obstacle they discover their father's have been kidnapped and labeled 'eco-terrorists'.

Should the boys alert the authorities or can they infiltrate the mining compound and expose the conspiracy? Tanner manages to rally his friends with the help of a special talent: A talent that sees him connecting to the power of the spiritual world and unleashing the energy within.

Hitting Shelves in the Fall 2016!!

About the Author

I'm a farm boy at heart. Slugging bales and milking cows during the summers of my youth in Southern Ontario. Palmerston to be exact. A place where the railroad birthed a town overnight only for the iron highway to slowly die out just a hundred years later. The tentacled stretches of the tracks drew me on their path and the long ride to who knows where has remained etched in my mind so long as the horizon hid their purpose.

It's no surprise I finished my arts degree at Wilfrid Laurier with the full intention of taking the film industry by storm in 1997. I was on a mission. To get into show business, gain enough knowledge to make my own film, and carve out a niche as a writer/director. I reached my goal in 2001 where *Shotgun Journalism* appeared in exactly ONE film festival. I had a decision to make: Now what? I remained a lighting technician, living with the ebb and flow of the cycle of work.

In the summer of 2001, a slowing film industry in Toronto sent me to Saint John, NB to work on a movie. It was there I met the love of my life, Sylvie Mazerolle, a make-up artist on the same project. At the end of that year, Sylvie moved to Toronto to live with me and pursue her dream of becoming a full-time make-up artist. Since then, Sylvie and I have lived, worked and travelled together until some startling news changed our lives.

Just two days before Christmas in 2007 Sylvie found out she was pregnant with our first child. As 2008 dawned and the housing crisis started to break down south of the border, we were starting to wonder how secure the investment our Toronto home had become. Feeling the pull of family and the chance to start a-new we sold our home and moved to Richibucto, New Brunswick and built a yurt.

ABOUT THE AUTHOR

From there, we reasoned, we would figure out "Life, the Yurt and Everything".

Seeking a more cosmopolitan atmosphere we eventually settled in Dieppe, the commercial hub of Acadia and a suburb of Moncton.